SOTHEBY'S

ART AT AUCTION

The Art Market Review 1993-94

SOTHEBY'S

ART AT AUCTION

The Art Market Review 1993-94

CONRAN OCTOPUS

First published in 1994 by
Conran Octopus Limited
37 Shelton Street
London WC2H 9HN

British Library Cataloguing in Publication Data
A catalogue record for this book is available from the
British Library

ISBN 1 85029 6464

Printed in Great Britain by
Butler & Tanner Ltd, Frome, Somerset

ENDPAPERS: Bible, the Latter Prophets,
Nevi'im Akhronim, with Masorah, in
Hebrew, illuminated manuscript on vellum
221 LEAVES, 17.2 x 16cm (6¾ x 6⁵⁄₁₆in)
London £210,500 ($334,700). 21.VI.94
From the library of the late David Solomon Sassoon

PAGE 1: A 'Universal Uhr' gold hunter
cased carillon clockwatch
UHRENFABRIK UNION, MOVEMENT SUPPLIED BY AUDEMARS PIGUET,
c. 1899, diameter 8.35cm (3¼in)
Geneva SFr883,500 (£397,975: $589,000).18.XI.93

PAGE 2: THOMAS GAINSBOROUGH
Portrait of Georgiana, Duchess of
Devonshire
OIL ON CANVAS, 127 x 101.5cm (50 x 40in)
London £265,500 ($416,800). 13.VII.94
From the Estate of Mabel Satterlee Ingall

PAGES 4 – 5: Painted grey pottery figure of a
female dancer
HAN DYNASTY, height 50.2cm (19¾in)
New York $81,700 (£53,900). 1.VI.94

CONTENTS

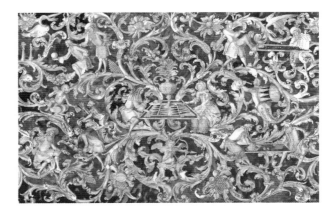

CONTRIBUTORS

ALEXANDER APSIS is a Senior Vice President and head of the Impressionist and Modern Paintings, Drawings and Sculpture department in New York. He joined Sotheby's London in 1974 where he worked in the Contemporary, Impressionist and Modern department before founding the Nineteenth-Century European Paintings department in 1978. He moved to New York to assume his current position in 1991.

TIM BARRINGER is Mobil Research Fellow in Victorian Studies in the Research Department of the Victoria and Albert Museum. He was educated at Cambridge University, as a Harkness Fellow at the Institute of Fine Arts, New York University, and at the University of Sussex. His book *The Cole Family: Painters of the English Landscape* was published to accompany a major exhibition at Portsmouth and Bradford in 1988. He is currently completing a book on representations of labour in British visual culture.

DAVID BENNETT joined Sotheby's in 1974 and was elected a Fellow of the Gemmological Association of Great Britain in 1980. He was appointed Senior Director, Head of European Jewellery sales, in 1989 and is co-author of *Understanding Jewellery* (1989).

JEREMY BLACK is Professor of History at the University of Durham, where he has taught since 1980. A graduate of Queens' Cambridge, he is a member of the Councils of the Royal Historical Society and the British Records Association. His eighteen books include *Culloden and the '45* (1990), *Eighteenth-Century Europe 1700-1789* (1990), *The British Abroad. The Grand Tour in the Eighteenth Century* (1992) and *The Politics of Britain 1688–1800* (1993).

DIANA D. BROOKS is President and Chief Executive Officer of Sotheby's Holdings, Inc., a position held since April 1994. She joined the firm in 1979 and in 1993 was appointed President and Chief Executive Officer of Sotheby's Worldwide Auction Operations. In both capacities she is closely involved with all major sales held by the company and has made a vital contribution to both the co-ordination and the integration of Sotheby's operations throughout the world.

JOSEPH FRIEDMAN works at Sotheby's London and is a partner in Historic Buildings Consultants. In 1985 he undertook a history and survey of Spencer House, which served as the basis of its restoration. He has also advised on the restoration of the British Embassy and the former residence of the Duke and Duchess of Windsor in Paris. His publications include *Inside London* (1988), *Inside Paris* (1989), *Inside New York* (1992) and, most recently, *Spencer House – Chronicle of a great London mansion* (1993).

WENDELL GARRETT is a Senior Vice President of American Decorative Arts at Sotheby's New York. He is also Editor-at-Large of the magazine *Antiques*. His most recent publication is entitled *Victorian America: Classical Romanticism to Gilded Opulence* (1993) and forthcoming is *Monticello and the Legacy of Thomas Jefferson*.

LESLIE GEDDES-BROWN is a journalist who specializes in the fields of antiquities, collecting and art criticism as well as houses and gardens. She is a regular contributor to *The Daily Telegraph* and a feature writer for *The World of Interiors, You* magazine and *Homes & Gardens*. She was previously Deputy Editor of *Country Life* and *The World of Interiors*.

SANDY MALLET joined the Marketing Department of Sotheby's London in 1993, having worked in advertising, television production, and as the editor of *Art at Auction*. His education includes a degree in art history from the University of East Anglia.

GERALDINE NORMAN is art market correspondent for *The Independent.* From 1969 to 1987 she was the saleroom correspondent for *The Times* newspaper. She is author of *The Sale of Works of Art* (1971), *Nineteenth-Century Painters and Painting* (1987) and *Biedermeier Painting* (1987).

ALAN PRYCE-JONES was Editor of the *Times Literary Supplement* from 1948 to 1959. He has contributed to numerous publications, including *The New York Times,* and has written widely on theatre and music, including a critical study of Beethoven. In addition, he is the author of the following travel books: *People in the South* and *The Spring Journey.*

DAVID N. REDDEN is a Senior Vice President and Director of Sotheby's North and South America and the Director of the Books and Manuscripts, Coins, Stamps, Collectibles and Arcade Division. He is also one of the firm's senior auctioneers. In his role as a senior director of Sotheby's, he has presided over some of Sotheby's most important sales, including the Library of H. Bradley Martin, which was dispersed in a series of nine sales from 1989 to 1990.

STEPHEN ROE joined Sotheby's London in 1980, with responsibility for the sale of printed and manuscript music. In 1994 he was made Head of Department for Printed Books and Manuscripts.

J. THOMAS SAVAGE, a consultant to the Miles Brewton house restoration scheme, is Curator and Director of the museum division of The Historic Charleston Foundation. He is a board member of the American Friends of the Attingham Summer School on the British Country House and a presidential appointee to the Committee for the Preservation of the White House.

JUDD TULLY has written widely on the international art market and the contemporary art world for publications such as *The Washington Post, Art & Auction, Architectural Digest, Artnews* and *Beaux Arts.* He is the author of *Red Grooms and Ruckus Manhattan* (1977).

MARINA VAIZEY was an art critic for twenty-one years, first for the *Financial Times,* then for *The Sunday Times,* and until 1994 was the editor of the *Art Quarterly* and *The Review* for the National Art Collections Fund. She has written several books including *100 Masterpieces of Art* and *The Artist as Photographer,* organized exhibitions, lectured and broadcast, and served as a member of the Arts Council and the Crafts Council. She is currently a trustee of several museums and galleries, including the Imperial War Museum, the Geffrye Museum and the National Museums and Galleries on Merseyside, and she is also a member of the British Council Visual Arts Advisory Committee.

RONALD VARNEY joined Sotheby's in 1989 and is a Vice President of Sotheby's New York. He has written extensively on the arts for *Esquire, Smithsonian* and *Connoisseur* magazines, as well as *The New York Times, The Los Angeles Times, The Wall Street Journal* and numerous quarterlies. He is also a regular contributor to *Art at Auction.*

ROBERT C. WOOLLEY is an Executive Vice President of Sotheby's North America and Director of the Decorative Arts Division of Sotheby's New York. He joined Sotheby's in 1968 and celebrated his 25th anniversary with the company in 1993. As well as being a specialist in Russian works of art and one of Sotheby's senior auctioneers, he is renowned as the leading charity auctioneer in America and has also lectured extensively throughout the United States on art and antiques.

INTRODUCTION *by Diana D. Brooks*

GUSTAV KLIMT
Dame mit Fácher
(detail)
OIL ON CANVAS, 100 x 100.3cm
(39⅜ x 39½in)
New York $11,662,500
(£7,827,200). 11.V.94 From
the Estate of Wendell Cherry
(LEFT)

While Sotheby's 250th anniversary began officially last January, unofficially it was inaugurated in late November 1993, in St James's Park, London. There a team of Sotheby's experts, led by the incoming Chairman of Sotheby's UK, Henry Wyndham, began to plant along The Mall one million daffodil bulbs, a presentation from Sotheby's to the people of London. In the ensuing months we have been pleased to extend the anniversary festivities to many other parts of the world, as colleagues, clients and friends of Sotheby's have gathered to celebrate the long and illustrious heritage of our firm.

In 1963, in an earlier version of Sotheby's Art at Auction *called* The Ivory Hammer, *we presented something quite unusual for this publication: a short story. How it came about was an exceptional case. The editor of the book in that year was a young member of our Impressionist and Modern Paintings department. His parents were close friends of novelist Ian Fleming, so the young expert decided to ask Fleming to write a story specially for the publication, involving Fleming's most famous literary creation, the dashing British agent 007. The resulting story, 'The Property of a Lady', which brings James Bond to Sotheby's on the trail of a Russian spy, was so popular that we have reprinted it here with specially commissioned illustrations. The young expert and editor was, I should add, Michel Strauss, now in his third decade at Sotheby's.*

In this special commemorative edition of Art at Auction *we have reviewed the 1993-94 season at Sotheby's, as well as examined the development of Sotheby's and the art market, through the prism of 250 years of history. As in recent editions of this book, we have invited a number of recognized scholars and journalists to contribute articles on themes related to art history, collecting and connoisseurship.*

A page from the original manuscript of 'The Property of a Lady' by Ian Fleming. (BELOW)

In the first section of the book, three of the articles – 'For King and Country', 'Storm Cloud of the Nineteenth Century' and 'Art, the Market and Modern Life' – give a panoramic view of the art world over the past two and a half centuries, charting major shifts in artistic taste, and the influence of major political, social and cultural events upon the art scene. In his article on the nineteenth century, for example,

THOMAS ROWLANDSON

An Auction Room – Selling a Library – Dispersal of Antique Library at Baker's Old Auction Room

c. 1880, WATERCOLOUR, PEN AND BLACK INK OVER PENCIL OUTLINE. (ABOVE)

Tim Barringer describes how Paris was acknowledged as the world's artistic capital of the day, and how Edouard Manet's Un Bar aux Folies-Bergère *was proclaimed by a critic as 'the most exactly modern' picture at the Paris Salon of 1882. (One of the highlights of the past auction season was the sale at Sotheby's London of Manet's first version of this great painting, now in the Courtauld Institute Galleries.) In her article, Marina Vaizey discusses the dramatic changes in civilization over the past 100 years and the attendant expansion, often breathtaking, of the world art market, particularly in the last twenty years. 'There is more', she writes in vividly summing up the current international art scene, 'more art, more materials, more media, more artists, more markets, more collectors, more museums, more galleries, more money and more public.'*

The Farquhar
Collection of
Natural History
Drawings of
Malacca

C. 1800, WATERCOLOUR OVER
TRACES OF PENCIL HEIGHTENED
WITH BODYCOLOUR, SOME
HEIGHTENED WITH GUM ARABIC,
WITH A BLACK LINE BORDER,
SOME ON LAID PAPER, BOUND IN
MARBLED BOARDS EDGED WITH
GREEN MOROCCO,
Each approximately 38 x 54cm
(15 x 21½in) or 54 x 38cm
(21½ x 15in)
London £1,343,500
($2,000,000). 20.X.93.
From the Property of the Royal
Asiatic Society, London
(BELOW)

These historical articles are followed by our traditional review of the art season. This section of the book comprises a visual gallery of highlights from the Sotheby's 1993-94 season, with commentary by senior specialists in London, Geneva and New York on the developments in every collecting category represented at Sotheby's.

As you will see, it was a season of often remarkable successes. Among these were the historic nine-day sale of the von Thurn und Taxis Collection at Schloss St Emmeram in Bavaria, the largest and most successful of its kind ever held in Germany; the Magnificent Jewellery sale in Geneva in November 1993, which established a world auction record for a jewellery sale and included a 100.36 carat diamond that sold for SF17,823,500; the Moller Collection sale in London in November, one of the most successful sales of English furniture in many years; the very strong American paintings sale in New York in May, which featured John Singer Sargent's Spanish Dancer, *from the Estate of Wendell Cherry, which brought $7.6 million, the second highest price ever paid at auction for a nineteenth-century American painting; and the sale in May in New York of the Collection of Mr and Mrs H Gates Lloyd, which included several major works by modern and contemporary artists and brought a total of $21.7 million. The reproductions of these and other highlights will, we hope, provide you with an insight into the many fine works of art that passed through our doors during the past season.*

Collectors have always been essential to the success of our firm, and over the past 250 years many prominent figures have assembled or dispersed collections through Sotheby's. In the eighteenth and nineteenth centuries, for example, when Sotheby's was known mainly as a leading bookseller, among the libraries we sold at auction were those of Prince Talleyrand, the Marquis of Lansdowne, the Dukes of Devonshire and Buckingham, and the Emperor Napoleon. In the twentieth century, the names of collectors buying and selling through Sotheby's read like a Who's Who in virtually every field of collecting, and every walk of life.

In the third and final section of the book, Art in Collections, we explore a number of themes, from the 'magnificent obsession' of collecting itself, as it is described by Alan Pryce-Jones, the history and development of corporate collecting, to the most prominent private collections offered at Sotheby's during the past season.

Housing one's works of art has always been a matter of great importance to collectors, and in her article Leslie Geddes-Brown tells the stories of four extraordinary homes belonging to renowned collectors in America and Europe, sold through Sotheby's International Realty. Continuing our anniversary theme for this volume, we present essays on two wonderful houses of the eighteenth century – Spencer House in London and the Miles Brewton House in Charleston, South Carolina – which epitomize the artistic and architectural achievements of the era in which Sotheby's was founded.

We hope you will enjoy reading this commemorative edition of Art at Auction *and we thank you for helping to make our anniversary a memorable one.*

A Regency silver-gilt
Egyptian-style
centrepiece
candelabrum
DIGBY SCOTT & BENJAMIN
SMITH, LONDON, 1806,
height 62.5cm (24⅜in)
New York $200,500
(£132,300). 20.V.94
From the Estate of Wendell
Cherry (BELOW)

x l p g t o b g t f i m b t d s m d p t a h

dg rz h y n g t r d y s b p b nd a b t x x m

g d t v b p z a r v a q n l g z g r c a d b s

s r t d g o s b a k t d e t c n g s a b z e

n s g b x k z a l v a e q h t d e t x s f a b

b a r c r d s b t c o u n t b h r s w c a v

c a t d e y u f u h i t f d e b s t k p d s v

v d e g m j g n d n f t d g t d w s c a x v d

b d t d m j k i y h t f b t g f e d t h f b k

c e t n f t b d r m k a w b f d d c r d s

v e t d e s d n g t t n t f d e

v e d n g s g f d k x n

b e f c e h g f i n v d g v s

b d t g k n u b f t c d t b t b r

b s d m d i m v d h l i n b y g d v

v e d v e l u g y t h b v r d k o

c e r s l v e t b n g c k a f b

m i f s b a z x h e g n s d c

t g e j d b t h p f c t h d x

THE PROPERTY OF A LADY *by Ian Fleming*

It was, exceptionally, a hot day in early June. James Bond put down the dark grey chalk pencil that was the marker for the dockets routed to the double O Section and took off his coat. He didn't bother to hang it over the back of his chair, let alone take the trouble to get up and drape the coat over the hanger Mary Goodnight had suspended, at her own cost (damn women!), behind the Office of Works' green door of his connecting office. He dropped the coat on the floor. There was no reason to keep the coat immaculate, the creases tidy. There was no sign of any work to be done. All over the world there was quiet. The In and Out signals had, for weeks, been routine. The daily top secret SITREP, even the newspapers, yawned vacuously – in the latter case scratchings at domestic scandals for readership, for bad news, the only news that makes such sheets readable, whether top secret or on sale for pennies.

Bond hated these periods of vacuum. His eyes, his mind, were barely in focus as he turned the pages of a jaw-breaking dissertation by the Scientific Research Station on the Russian use of cyanide gas, propelled by the cheapest bulb-handled children's water pistol, for assassination. The spray, it seemed, directed at the face, took instantaneous effect. It was recommended for victims from 25 years upwards, on ascending stairways or inclines. The verdict would then probably be heart-failure.

The harsh burr of the red telephone sprayed into the room so suddenly that James Bond, his mind elsewhere, reached his hand automatically towards his left arm-pit in self-defence. The edges of his mouth turned down as he recognized the reflex. On the second burr he picked up the receiver.

'Sir?'

'Sir.'

He got up from his chair and picked up his coat. He put on the coat and at the same time put on his mind. He had been dozing in his bunk. Now he had to go up on the bridge. He walked through the connecting office and resisted the impulse to ruffle up the inviting nape of Mary Goodnight's golden neck.

He told her 'M' and walked out into the close-carpeted corridor and along, between the muted whizz and zing of the Communications Section, of which his Section was a neighbour, to the lift and up to the eighth.

Miss Moneypenny's expression conveyed nothing. It usually conveyed something if she knew something – private excitement, curiosity, or, if Bond was in trouble, encouragement or even anger. Now the smile of welcome showed disinterest. Bond registered that this was going to be some kind of a routine job, a bore, and he adjusted his entrance through that fateful door accordingly.

There was a visitor – a stranger. He sat on M's left. He only briefly glanced up as Bond came in and took his usual place across the red leather-topped desk.

M said, stiffly, 'Dr Fanshawe, I don't think you've met Commander Bond of my Research Department.'

Bond was used to these euphemisms.

He got up and held out his hand. Dr Fanshawe rose, briefly touched Bond's hand and sat quickly down as if he had just touched paws with a Gila monster.

If he looked at Bond, inspected him and took him in as anything more than an anatomical silhouette, Bond thought that Dr Fanshawe's eyes must be fitted with a thousandth of a second shutter. So this was obviously some kind of an expert – a man whose interests lay in facts, things, theories – not in human beings. Bond wished that M had given him some kind of a brief, hadn't got this puckish, rather childishly malign desire to surprise – to spring the jack-in-a-box on his staff. But Bond, remembering his own boredom of ten minutes ago, and putting himself in M's place, had the intuition to realize that M himself might have been subject to the same June heat, the same oppressive vacuum in his duties, and, faced by the unexpected relief of an emergency, a small one perhaps, had decided to extract the maximum effect, the maximum drama, out of it to relieve his own tedium.

The stranger was middle-aged, rosy, well-fed, and clothed rather foppishly in the neo-Edwardian fashion – turned up cuffs to his dark blue, four-buttoned coat, a pearl pin in a heavy silk cravat, spotless wing collar, cuff links formed of what appeared to be antique coins, pince-nez on a thick black ribbon. Bond summed him up as something literary, a critic perhaps, a bachelor – possibly with homosexual tendencies.

M said, 'Dr Fanshawe is a noted authority on antique jewellery. He is also, though this is confidential, adviser to H.M. Customs and to the C.I.D. on such things. He has in fact been referred to me by our friends at M.I.5. It is in connection with our Miss Freudenstein.'

Bond raised his eyebrows. Maria Freudenstein was a Secret Agent working for the Soviet K.G.B. in the heart of the Secret Service. She was in the Communications Department, but in a watertight compartment of it that had been created especially for her, and her duties were confined to operating the Purple Cipher – a cipher which had also been created especially for her. Six times a day she was responsible for encoding and dispatching lengthy SITREPS in this cipher to the C.I.A. in Washington. These messages were the output of Section 100 which was responsible for running double agents. They were an ingenious mixture of true fact, harmless disclosures and an occasional nugget of the grossest misinformation. Maria Freudenstein, who had been known to be a Soviet agent when she was taken into the Service, had been allowed to steal the key to the Purple Cipher with the intention that the Russians should have complete access to these SITREPS – be able to intercept and decipher them – and thus, when appropriate, be fed false information. It was a highly secret operation which needed to be handled with extreme delicacy, but it had now been running smoothly for three years and, if Maria Freudenstein also picked up a certain amount of canteen gossip at Headquarters, that was a necessary risk, and she was not attractive enough to form liaisons which could be a security risk.

M turned to Dr Fanshawe, 'Perhaps Doctor, you would care to tell Commander Bond what it is all about.'

'Certainly, certainly.' Dr Fanshawe looked quickly at Bond and then away again. He addressed his boots. 'You see, it's like this, er, Commander. You've heard of a man called Fabergé, no doubt. Famous Russian jeweller.'

'Made fabulous Easter eggs for the Czar and Czarina before the revolution.'

'That was indeed one of his specialities. He made many other exquisite pieces of what we may broadly describe as objects of vertu. Today, in the sale rooms, the best examples fetch truly fabulous prices – £50,000 and more. And recently there entered this country the most amazing specimen of all – the so-called Emerald Sphere, a work of supreme art hitherto known only from a sketch by the great man himself. This treasure arrived by registered post from Paris and it was addressed to this woman of whom you know, Miss Maria Freudenstein.'

'Nice little present. Might I ask how you learned of it, Doctor?'

'I am, as your Chief has told you, an adviser to H.M. Customs and Excise in matters concerning antique jewellery and similar works of art. The declared value of the package was £100,000. This was unusual. There are methods of opening such packages clandestinely. The package was opened – under a Home Office Warrant, of course – and I was called in to examine the contents and give a valuation. I immediately recognized the Emerald Sphere from the account and sketch of it given in Mr Kenneth Snowman's definitive work on Fabergé. I said that the declared price might well be on the low side. But what I found of particular interest was the accompanying document which gave, in Russian and French, the provenance of this priceless object.' Dr Fanshawe gestured towards a photostat of what appeared to be a brief family tree that lay on the desk in front of M. 'That is a copy I had made. Briefly, it states that the Sphere was commissioned by Miss Freudenstein's grandfather directly from Fabergé in 1917 – no doubt as a means of turning some of his roubles into something portable and of great value. On his death in 1918 it passed to his brother and thence, in 1950, to Miss Freudenstein's mother. She, it appears, left Russia as a child and lived in White Russian émigré circles in Paris. She never married, but gave birth to this girl, Maria, illegitimately. It seems that she died last year and that some friend or executor, the paper is not signed, has now forwarded the Sphere to the rightful owner, Miss Maria Freudenstein. I had no reason to question this girl, although as you can imagine my interest was most lively, until last month Sotheby's announced that they would auction the piece, described as "the property of a lady", in a week from today. On behalf of the British Museum and, er, other interested parties, I then made discreet enquiries and met the lady, who, with perfect composure, confirmed the rather unlikely story contained in the provenance. It was then that I learned that she worked for the Ministry of Defence and it crossed my rather suspicious mind that it was, to say the least of it, odd that a junior clerk, engaged presumably on sensitive duties, should suddenly receive a gift to the value of £100,000 or more from abroad. I spoke to a senior official in M.I.5 with whom I have some contact through my work for H.M. Customs and I was in due course referred to this, er, department.' Dr Fanshawe spread his hands and gave Bond a brief glance, 'And that, Commander, is all I have to tell you.'

M broke in, 'Thank you, Doctor. Just one or two final questions and I won't detain you any further. You have examined this emerald ball thing and you pronounce it genuine?'

Dr Fanshawe ceased gazing at his boots. He looked up and spoke to a point somewhere above M's left shoulder. 'Certainly. So does Mr Snowman of Wartski's, the greatest Fabergé experts and dealers in the world. It is undoubtedly the missing masterpiece of which hitherto Carl Fabergé's sketch was the only record.'

'What about the provenance? What do the experts say about that?'

'It stands up adequately. The greatest Fabergé pieces were nearly always privately commissioned. Miss Freudenstein says that her grandfather was a vastly rich man before the revolution – a porcelain manufacturer. Ninety-nine per cent of all Fabergé's output has found its way abroad. There are only a few pieces left in the Kremlin – described simply as "pre-revolutionary examples of Russian jewellery". The official Soviet view has always been that they are merely capitalist baubles. Officially they despise them as they officially despise their superb collection of French Impressionists.'

'So the Soviet still retain some examples of the work of this man Fabergé. Is it possible that this emerald affair could have lain secreted somewhere in the Kremlin through all these years?'

'Certainly. The Kremlin treasure is vast. No one knows what they keep hidden. They have only recently put on display what they have wanted to put on display.'

M drew on his pipe. His eyes through the smoke were bland, scarcely interested. 'So that, in theory, there is no reason why this emerald ball should not have been unearthed from the Kremlin, furnished with a fake history to establish ownership, and transferred abroad as a reward to some friend of Russia for services rendered?'

'None at all. It would be an ingenious method of greatly rewarding the beneficiary without the danger of paying large sums into his, or her, bank account.'

'But the final monetary reward would of course depend on the amount realized by the sale of the object – the auction price for instance?'

'Exactly.'

'And what do you expect this object to fetch at Sotheby's?'

'Impossible to say. Wartski's will certainly bid very high. But of course they wouldn't be prepared to tell anyone just how high – either on their own account for stock, so to speak, or acting on behalf of a customer. Much would depend on how high they are forced up by an underbidder. Anyway, not less than £100,000 I'd say.'

'Hm.' M's mouth turned down at the corners. 'Expensive hunk of jewellery.'

Dr Fanshawe was aghast at this bare-faced revelation of M's philistinism. He actually looked M straight in the face. 'My dear sir', he expostulated, 'do you consider the stolen Goya, sold at Sotheby's for £140,000, that went to the National Gallery, just an expensive hunk, as you put it, of canvas and paint?'

M said placatingly, 'Forgive me, Dr Fanshawe. I expressed myself clumsily. I have never had the leisure to interest myself in works of art nor, on a naval officer's pay, the money to acquire any. I was just registering my dismay at the runaway prices being fetched at auction these days.'

'You are entitled to your views, sir', said Dr Fanshawe stuffily.

Bond thought it was time to rescue M. He also wanted to get Dr Fanshawe out of the room so that they could get down to the professional aspects of this odd business. He got to his feet. He said to M, 'Well, sir, I don't think there is anything else I need to know. No doubt this will turn out to be perfectly straight forward (like hell it would!) and just a matter of one of your staff turning out to be a very lucky woman. But it's very kind of Dr Fanshawe to have gone to so much trouble.' He turned to Dr Fanshawe. 'Would you care to have a staff car to take you wherever you're going?'

'No thank you, thank you very much. It will be pleasant to walk across the park.'

Hands were shaken, goodbyes said and Bond showed the doctor out. Bond came back into the room. M had

taken a bulky file, stamped with the top secret red star, out of a drawer and was already immersed in it. Bond took his seat again and waited. The room was silent save for the riffling of paper. This also stopped as M extracted a foolscap sheet of blue cardboard used for confidential staff records and carefully read through the forest of close type on both sides.

Finally he slipped it back in the file and looked up. 'Yes', he said and the blue eyes were bright with interest. 'It fits all right. The girl was born in Paris in 1935. Mother very active in the Resistance during the war. Helped run the Tulip Escape Route and got away with it. After the war, the girl went to the Sorbonne and then got a job in the Embassy, in the Naval Attaché's office, as an interpreter. You know the rest. She was compromised – some unattractive sexual business – by some of her mother's old Resistance friends who by then were working for the N.K.V.D., and from then on she has been working under Control. She applied, no doubt on instruction, for British citizenship. Her clearance from the Embassy and her mother's Resistance record helped her to get that by 1959, and she was then recommended to us by the F.O. But it was there that she made her big mistake. She asked for a year's leave before coming to us and was next reported by the Hutchinson network in the Leningrad espionage school. There she presumably received the usual training and we had to decide what to do about her. Section 100 thought up the Purple Cipher operation and you know the rest. She's been working for three years inside headquarters for the K.G.B. and now she's getting her reward – this emerald ball thing worth £100,000. And that's interesting on two counts. First it means that the K.G.B. is totally hooked on the Purple Cipher or they wouldn't be making this fantastic payment. That's good news. It means that we can hot up the material we're passing over – put across some Grade 3 deception material and perhaps even move up to Grade 2. Secondly, it explains something we've never been able to understand – that this girl hasn't hitherto received a single payment for her services. We were worried by that. She had an account at Glyn, Mills that only registered her monthly pay cheque of around £50. And she's consistently lived within it. Now she's getting her pay-off in one large lump sum via this bauble we've been learning about. All very satisfactory.'

M reached for the ashtray made out of a twelve-inch shell base and rapped out his pipe with the air of a man who has done a good afternoon's work.

Bond shifted in his chair. He badly needed a cigarette, but he wouldn't have dreamed of lighting one. He wanted one to help him focus his thoughts. He felt there were some ragged edges to this problem – one particularly. He said, mildly, 'Have we ever caught up with her local Control, sir? How does she get her instructions?'

'Doesn't need to', said M impatiently, busying himself with his pipe. 'Once she'd got hold of the Purple Cipher all she needed to do was hold down her job. Damn it man, she's pouring the stuff into their lap six times a day. What sort of instructions would they need to give her? I doubt if the K.G.B. men in London even know of her existence – perhaps the Resident Director does, but as you know we don't even know who he is. Give my eyes to find out.'

Bond suddenly had a flash of intuition. It was as if a camera had started grinding in his skull, grinding out a length of clear film. He said quietly, 'It might be that this business at Sotheby's could show him to us – show us who he is'.

'What the devil are you talking about, 007? Explain yourself.'

'Well sir', Bond's voice was calm with certainty, 'You remember what this

Dr Fanshawe said about an underbidder – someone to make these Wartski merchants go to their very top price. If the Russians don't seem to know or care very much about Fabergé, as Dr Fanshawe says, they may have no very clear idea what this thing's really worth. The K.G.B. wouldn't be likely to know about such things anyway. They may imagine it's only worth its break-up value – say ten or twenty thousand pounds for the emerald. That sort of sum would make more sense than the small fortune the girl's going to get if Dr Fanshawe's right. Well, if the Resident Director is the only man who knows about this girl, he will be the only man who knows she's been paid. So he'll be the underbidder. He'll be sent to Sotheby's and told to push the sale through the roof. I'm certain of it. So we'll be able to identify him and we'll have enough on him to have him sent home. He just won't know what's hit him. Nor will the K.G.B. If I can go to the sale and bowl him out and we've got the place covered with cameras, and the auction records, we can get the F.O. to declare him persona non grata inside a week. And Resident Directors don't grow on trees. It may be months before the K.G.B. can appoint a replacement.'

M said, thoughtfully, 'Perhaps you've got something there.' He swivelled his chair round and gazed out of the big window towards the jagged skyline of London. Finally he said, over his shoulder, 'All right, 007. Go and see the Chief of Staff and set the machinery up. I'll square things with Five. It's their territory, but it's our bird. There won't be any trouble. But don't go and get carried away and bid for this bit of rubbish yourself. I haven't got the money to spare.'

Bond said, 'No sir.' He got to his feet and went quickly out of the room. He thought he had been very clever and he wanted to see if he had. He didn't want M to change his mind.

Wartski has a modest, ultra modern frontage at 138 Regent Street. The window, with a restrained show of modern and antique jewellery, gave no hint that these were the greatest Fabergé-dealers in the world. The interior – grey carpet, walls panelled in sycamore, a few unpretentious vitrines – held none of the excitement of Cartier's, Boucheron or Van Cleef, but the group of framed Royal Warrants from Queen Mary, the Queen Mother, the Queen, King Paul of Greece and the unlikely King Frederick IX of Denmark, suggested that this was no ordinary jeweller.

James Bond asked for Mr Kenneth Snowman. A good looking, very well-dressed man of about 40 rose from a group of men sitting with their heads together at the back of the room and came forward.

Bond said quietly, 'I'm from the C.I.D. Can we have a talk? Perhaps you'd like to check my credentials first. My name's James Bond. But you'll have to go direct to Sir Ronald Vallance or his P.A. I'm not directly on the strength at Scotland Yard. Sort of liaison job.'

The intelligent, observant eyes didn't appear even to look him over. The man smiled. 'Come on downstairs. Just having a talk with some American friends – sort of correspondents really. From "Old Russia" on Fifth Avenue.'

'I know the place', said Bond. 'Full of rich-looking icons and so on. Not far from the Pierre.'

'That's right.' Mr Snowman seemed even more reassured. He led the way down a narrow, thickly carpeted stairway into a large and glittering showroom which was obviously the real treasure house of the shop. Gold and diamonds and cut stones winked from lit cases round the walls.

'Have a seat. Cigarette?'

Bond took one of his own. 'It's about this Fabergé piece that's coming up at Sotheby's tomorrow – this Emerald Sphere.'

'Ah, yes'. Mr Snowman's clear brow furrowed anxiously. 'No trouble about it I hope?'

'Not from your point of view. But we're very interested in the actual sale. We know about the owner, Miss Freudenstein. We think there may be an attempt to raise the bidding artificially. We're interested in the underbidder – assuming, that is, that your firm will be leading the field, so to speak.'

'Well, er, yes', said Mr Snowman with rather careful candour. 'We're certainly going to go after it. But it'll sell for a huge price. Between you and me, we believe the V and A are going to bid, and probably the Metropolitan. But is it some crook you're after? If so you needn't worry. This is out of their class.'

Bond said, 'No. We're not looking for a crook.' He wondered how far to go with this man. Because people are very careful with the secrets of their own business doesn't mean that they'll be careful with the secrets of yours. Bond picked up a wood and ivory plaque that lay on the table. It said:

'It is naught, it is naught, saith the buyer. But when he is gone his way, he boasteth.
PROVERBS XX,14'

Bond was amused. He said so. 'You can read the whole history of the bazaar, of the dealer and the customer, behind that quotation', he said. He looked Mr Snowman straight in the eyes. 'I need that sort of nose, that sort of intuition in this case. Will you give me a hand?'

'Certainly. If you'll tell me how I can help.' He waved a hand. 'If it's secrets you're worried about, please don't worry. Jewellers are used to them. Scotland Yard will probably give my firm a clean bill in that respect. Heaven knows we've had enough to do with them over the years.'

'And if I told you that I'm from the Ministry of Defence?'

'Same thing', said Mr Snowman. 'You can naturally rely absolutely on my discretion!'

Bond made up his mind. 'All right. Well, all this comes under the Official Secrets Act, of course. We suspect that the underbidder, presumably to you, will be a Soviet Agent. My job is to establish his identity. Can't tell you any more, I'm afraid. And you don't actually need to know any more. All I want is to go with you to Sotheby's tomorrow night and for you to help me spot the man. No medals, I'm afraid, but we'd be extremely grateful.'

Mr Kenneth Snowman's eyes glinted with enthusiasm. 'Of course. Delighted to help in any way. But,' he looked doubtful, 'you know it's not necessarily going to be all that easy. Peter Wilson, the head of Sotheby's, who'll be taking the sale, would be the only person who could tell us for sure – that is, if the bidder wants to stay secret. There are dozens of ways of bidding without making any movement at all. But if the bidder fixes his method, his code so to speak, with Peter Wilson before the sale, Peter wouldn't think of letting anyone in on the code. It would give the bidder's game away to reveal his limit. And that's a close secret, as you can imagine, in the rooms. And a thousand times not if you come with me. I shall probably be setting the pace. I already know how far I'm going to go – for a client by the way – but it would make my job vastly easier if I could tell how far the underbidder's going to go. As it is, what you've told me has been a great help. I shall warn my man to put his sights even higher. If this chap of yours has got a strong nerve, he may push me very hard indeed. And there will be others in the field of course. It sounds as if this is going to be quite a night. They're putting it on television and asking all the millionaires and dukes and duchesses for the sort of gala performance Sotheby's do rather well. Wonderful publicity of course. By jove, if they knew there was cloak-and-dagger stuff mixed up with the sale, there'd be a riot! Now then, is there anything else to go into? Just spot this man and that's all?'

'That's all. How much do you think this thing will go for?'

Mr Snowman tapped his teeth with a gold pencil. 'Well now, you see that's where I have to keep quiet. I know how high I'm going to go, but that's my client's secret.' He paused and looked thoughtful, 'Let's say that if it goes for less than £100,000 we'll be surprised.'

'I see', said Bond. 'Now then, how do I get into the sale?'

Mr Snowman produced an elegant alligator-skin notecase and extracted two engraved bits of pasteboard. He handed one over. 'That's my wife's. I'll get her one somewhere else in the rooms. B.5 – well placed in the centre front. I'm B.6.'

Bond took the ticket. It said:

Sotheby & Co
Sale of
A Casket of Magnificent Jewels
and
A Unique Object of Vertu by Carl Fabergé
The Property of a Lady
Admit one to the Main Sale Room
Tuesday, 20 June, at 9.30pm precisely
Entrance in St George Street

'It's not the old Georgian entrance in Bond Street', commented Mr Snowman. 'They have an awning and red carpet out from their back door now that Bond Street's one-way. Now,' he got up from his chair, 'would you care to see some Fabergé? We've got some pieces here my father bought from the Kremlin around 1927. It'll give you some idea of what all the fuss is about, though of course the Emerald Sphere's incomparably finer than anything I can show you by Fabergé, apart from the Imperial Easter Eggs.'

Later, dazzled by the diamonds, the multi-coloured gold, the silken sheen of translucent enamels, James Bond walked up and out of the Aladdin's Cave under Regent Street and went off to spend the rest of the day in drab offices around Whitehall planning drearily minute arrangements for the identification and photographing of a man in a crowded room who did not yet possess a face or an identity but who was certainly the top Soviet spy in London.

Through the next day, Bond's excitement mounted. He found an excuse to go into the Communications Section and wander into the little room where Miss Maria Freudenstein and two assistants were working the cipher machines that handled the Purple Cipher dispatches. He picked up the *en clair* file – he had freedom of access to most material at headquarters – and ran his eye down the carefully edited paragraphs that, in half an hour or so, would be spiked, unread, by some junior C.I.A. clerk in Washington and, in Moscow, be handed, with reverence, to a top-ranking officer of the K.G.B. He joked with the two junior girls, but Maria Freudenstein only looked up from her machine to give him a polite smile and Bond's skin crawled minutely at this proximity to treachery and at the black and deadly secret locked up beneath the frilly white blouse. She was an unattractive girl with a pale, rather pimply skin, black hair and a vaguely unwashed appearance. Such a girl would be unloved, make few friends, have chips on her shoulder – more particularly in view of her illegitimacy – and a grouse against society. Perhaps her only pleasure in life was the triumphant secret she harboured in that flattish bosom – the knowledge that she was cleverer than all those around her, that she was, every day, hitting back against the world – the world that despised, or just ignored her, because of her plainness – with all her might. One day they'd be sorry! It was a common neurotic pattern – the revenge of the ugly duckling on society.

Bond wandered off down the corridor to his own office. By tonight that girl would have made a fortune, been paid her thirty pieces of silver a thousandfold. Perhaps the money would change her character, bring her happiness. She would be able to afford the best beauty specialists, the best clothes, a pretty flat. But M had said he was now going to hot up the Purple Cipher Operation, trying a more dangerous level of deception. This would be dicey work. One false step, one incautious lie, an ascertainable falsehood in a message, and the K.G.B. would smell a rat. One more, and they would know that they were being hoaxed and probably had been ignominiously hoaxed for three years. Such a shameful revelation would bring quick revenge. It would be assumed that Maria Freudenstein had been acting as a double agent, working for the British as well as the Russians. She would inevitably and quickly be liquidated – perhaps with the cyanide pistol Bond had been reading about only the day before.

James Bond, looking out of the window across the trees in Regent's Park, shrugged. Thank God it was none of his business. The girl's fate wasn't in his hands. She was caught in the grimy machine of espionage and she would be lucky if she lived to spend a tenth of the fortune she was going to gain in a few hours in the auction rooms.

There was a line of cars and taxis blocking St George Street behind Sotheby's. Bond paid off his taxi and joined the crowd filtering under the awning and up the steps. He was handed a catalogue by the uniformed Commissionaire who inspected his ticket, and went up the broad stairs with the fashionable, excited crowd and along a gallery and into the main auction room that was already thronged. He found his seat next to Mr Snowman, who was writing figures on a pad on his knee, and looked round him.

The lofty room was perhaps as large as a tennis court. It had the look and the smell of age and the two large chandeliers, to fit in with the period, blazed warmly in contrast to the strip lighting along the vaulted ceiling whose glass roof was partly obscured by a blind, still half-drawn against the sun that would have been blazing down on the afternoon's sale. Miscellaneous pictures and tapestries hung on the olive green walls and batteries of television and other cameras (amongst them the M.I.5 cameraman with a press pass from *The Sunday Times*) were clustered with their handlers on a platform built out from the middle of a giant tapestried hunting scene. There were perhaps a hundred dealers and spectators sitting attentively on small gilt chairs. All eyes were focused on the slim, good looking auctioneer talking quietly from the raised wooden pulpit. He was dressed in an immaculate dinner jacket with a red carnation in the buttonhole. He spoke unemphatically and without gestures.

'Fifteen thousand pounds. And sixteen', a pause. A glance at someone in the front row. 'Against you, sir.' The flick of a catalogue being raised. 'Seventeen thousand pounds I am bid. Eighteen. Nineteen. I am bid twenty thousand pounds.' And so the quiet voice went, calmly, unhurriedly on while down among the audience the equally impassive bidders signalled their responses to the litany.

Sotheby & Co

Sale of

A Casket of Magnificent Jewels

and

A Unique Object of Vertu by Carl Fabergé

The Property of a Lady

to the Main Sale Room

at 9.30 pm pre

'What is he selling?' asked Bond opening his catalogue.

'Lot 40', said Mr Snowman. 'That diamond rivière the porter's holding on the black velvet tray. It'll probably go for about twenty-five. An Italian is bidding against a couple of Frenchmen. Otherwise they'd have got it for twenty. I only went to fifteen. Liked to have got it. Wonderful stones. But there it is.'

Sure enough, the price stuck at twenty-five thousand and the hammer, held by its head and not by its handle, came down with soft authority, 'Yours, sir', said Mr Peter Wilson and a sales clerk hurried down the aisle to confirm the identity of the bidder.

'I'm disappointed', said Bond.

Mr Snowman looked up from his catalogue, 'Why is that?'

'I've never been to an auction before and I always thought the auctioneer banged his gavel three times and said going, going, gone, so as to give the bidders a last chance.'

Mr Snowman laughed. 'You might still find that operating in the Shires or in Ireland, but it hasn't been the fashion at London sale rooms since I've been attending them.'

'Pity. It adds to the drama.'

'You'll get plenty of that in a minute. This is the last lot before the curtain goes up.'

One of the porters had reverently uncoiled a glittering mass of rubies and diamonds on his black velvet tray. Bond looked at the catalogue. It said 'Lot 41' which the luscious prose described as:

> A pair of fine and important ruby and diamond bracelets
>
> THE FRONT OF EACH IN THE FORM OF AN ELLIPTICAL CLUSTER COMPOSED OF ONE LARGER AND TWO SMALLER RUBIES WITHIN A BORDER OF CUSHION-SHAPED DIAMONDS, THE SIDES AND BACK FORMED OF SIMPLER CLUSTERS ALTERNATING WITH DIAMOND OPENWORK SCROLL MOTIFS SPRINGING FROM SINGLE-STONE RUBY CENTRES MILLEGRIFFE-SET IN GOLD, RUNNING BETWEEN CHAINS OF RUBIES AND DIAMONDS LINKED ALTERNATELY, THE CLASP ALSO IN THE FORM OF AN ELLIPTICAL CLUSTER.
>
> According to family tradition, this lot was formerly the property of Mrs Fitzherbert (1756–1837) whose marriage to The Prince of Wales afterwards Geo.IV was definitely established when in 1905 a sealed packet deposited at Coutts Bank in 1833 and opened by Royal permission disclosed the marriage certificate and other conclusive proofs. These bracelets were probably given by Mrs Fitzherbert to her niece, who was described by the Duke of Orleans as 'the prettiest girl in England'.

While the bidding progressed, Bond slipped out of his seat and went down the aisle to the back of the room where the overflow audience spread out into the New Gallery and the Entrance Hall to watch the sale on closed circuit television. He casually inspected the crowd, seeking any face he could recognize from the 200 members of the Soviet embassy staff whose photographs, clandestinely obtained, he had been studying during the past days. But amidst an audience that defied classification – a mixture of dealers, amateur collectors and what could be broadly classified as rich pleasure-seekers – was not a feature, let alone a face, that he could recognize except from the gossip columns. One or two sallow faces might have been Russian, but equally they might have belonged to half a dozen European races. There was a scattering of dark glasses, but dark glasses are no longer a disguise. Bond went back to his seat. Presumably the man would have to divulge himself when the bidding began.

'Fourteen thousand I am bid. And fifteen. Fifteen thousand.' The hammer came down. 'Yours, sir.'

There was a hum of excitement and a fluttering of catalogues. Mr Snowman wiped his forehead with a white silk handkerchief. He turned to Bond. 'Now I'm afraid you are more or less on your own. I've got to pay attention to the bidding and anyway for some unknown reason it's considered bad form to look over one's shoulder to see who's bidding against you – if you're in the trade that's to say – so I'll only be able to spot him if he's somewhere up front here, and I'm afraid that's unlikely. Pretty well all dealers, but you can stare around as much as you like. What you've got to do is watch Peter Wilson's eyes and then try and see who he's looking at, or who's looking at him. If you can spot the man, which may be quite difficult, note any movement he makes, even the very smallest. Whatever the man does – scratching his head, pulling at the lobe of his ear or whatever, will be the code he's arranged with Peter Wilson. I'm afraid he won't do anything obvious like raising his catalogue. Do you get me? And don't forget that he may make absolutely no movement at all until right at the end when he's pushed me as far as he thinks I'll go, then he'll want to sign off. Mark you,' Mr Snowman smiled, 'when we get to the last lap I'll put plenty of heat on him and try and make him show his hand. That's assuming of course that we are the only two bidders left in.' He looked enigmatic, 'And I think you can take it that we shall be.'

From the man's certainty, James Bond felt pretty sure that Mr Snowman had been given instructions to get the Emerald Sphere at any cost.

A sudden hush fell as a tall pedestal draped in black velvet was brought in with ceremony and positioned in front of the auctioneer's rostrum. Then a handsome oval case of what looked like white velvet was placed on top of the pedestal and, with reverence, an elderly porter in grey uniform with wine red sleeves, collar and black belt, unlocked it and lifted out Lot 42, placed it on the black velvet and removed the case. The cricket ball of polished emerald on its exquisite base glowed with a supernatural green fire and the jewels on its surface and on the opalescent meridian winked their various colours. There was a gasp of admiration from the audience and even the clerks and experts behind the rostrum and sitting at the tall counting-house desk beside the auctioneer, accustomed to the Crown jewels of Europe parading before their eyes, leaned forward to get a better look.

James Bond turned to his catalogue. There it was, in heavy type and in prose as stickily luscious as a butterscotch sundae:

The Terrestrial Globe

DESIGNED IN 1917 BY CARL FABERGÉ FOR A RUSSIAN GENTLEMAN AND NOW THE PROPERTY OF HIS GRANDDAUGHTER

42   A very important Fabergé terrestrial globe. A sphere carved from an extraordinarily large piece of Siberian emerald matrix weighing approximately one thousand three hundred carats and of a superb colour and vivid translucence, represents a terrestrial globe supported upon an elaborate *rocaille* scroll mount finely chased in *quatre-couleur* gold and set with a profusion of rose-diamonds and small emeralds of intense colour, to form a table-clock.
Around this mount six gold *putti* disport themselves among cloudforms which are naturalistically rendered in carved rock-crystal finished matt and veined with fine lines of tiny rose-diamonds.
The globe itself, the surface of which is meticulously engraved with a map of the world with the principal cities indicated by brilliant diamonds embedded within gold collets, rotates mechanically on an axis controlled by a small clock-movement, by G Moser, signed, which is concealed in the base, and is girdled by a fixed gold belt enamelled opalescent oyster along a reserved path in *champlevé* technique over a moiré *guillochage* with painted Roman numerals in pale sepia enamel serving as the dial of the clock, and a single triangular pigeon-blood Burma ruby of about five carats set into the surface of the orb, pointing the hour. Height: 7½in. *Workmaster, Henrik Wigström.* In the original double-opening white velvet, satin lined, oviform case with the gold key fitted in the base.
The theme of this magnificent sphere is one that had inspired Fabergé some fifteen years earlier, as evidenced in the miniature terrestrial globe which forms part of the Royal Collection at Sandringham. (*See* plate 280 in *The Art of Carl Fabergé,* by A. Kenneth Snowman.)

After a brief and searching glance around the room, Mr Wilson banged his hammer softly. 'Lot 42 – an object of vertu by Carl Fabergé.' A pause. 'Twenty thousand pounds I am bid.'

Mr Snowman whispered to Bond. 'That means he's probably got a bid of at least fifty. This is simply to get things moving.'

Catalogues fluttered. 'And thirty, forty, fifty thousand pounds I am bid. And sixty, seventy and eighty thousand pounds. And ninety.' A pause and then: 'One hundred thousand pounds I am bid.'

There was a rattle of applause around the room. The cameras had swivelled to a youngish man, one of three on a raised platform to the left of the auctioneer who were speaking softly into telephones. Mr Snowman commented, 'That's one of Sotheby's young men. He'll be on an open line to America. I should think that's the Metropolitan bidding, but it might be anybody. Now it's time for me to get to work.' Mr Snowman flicked up his rolled catalogue.

'And ten', said the auctioneer. The man spoke into his telephone and nodded. 'And twenty.'

Again a flick from Mr Snowman.

'And thirty.'

The man on the telephone seemed to be speaking rather more words than before into his mouthpiece – perhaps giving his estimate of how much further the price was likely to go. He gave a slight shake of his head in the direction of the auctioneer and Peter Wilson looked away from him and round the room.

'One hundred and thirty thousand pounds I am bid', he repeated quietly.

Mr Snowman said, softly, to Bond, 'Now you'd better watch out. America seems to have signed off. It's time for your man to start pushing me.'

James Bond slid out of his place and went and stood amongst a group of reporters in a corner to the left of the rostrum. Peter Wilson's eyes were directed towards the far right hand corner of the room. Bond could detect no movement, but the auctioneer announced 'And forty thousand pounds.' He looked down at Mr Snowman. After a long pause Mr Snowman raised five fingers. Bond guessed that this was part of his process of putting the heat on. He was showing reluctance, hinting that he was near the end of his tether.

'One hundred and forty-five thousand.' Again the piercing glance towards the back of the room. Again no movement. But again some signal had been exchanged. 'One hundred and fifty thousand pounds.'

There was a buzz of comment and some desultory clapping. This time Mr Snowman's reaction was even slower and the auctioneer twice repeated the last bid. Finally he looked directly at Mr Snowman, 'Against you, sir.' At last Mr Snowman raised five fingers.

'One hundred and fifty-five thousand pounds.'

James Bond was beginning to sweat. He had got absolutely nowhere and the bidding must surely be coming to an end. The auctioneer repeated the bid.

And now there was the tiniest movement. At the back of the room, a chunky-looking man in a dark suit reached up and unobtrusively took off his dark glasses. It was a smooth, nondescript face – the sort of face that might belong to a bank manager, a member of Lloyd's, or a doctor. This must have been the prearranged code with the auctioneer. So long as the man wore his dark glasses he would raise in tens of thousands. When he took them off, he had quit.

Bond shot a quick glance towards the bank of cameramen. Yes, the M.I.5 photographer was on his toes. He had also seen the movement. He lifted his camera deliberately and there was the quick glare of a flash. Bond got back to his seat and whispered to Snowman. 'Got him. Be in touch with you tomorrow. Thanks a lot.' Mr Snowman only nodded. His eyes remained glued on the auctioneer.

Bond slipped out of his place and walked swiftly down the aisle as the auctioneer said for the third time, 'One hundred and fifty-five thousand pounds I am bid', and then softly brought down his hammer, 'Yours, sir.'

Bond got to the back of the room before the audience had risen, applauding, to its feet. His quarry was hemmed in amongst the gilt chairs. He had now put on his dark glasses again and Bond put on a pair of his own. He contrived to slip into the crowd and get behind the man as the chattering crowd streamed down the stairs. The hair grew low down on the back of the man's rather squat neck and the lobes of his ears were pinched in close to his head. He had a slight hump, perhaps only a bone deformation, high up on his back. Bond suddenly remembered. This was Piotr Malinowski, with the official title on the Embassy staff of 'Agricultural Attaché'. So!

Outside, the man began walking swiftly towards Conduit Street. James Bond got unhurriedly into a taxi with its engine running and its flag down. He said to the driver, 'That's him. Take it easy.'

'Yes, sir', said the M.I.5 driver, pulling away from the curb.

The man picked up a taxi in Bond Street. The tail in the mixed evening traffic was easy. Bond's satisfaction mounted as the Russian's taxi turned up north of the Park and along Bayswater. It was just a question whether he would turn down the private entrance into Kensington Palace Gardens, where the first mansion on the left is the massive building of the Soviet Embassy. If he did, that would clinch matters. The two patrolling policemen, the usual Embassy guards, had been specially picked that night. It was their job just to confirm that the occupant of the leading taxi actually entered the Soviet Embassy.

Then, with the Secret Service evidence and the evidence of Bond and the M.I.5 cameraman, there would be enough for the Foreign Office to declare Comrade Piotr Malinowski persona non grata on the grounds of espionage activity and send him packing. In the grim chess game that is secret service work, the Russians would have lost a queen. It would have been a very satisfactory visit to the auction rooms.

The leading taxi *did* turn in through the big iron gates.

Bond smiled with grim satisfaction. He leant forward, 'Thanks, driver. Headquarters please.'

I
Art
in
Time

FOR KING AND COUNTRY *by Jeremy Black*

The year in which Sotheby's was founded, 1744, was a year of crisis in Britain, as the diary entry of Dudley Ryder, the Attorney General, makes clear:

'Certain news that the French intend a descent, and the Brest squadron is reported to be now in the Downs, and they intended to come up the river…. We are now very bare of soldiers.'

The French invasion attempt was thwarted by a savage storm and French commander, Marshall Saxe, informed Prince Charles Edward Stuart ('Bonnie Prince Charlie') that the expedition had to be abandoned. Nevertheless, in 1745 Charles evaded British warships, landed in Scotland and brought his Highland army as far south as Derby. Jacobite hopes, long expressed surreptitiously, seemed near to fulfilment. However, the Highlanders' nerves cracked, forcing Charles to turn back. George II seized the opportunity, and his second son, William, Duke of Cumberland, crushed the rebellion at Culloden.

What was the country that they secured like? Eighteenth-century Britain presented different aspects of a sophisticated society. The prints of Hogarth depict the vigorous, if not seamy, side of life in London, a thriving metropolis where organized crime, prostitution and squalor were ever present. Serious disease played a major role in what was a hostile environment.

Yet this was also the age of ease and elegance, of city bustle and balance, a land of stately homes and urban squares, Castle Howard, Blenheim Palace, the City of Bath and the New Town of Edinburgh. Brick buildings with large windows were built in a regular 'classical' style on new boulevards, squares and circles. Parks and theatres, assembly rooms, racecourses and other leisure facilities were opened in many towns. In London, the fashionable set came to the pleasure gardens of Vauxhall, Marylebone and Ranelagh, to see and be seen, inspire and spot fashions, find spouses or whores. Horace Walpole noted, 'The company is universal: from his Grace of Grafton down to children out of the Foundling Hospital.'

The stately homes of town and country were a testimony to personal, family and national wealth and confidence. Sir John Vanbrugh, the prime exponent of the baroque style in England, displayed at Blenheim Palace and Seaton Delaval a degree of spatial enterprise similar to the architects of princely palaces on the Continent. Robert Adam, inspired by classical themes, rebuilt or redesigned many stately homes, including Harewood House, Kedleston Hall and Kenwood House. Landscape gardening, inescapably linked to wealthy landed patronage, flourished and was influential abroad. William Kent developed and decorated parks to provide an appropriate setting for buildings. Lancelot 'Capability' Brown rejected the rigid formality associated with continental models, contriving a setting that appeared natural but was, nevertheless, carefully designed for

The Beheading of the Rebel Lords on Great Tower Hill
1746, AQUATINT.
Museum of London
After his victory at Culloden, the Duke of Cumberland ordered the deaths of the rebel Highlanders. (BELOW)

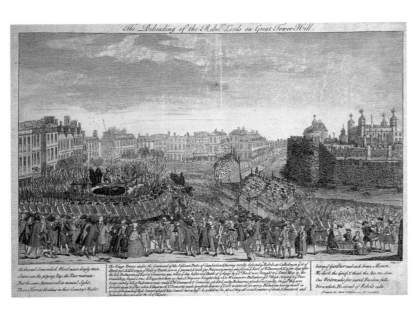

effect. Brown's ideas were developed further by Humphry Repton in accordance with the concept of the 'picturesque', which stressed the individual character of each landscape and the need to retain it, while making improvements to remove what were judged blemishes and obstructions and to open up vistas. Landscape gardening and decoration was of direct interest to some members of the nobility, most notably Richard, 1st Viscount Cobham, at Stowe, and his protégé William Pitt the Elder, who helped lay out the grounds of his friends' seats, and erected a garden pyramid and a temple dedicated to Pan at his house in South Lodge, Enfield.

In architecture, the British gentry were greatly influenced by what they had seen on the Grand Tour. It became fashionable for the young male members of the social élite to see Paris and the splendours of Italian civilization. The classical style of Andrea Palladio's villas were studied first-hand by British patrons and architects: Lord Burlington's villa at Chiswick and Colen Campbell's remodelling of Stourhead are prime examples. The gardens at Stourhead were laid out in 1741–80 by Henry Hoare, the owner of the house, and were planned as a neo-classical scene, an English realization of the landscape of Roman

Italy as seen in the paintings of Claude Lorrain.

In the 1730s and 1740s artistic life was heavily influenced by French artists, who introduced the rococo style to England. The wealthy commissioned and purchased works of great elegance for their houses, making England very much part of the rococo movement. Andien de Clermont worked in England producing decorative paintwork at Kew, Strawberry Hill and Wilton. The portrait painter Jean Van Loo arrived in London in 1737 and spent a lucrative five years taking commissions from resentful English rivals. The draughtsman Hubert-François Gravelot worked in England from 1732 until the 1745 uprising led him to return to France. As a teacher at the St Martin's Lane Academy, he trained a whole generation of British artists including Gainsborough.

Britain was open to continental cultural developments. Foreign porcelain, such as that from Meissen, and furniture, particularly from France, were purchased. The Venetian artist Canaletto came to London in the 1740s and produced splendid scenes of the city for British patrons, who were also keen collectors of paintings from the renaissance and baroque periods, acquired while touring in Italy. Throughout the eighteenth century London, along with Paris, was the largest

View of the interior of the library at Kenwood House, Highgate, designed by Robert Adam. (ABOVE LEFT)

View of the Pantheon from across the lake at Stourhead. (ABOVE)

and most prosperous musical centre in Europe. The public concerts and clubs, and its tradition of music in private circles, attracted Georg Friedrich Handel to London, where in 1750 he conducted a concert of the *Messiah* at the Foundling Hospital; the young Mozart arrived with his father and sister in 1764, and Haydn visited in 1791.

At the same time there was a vital domestic cultural tradition which became stronger in the second half of the century. British artists and craftsmen developed products of excellence in areas formerly dominated by foreign work: English silverware gained in importance and ceramics produced in London and Staffordshire were admired for their beauty. In painting, a modernized classical style was popularized by Sir Joshua Reynolds and taught at the Royal Academy, founded in 1768. The actor David Garrick developed a naturalistic school of acting, believed to be superior to continental acting methods.

GIOVANNI ANTONIO
CANALE, CALLED
CANALETTO
Old Horse's Guard
Parade
Private collection.
(LEFT ABOVE)

FRANCIS HAYMAN
Portrait of David
Garrick and
William Windham
C.1745, OIL ON CANVAS,
84.5 x 100cm (33¼ x 39½in),
London £161,000 ($238,280).
10.XI.93 (LEFT)

BENJAMIN WEST
Death of General
Wolfe
1759, OIL ON CANVAS,
151.1 x 213.4cm (59½ x 84in)
National Gallery of Canada,
Ottawa (ABOVE)

There was a certain amount of cultural tension. James Smythe, in his comedy *The Rival Modes*, presented the Earl of Late-Airs and his son Lord Toupet, the latter of whom had 'always avoided aucune chose de Bourgeois', and declared, 'Is it possible to conceive that after one's Travels…any English Things should make a part in my dress, from the Brilliant in my shoe to the patch that embraces my upper lip?' A preference for French cooking was deplored, as was the effeminacy of French men and their customary greeting of kissing each other. The Anti-Gallican Association was founded in 1745 'to oppose the insidious arts of the French Nation' and also 'to promote British manufactures…discourage the introduction of French modes and oppose the importation of French commodities.'

A greater emphasis on British culture became more apparent, especially from the early 1760s, possibly because of the ebbing of the rococo, the less obvious influence of French culture in the age of Reynolds and Gainsborough. The Seven Years' War (1756-63) also resulted in increased national confidence and pride.

The victories of that war are a reminder that the age of refinement was also an age of the empire. Canada was conquered, Quebec falling in 1759. The French were defeated in India, Africa and the West Indies, and their plans to invade Britain were smashed by the naval victories of Lagos and Quiberon Bay (1759). When Spain entered the war on the side of France, the British took Havana and Manila in 1762. These victories owed much to Pitt's leadership in 1757–61 and it is fitting that his monument in Westminster Abbey declared that during his administration Britain was 'exalted…to an height of prosperity and glory unknown to any former age'.

Pitt's Britain was soon to be shaken by the spirit of revolution – social, political and cultural – which was brewing on the Continent and which would erupt in Paris in 1789.

STORM CLOUD OF THE NINETEENTH CENTURY

by Tim Barringer

Emerging from a period of mental illness in 1884, the critic of art and society, John Ruskin, reflected on the century in which he lived in an essay entitled 'The Storm Cloud of the Nineteenth Century'. In opposition to the liberal belief in progress dominant in the political thought of the Victorian era, Ruskin questioned the whole venture of modernity with its uneasy quest for ever more rapid change. The image of the storm cloud as an emblem of modernity derives its power from the relationship it suggests between nature and history, two forces central to the art and culture of the nineteenth century. Ruskin's storm cloud is both a physical and a symbolic phenomenon: as a scientific observer, Ruskin recognised in the 'dense manufacturing mist' a result of the industrial pollution which was one cost of the nineteenth century's frenzied drive for material progress. But Ruskin the visionary saw in it also a 'moral gloom', symbolic of the tempestuous political, social and cultural developments which had transformed the world in his century; it was a sign of the times. Possessed of a vivid sense of history informed by his study of medieval architecture, Ruskin had explored the contrasts between past and present in *The Stones of Venice* (1851-3), in which he found nineteenth-century England wanting in comparison with the earlier Italian seafaring empire; historical narratives, like the storm cloud, were both real and allegorical.

Ruskin's essay may be seen as the nineteenth century's lament for the passing of the rural world, which the new forces of industrialization and urbanization had overtaken. But Ruskin's writing, like his century, encapsulates the modern as well as the traditional; in his expressive style and vivid imagery, and its linkage of psychological crisis with world history, we find a blurring of interior and exterior worlds typical of much of the art of the nineteenth century. This interpreta-tion of the art of a profoundly complex century explores the themes raised by Ruskin; nature and history, historicism and modernity.

The Western world began the nineteenth century in a turmoil which engulfed the artistic and cultural as well as the political. Three historical developments which affected the century's course had already occurred before 1800: the American Revolution of 1776, the French Revolution which began in 1789, and the Industrial Revolu-tion which in Britain had begun by the 1780s. Each of these reflected a triumph of the bour-geoisie, the middle class which was to provide the dominant social and political force in nineteenth-century Europe and America. While the Ameri-can Revolution acted out the Enlightenment principles of individual liberty and the language of rights, the French Revolution put these dra-matically into action by ending the traditional order in Europe through its declaration of 1789: 'men are born and live free and equal under the laws'. Not for a long time was a revolution to have such an impact on the people as this one.

The most vivid of all visual responses to the spirit of revolution is Eugène Delacroix's paint-ing, *The 28th July: Liberty Leading the People*, which recalled the 'three glorious days' of popular uprising in 1830. The foreground strewn with dead bodies and the carefully differentiated types of each class among the revolutionaries – prole-tarian, bourgeois, street child – document the specifics of the events. Yet, the painting's impact depends upon the central figure, occupying that ambiguous area between the literal and symbolic so central to nineteenth-century art; a working-class woman brandishing the tricolour on the barricades is simultaneously a classical nude personifying liberty and revolution itself.

While there can be no doubt of the epochal significance of the events which began in 1789, by the opening of the nineteenth century, France

was governed by a new regime led by a military hero, Napoleon Bonaparte. In 1800 Bonaparte was portrayed as First Consul by Jacques-Louis David, who had built a reputation as the leading history painter both under the old regime and during the revolution. *Napoleon Crossing the Saint-Bernard* strikes a heroic note, picturing an idealized figure of Bonaparte with his armies crossing the Alps. As with Ruskin's portentous cloud, nature and history – the epic history which was being forged in the present day – are here dramatically juxtaposed, the stormy landscape behind commenting upon the pictorial narrative. The Consul appears on a rearing charger, his hand raised in a gesture of leadership drawn from classical equestrian portraiture; inscribed on the rocks beneath him are the names of two great heroes of the past, Hannibal and Charlemagne, who followed the same mountain route to victory in Italian campaigns. Although David came to doubt the legitimacy of the Napoleonic regime, his portrait constitutes an emblem of a new and heroic concept of masculine individuality. Different from the measured Enlightenment ideal of the individual within civil society, the Romantic idea of the individual incorporated elements of the irrational, with a new emphasis on individual subjectivity and creativity. The biographies of powerful and charismatic individuals, such as Cromwell and Frederick the Great, were studied

with enthusiasm, while exemplars of the Romantic artist include Beethoven, Blake, Byron, Keats and Géricault. Each was unconventional in his style of life, turbulent in his relations with patrons; most were derided as madmen before their genius was belatedly, or posthumously, recognized.

The German landscape painter Caspar David Friedrich, a reticent and pious man unmoved by the Bohemian and avant-garde tendencies of younger Romantic artists, produced images which combine the sense of the individual's spiritual quest – the new subjectivity of the nineteenth century – with a heightened feeling for the religious significance of nature. Friedrich's *The Wanderer above the Mists* operates at the limits of naturalistic representation, offering both a reported and a transcendental truth. The foreground is clearly based on careful studies of rock formations and mountain mists, but it is in the central figure of the lone male traveller, his head turned away from us, reverentially contemplating nature, that we can discern the uniquely Romantic note. For Friedrich, the experience of nature was not solely that of observing a compendium of natural phenomena; rather it was a form of divine revelation accessible not through organized religion but through private contemplation. Friedrich's art was closely in tune with contemporary developments in German philosophy, as expressed by the philospher Friedrich Schelling's belief that 'The

EUGÈNE DELACROIX
The 28th July: Liberty Leading the People
1831, OIL ON CANVAS, 2.59 x 3.25m (8ft 6in x 10ft 7in), Louvre, Paris. (ABOVE LEFT)

JACQUES-LOUIS DAVID
Napoleon Crossing the Saint-Bernard
1800, OIL ON CANVAS, 2.60 x 2.21m (8ft 6½in x 7ft 2½in), Palace of Versailles, Paris. (ABOVE RIGHT)

CASPAR DAVID
FRIEDRICH

The Wanderer
above the Mists
c. 1817-18, OIL ON CANVAS,
74.8 x 94.8cm (29½ x 37¼in),
Kunsthalle, Hamburg.
(ABOVE)

represent great historical and literary narratives, and derive much of their meaning from human associations of places and events. In *Snow Storm: Hannibal Crossing the Alps,* history and natural forces are again drawn together in an epic canvas. This time, however, man's activities are dwarfed by the sheer immensity of nature, with the great vortex of storm clouds and the sun reminding us of the triviality of human life. These contrasts of scale present the viewer with a shock or thrill at the power of nature, the experience of the sublime which was fundamental to early nineteenth-century aesthetics. According to one account, the painting was conceived when Turner sketched a fierce snowstorm near Farnley Hall in Wharfedale in 1810, telling his patron Walter Fawkes, 'in two years you will see this sketch again, and call it Hannibal Crossing the Alps.' The finished work is replete with political and historical significance: Turner had seen David's *Napoleon Crossing the Saint-Bernard* in 1802 and probably saw a parallel between the struggle of Rome and Carthage and that of England and Napoleon's France, which was raging as he painted. The heroic parallel between Napoleon and Hannibal is, of course, inflected differently by the English painter; the accompanying verse from Turner's fragmentary epic poem *The Fallacies of Hope* alludes to the hubris of the Carthaginian leader and the potential enervating effects of Italian conquests.

Landscapes of a different, though no less heroic, kind emerged from the New World. Though closer to English prototypes than art historians have generally acknowledged, the paintings of the early Hudson River artists, notably Thomas Cole and Frederick Edwin Church, evince an iconography of landscape whose novelty and whose epic quality was drawn from the character of the vast and largely virgin territories of the United States. Whereas European landscapes were inscribed with historical memories, Cole argued that 'American associations are not so much of the past as of the present and the future'. Indeed, the American scene with its limitless scale and resources seemed to offer a future of indefinite expansion, and presented vistas as grandiose as any in Europe. Thomas Cole's image of *The Oxbow (see* p. 38) once again memorializes nature

artist should not only paint what he sees before him, but what he sees within him.'

The development of landscape painting became a significant feature of British art from the late-eighteenth century, but it was only during the nineteenth century that landscape came to theoretical respectability through the advocacy of Ruskin in *Modern Painters* (1843-60). Ruskin began the work as a statement in defence of Joseph Mallord William Turner, whom he presented as a great observer of nature. (Today, by contrast, his works are often considered solely as exercises in light and colour.) Yet neither Ruskin nor the modernist critics fully acknowledge that the paintings Turner chose to exhibit frequently and history; the storm clouds of untamed nature to the left blend with the smoke of hearths and forges in the cultivated vista around the Connecticut River to the right, a fusion of the modern and the natural which Ruskin also noticed later in the century. But Cole was celebrating man's transformation of nature as a symbol of the spread of civilization rather than its decline, mapping out the as yet unwritten history of a new nation forged by the axe and steam locomotive.

As the century progressed, industrialization proceeded at great speed in Germany and in America; but it was Britain which became the first modern capitalist economy. By the time of the 1851 census more people lived in cities than in the country. The pace of life increased dramatically, assisted by new technologies, especially the railways which snaked across Europe and America during the 1840s and 1850s. Economic growth spiralled, manufactured goods were more plentiful, diverse and cheaper than ever before. This was achieved, however, at the cost of the exploitation of a large unskilled urban working class, housed mainly in unplanned and insanitary city developments. A mass working-class movement in Britain, Chartism, grew to a position of great strength in the 'hungry forties', demanding political reforms including manhood suffrage (although not the vote for women). It collapsed, however, in 1848, the year of European revolutions when Karl Marx and Friedrich Engels published a brilliant critique of capitalism in *The Communist Manifesto*. Initially ignored, the ideas outlined in this and later works by Marx would ultimately dominate the political systems of half the globe.

One of the most spectacular events of the nineteenth century was mounted specifically to celebrate and promote the triumph of British industry and commerce. Described as 'a precipice in time', the Great Exhibition of the Industry of All Nations was held in Hyde Park in 1851: it was a hymn to modernity itself. The structure erected by Joseph Paxton to house the exhibition, soon popularly known as the Crystal Palace, was uncompromising in its modernity, replacing traditional materials with iron and glass and departing radically from the dominant classical and gothic styles of the period. The exhibition proudly placed on show an unprecedented array of commodities, from raw materials to luxury goods, from hand-crafted objects to the most

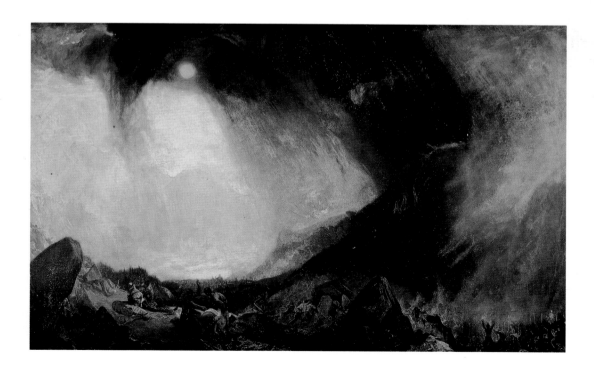

JOSEPH MALLORD WILLIAM TURNER

Snow Storm: Hannibal and his Army Crossing the Alps
1812, OIL ON CANVAS, 1.46 x 2.375m (4ft 9½in x 7ft 9½in). Tate Gallery, London. (LEFT)

THOMAS COLE
The Oxbow (The
Connecticut River
near Northampton)
1836, OIL ON CANVAS,
130.8 x 193cm (51½ x 76in),
The Metropolitan Museum of
Art, gift of Mrs Russell Sage.
(ABOVE)

recent examples of mass production and the machines which made them, all of them ordered by type into taxonomies. It seemed that industrial progress had brought the natural world to order. It was a truly global enterprise, presenting the produce of thirty-two nations from Europe, America, Africa and the Far East, with prominence given to Britain's colonial possessions in Australia, Canada, Africa, Asia and, above all, India. The increasing political and economic expansionism of European nations, often achieved by military conquest aided by technological superiority, had profound repercussions on European culture, as well as often disastrous effects for the colonized peoples. Increased trade with the East resulted in a vogue for Japanese art in the late nineteenth century while Indian and Islamic fabrics, for example, became fashionable in Europe, later being imitated by enterprising manufacturers such as Arthur Lasenby Liberty.

The Crystal Palace did not contain an exhibition of the fine arts, which would however be included in later international exhibitions in Paris in 1855 and 1867. The organizers of the 1851

exhibition, led by Henry Cole and Prince Albert, pursued instead an agenda for design reform, dedicated to improving the aesthetic and technical quality of the products of British industry. The Exhibition demonstrated the superior quality of French goods, and measures were taken to reform design education in Britain, notably the founding of a Museum of Manufactures, which in 1857 became the South Kensington Museum. By 1899, when it was finally renamed the Victoria and Albert Museum, it had amassed a great collection of decorative arts and sculpture, particularly from the medieval period and the Renaissance, but also from non-European origin, which were intended as a store-house of examples and ideas for industrial designers.

Conspicuous at the Great Exhibition had been the Medieval Court, organized by the Gothic Revival architect and designer, Augustus Welby Northmore Pugin. Pugin's historicism was characteristic of the nineteenth century's passion for reviving the art of the past, one symptom of its deep engagement with history. His Court was packed with furnishings for homes and churches, fashioned in the richly decorated Gothic Revival style which, for church building in particular, was to attain wide popularity across Europe and America in the second half of the nineteenth century. From 1836 until his premature death in 1852, Pugin worked on the design of the interior and exterior decoration of the new Palace of Westminster in a sumptuous neo-gothic style. An ardent Catholic, Pugin's commitment to the revival of the gothic was based on what he saw as the spiritual qualities of pre-Reformation society and its buildings. His book *Contrasts: or, a parallel between the noble edifices of the fourteenth and fifteenth centuries, and similar buildings of the present day: shewing the present decay of taste* provided an important precedent for Ruskin's arguments in *The Stones of Venice*, which, in turn, was fundamental to the intellectual development of the English craftsman and social reformer William Morris. Impressed by Ruskin's account of the gothic workman, Morris developed an ideal of handicraft production in opposition to mechanization and capitalism. His designs for textiles, wallpaper and furniture, though startling in their originality, were often suggested by historical examples, such as those he saw in the South Kensington Museum.

Painters, too, explored historical styles and subjects throughout the nineteenth century, partly as a result of the increasing availability of fine examples of earlier art in public museums such as the Louvre in Paris, the National Gallery in London and the Altes Museum in Berlin. A group of German artists living in Rome in the early years of the nineteenth century, known as the Nazarenes, ran counter to their academic art education by painting religious subjects in styles derived directly from Italian and Northern Renaissance painting. The revival of interest in medieval subjects, such as the myths of King Arthur and the Song of the Niebelung, had a profound impact on nineteenth-century culture, across the fine and decorative arts, poetry and opera. The young English painters who formed the Pre-Raphaelite Brotherhood, influenced by Ruskin's works, decided like the Nazarenes to turn away from the academic traditions and techniques of painting and return to working directly from nature, as they supposed the painters of the fifteenth century, before Raphael, to have done.

The Pre-Raphaelites also signalled their wish to create an art which was both religious and relevant to the present day. In this aim their associate Ford Madox Brown succeeded pre-eminently in *Work*, which is both an elaborately detailed representation of everyday life in a suburb of Victorian London and an allegory on the solution of the social problems of the day. The arched frame bearing biblical texts and the formalized composition signal the quasi-religious seriousness of Brown's painting; yet its obsessive verisimilitude of detail pins it down to the specifics of the here and now. The intense study of 'nature' or, at least, real life provided an image which historicized the present day, endowing the humdrum event of roadworks in Hampstead with a transcendental significance. This was achieved through the painting's central moral – that hard work will lead to salvation. Here, history is being made in the streets not through the revolutionary upheavals of Delacroix's *The 28th July* but

The Transept of the Crystal Palace, designed by Joseph Paxton. LITHOGRAPH, SKETCHED AND DRAWN BY C. BURTON. (TOP)

The Green Dining Room by William Morris. (BOTTOM LEFT)

Interior of the House of Commons by Augustus Welby Northmore Pugin. (BOTTOM RIGHT)

FORD MADOX BROWN
Work
1852–63, OIL ON CANVAS, 137 x 197.3cm (53¹⁹⁄₆₀ x 77¹¹⁄₆₀in).
Manchester City Art Gallery. (TOP)

EDOUARD MANET
Un Bar aux Folies-Bergère
1882, OIL ON CANVAS, 96 x 103cm (37⅞ x 40½in),
Courtauld Institute Galleries, London. (ABOVE)

through the gradual promotion of a coherent social fabric of the Victorian settlement of capitalism.

If London was the centre of the world economy, Paris was acknowledged as the world's artistic capital. After 1852, the medieval city of Paris was transformed into a modern city whose wide geometric boulevards became an important place of social display and interaction. As in *Work*, looking at people and studying them for signs of character and social position became an obsessive social practice. In Parisian culture, however, the object of the exercise was pleasure, licit or illicit, rather than stern Victorian moralizing. The painter who provided an art that captured the epic quality of this modern life was Edouard Manet, whose *Un Bar aux Folies-Bergère* was described by a critic as 'the most exactly modern' picture at the Paris Salon of 1882. The scene is one of popular entertainment in a smoke-filled bar, garishly lit by electricity. The mirror behind the barmaid captures the face of a man of substance, and there is a strong suggestion of the prostitution for which the Folies-Bergère was famous. Of course it was not only the risqué subject matter which made Manet's work notorious; it flouted academic convention in both composition (the curiously distorted reflection, the legs of a trapeze artist visible in the upper left) and in style (the allusive and visible brushwork, the white smudges depicting the smoke).

While art history has championed the works of artists who rebelled against the traditional standards of the academies in London and Paris, we should not ignore the quality of artists whose work was achieved within an academic context. Frederic Leighton, for example, who as President guided the Royal Academy from 1878 to 1896, produced works of supreme accomplishment such as *Captive Andromache,* in which a sophisticated rendering of myth is articulated through a mastery of the human form and drapery: the possible stuffiness of such formal classicism is offset by an opulent handling of colour and an underlying current of hedonism. If Leighton's work reaches back to Classical Greece, its melancholy atmosphere and eroticized figures also provide a link to the so-called decadent works of the last decade of the century.

FREDERIC LEIGHTON
Captive Andromache
*c.*1888, OIL ON CANVAS,
197 x 407cm (77‰ x 160¼in).
Manchester City Art Gallery.
(LEFT)

By the late 1880s the attractions of the modern city were increasingly rejected by advanced young artists in France. Paul Gauguin sought an alternative, initially in the peasant culture of rural France, and subsequently in what were thought of as 'primitive' non-Western cultures, a concept which implied a natural state of mankind outside history. Gauguin left France for Tahiti in 1891, where, in spite of increasing Westernization, he encountered a radically different culture. In *Manao Tupapau*, a reclining nude in the Western tradition is set against an expression of a Polynesian spirituality in the form of the figure of the Spirit of the Dead, visible only through the culture and imagination of the Tahitian girl. For all its formal and colouristic daring, Gauguin's work can be seen as a late manifestation of the nineteenth-century penchant for the juxtaposition of naturalism and allegory within a single image.

PAUL GAUGUIN
**Manao Tupapau
(The Spirit of the
Dead Keeps Watch)**
c. 1892, OIL ON CANVAS,
73 x 91.5cm (28¾ x 36in).
The Albright-Knox Gallery,
Buffalo, New York. (ABOVE)

If at the beginning of the nineteenth century few viewed their era with the despair of the ageing Ruskin, by the end of the century few held the confident belief in infinite progress which underpinned the Great Exhibition in 1851. Moreover, if Ruskin's prophetic imagery of the storm cloud seemed unduly pessimistic in his own time, it has undeniable resonance for the post-industrial present. His prescient concern for ecology foreshadowed a major preoccupation of today, one which echoes the nineteenth-century cult of nature. The clash between modernity and historicism, which for so long seemed to have ended in a victory for the ideologies of the modern and styles of modernism, has returned, at the end of the twentieth century, in the smouldering and eclectic truce of post-modernism. With so many of its debates yet to be played out, perhaps it is still too soon to offer a final assessment of the art and culture of the nineteenth century.

ART, THE MARKET AND MODERN LIFE *by Marina Vaizey*

Art reproductions are now available on the latest technology: the collection of the National Gallery in London is one of many available on CD-ROM. (BELOW)

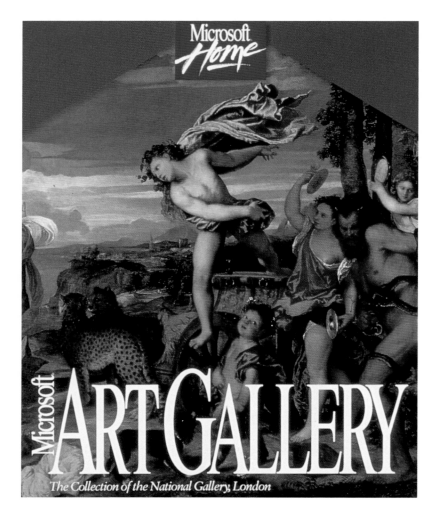

Apocalypse, cataclysm, triumph and apotheosis: the twentieth century – the era of the avant-garde and modernism – has witnessed both worldwide calamity and massive advances in human welfare. It has been marked both by extensive destruction – the Gulag, the holocaust, two world wars and countless conflicts – and by greater medical power to save the lives of millions, greater affluence for more people, greater freedom to travel, greater communications, greater human ease. While the scale of events of this century has expanded to a truly global and even extra-terrestrial dimension, so too has our access to information. We talk about information technology or IT, information networks, information highways, satellite and cable television, E-mail, and more recently about a 'virtual reality' which threatens to take the place of real objects and real time and space.

No one is quite sure what the electronic revolution will bring, whether we will see the technologically advanced races withdraw to their screens and become isolated from social contact and real life, or whether the new mediums will whet the appetite to see and experience more. In the field of art, the latest innovations in computer technology are being offered as new products by our cultural institutions. The National Gallery in London, for example, helped by Apple Computer, Inc and the American Express Company – an example of the increasing collaboration between commercial enterprises and publicly subsidized institutions in the promotion of culture – has produced a CD-ROM which gives access to reproductions of the Gallery's paintings on the home computer screen. It also provides information on each of the images, from a town map of Renaissance Siena to a description of the meanings behind a still life. This piece of technology sells for less than £50 and is the latest manifestation of the reproduction of our culture, of art history taught through slide and photograph. The growth of art reproductions has hitherto coincided with a passion for seeing the real thing. Indeed, the phenomenon of cultural tourism has been as important a symptom of the growing interest in the visual arts as the unprecedented growth of art history scholarships, courses and education programmes and what has been accurately described as the explosion in the number of museums and galleries.

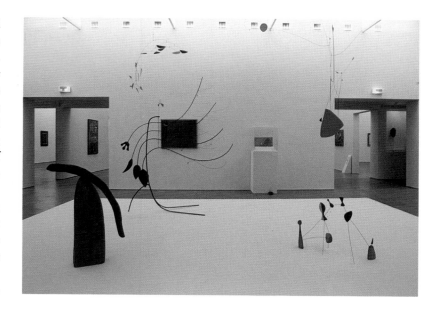

Some of the most spectacular architectural projects worldwide have been concerned with the expansion and building of museums and galleries. The very nature of the museum and art gallery was set for debate with the construction of the National Pompidou Centre for Arts and Culture in Paris in 1977, designed by Renzo Piano and Richard Rogers, complete with Vasarely's portrait of Georges Pompidou hanging from the ceiling of the foyer. The response has been phenomenal: Mies van der Rohe's National Gallery in Berlin, Robert Venturi's Sainsbury Wing of the National Gallery in London, I M Pei's glass pyramids at the Louvre, Gae Aulenti's conversion of the Gare d'Orsay into the Musée d'Orsay in Paris, the same architect's conversion of the Palazzo Grassi in Venice for Fiat, Cesare Pelli's expansion of the Museum of Modern Art in New York, Renzo Piano's Menil Collection in Houston, Arata Isozaki's Museum of Contemporary Art in Los Angeles, the same architect's new wing for the Brooklyn Museum, Mario Botta's new San Francisco Museum of Modern Art (the second largest building for modern art in America, as well as the largest museum building of the decade), the Van Gogh Museum in Amsterdam, the Reina Sophia in Madrid, the Picasso, Miró and Tapies museums in Barcelona, the Houston Museum of Fine Art's latest commission for a new building, the proposed new Tate Gallery of Modern Art in London, Barry Gasson's Burrell Collection in Glasgow, a new Museum of Scotland in Edinburgh to open in two years' time, and literally hundreds of new museums and sculpture parks in Japan...the list is long.

Moreover, there is speculation about franchising and setting up branches of museums, such as the Tate Gallery in Liverpool, England, and the overseas branches of New York's Guggenheim. There is also increased specialization within the museums and galleries network, from Britain's National Museum of Photography, Film and Television in Bradford and the Museum of the Moving Image in London, to Washington's Museum of Women's Art. Existing institutions are also setting up their own sub-divisions, particularly Western institutions keen to expand into Asian and African art.

This immense industry depends on – to use the market vocabulary – product: the product of the past, and the product of newly discovered worlds. In the West the visual arts have witnessed both a series of major re-assessments of the past and its own dizzying succession of styles and 'isms', from nineteenth-century salon painting, realism and impressionism to American and European symbolism, German expressionism, turn-of-the-century Vienna, and nineteenth-century Scandinavian art. And as testimony to changing economic status, more galleries in the West – and dealers worldwide – are looking at the art of Asia.

This diversity in art culture has taken place in accord with the changing kaleidoscopic pattern of world events, their economic and political effects, and the resulting shift in cultural power and prestige. The end of World War II marked the biggest shift in the making, collecting and patronage of art in the West. In the 1930s, the exodus of intellectuals and artists from Europe, mainly Nazi Germany, to America included Max Beckmann, George Grosz and some of the leading Bauhaus figures (Walter Gropius, Mies van der Rohe, László Moholy-Nagy). By the 1940s a further influx of refugees from France, among them Fernand Léger, Piet Mondrian, Max Ernst and Salvador Dali, settled in New York. New

Interior view of the Pompidou Centre in Paris. (TOP)

The Museum of Mankind in London features an exhibition of traditional costume art from Palestine. (ABOVE)

York superceded Paris and Berlin as the focal point of new art in the West. This position was underpinned by the serious concern shown for contemporary art in the founding of New York's Museum of Modern Art in 1929, and the Guggenheim a decade later.

Patronage, too, has undergone change. The state, in terms of taxes foregone (the American model) and massive subsidy (France in the postwar period), has been a major player. So, too, has the private patron, notably in America, where benefactors such as Andrew and Paul Mellon have founded important collections. America has also recognized the power of collective patronage. This was first, and perhaps most imaginatively, exemplified in President Roosevelt's New Deal policy during the Great Depression in support of the work of artists. By the end of the 1930s 'advanced' art truly originated in North America.

The shift to a new market was not just a geographical transition; in terms of economic power America has increasingly grown in importance, and its status is evidenced in the extent of American ownership and direction, not least in the ownership of Sotheby's itself. London, long the leading art market in the world, is now *primus inter pares*.

ANDY WARHOL
210 Coca-Cola Bottles
1962, SILK SCREEN INK
ON SYNTHETIC POLYMER
PAINT ON CANVAS.
The Andy Warhol Foundation
for the Visual Arts (BELOW)

At the same time greater individual economic power has brought freedom to exercise individual taste, as well as greater conformity and, in some parts of the world, savage political repression. The contradiction is embodied in the life and works of Pablo Picasso, acknowledged as the colossus of the entire modern period. A traditionalist, who did not mind stealing from the art of the past in order to make a new and highly personal art, his work reflects the artist as biographer and autobiographer and as non-conformist. The other side of the modern era shows the striking standardization of art brought about by mass production and mass export of consumer goods and culture alike, from Hollywood to Coca-Cola. This 'en masse' distribution of culture has come to be called the 'americanization' of culture.

World War I held up by a decade the rise of an avant-garde distinguished by its ferocity of visual invention and its questioning of shared assumptions about the values of society. Even so, the burgeoning of art during the course of the conflict was a fact of the life and death of the artist. The twentieth century had kicked off with the birth of a new and abstract idiom in painting, which was echoed by striking innovation in the decorative, applied and architectural arts. The period up to World War I was one of the most adventurous in the history of Western art, and was characterized by the work of those who are still seen as both idiosyncratic precursors and pioneers, from Frank Lloyd Wright and Adolf Loos to Charles Rennie Mackintosh and Antoni Gaudí. Even more daring were the foundation stones of what we have come to think of as modernism, characterized by a violent, quite arbitrary and non-naturalistic use of colour. The Fauves, Henri Matisse among them, were given the name 'wild beasts' for their part, and the anarchic theories of vorticism and futurism were led by a sense of the untame. Indeed, it can be said that Picasso's seminal painting of 1907, *Les Demoiselles d'Avignon*, almost literally set the scene.

Though it is perhaps glib to talk of cultural diversity at the start of the twentieth century, Picasso and his peers made consciously innovative use of ancient and so-called 'primitive' art. New exhibitions of ancient and non-Western tribal art became interesting to both the public and practitioners, with the result that artists and tourists alike set off to travel in search of light, motif and inspiration. Matisse is the prime example. An artist who always took great hedonistic pleasure in colour and shape, he eventually travelled to North Africa to be closer to a more primitive way of life, and was so stimulated by the great exhibition of Islamic Art in Munich in 1910 that he allowed it to have a formative role in his own work. It was also in 1910 that the controversial showing of Manet's work and Post-Impressionism was mounted in London under the direction of Roger Fry. Ironically, this art, which at the time was so subversive, has now come to be collected by the very capitalistic institutions that some of the artists questioned.

Perhaps the entire thrust of the twentieth century has been summed up with the phrase 'the shock of the new'. The statement was made by auctioneer, dealer and critic Ian Dunlop in a book which charted the impact of a number of seminal exhibitions, including the Armory Show in New York in 1913 (the début of European modernism across the Atlantic marked by the showing of Marcel Duchamp's *Nude Descending a Staircase*), and the International Surrealist Show in Paris in 1925. The phrase was later adopted by the critic and scholar Robert Hughes for the title of his television programme on the visual arts in the twentieth century.

What has been perhaps surprising in view of the extraordinary conflicts and upheavals worldwide is the comparative paucity of overtly political

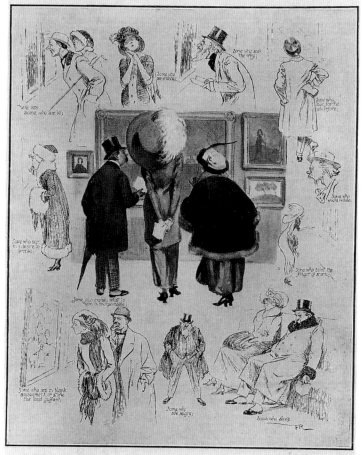

POST-IMPRESSIONIST EXPRESSIONS—SKETCHES BY FRANK REYNOLDS.

GAZERS AT PAINTINGS FEW APPRECIATE AND FEWER UNDERSTAND: STUDIES AT THE GRAFTON GALLERIES.

'Post-Impressionist Expressions'
Illustrated London News,
3 December 1910
The term 'Post-Impressionism' was coined by two English critics, Roger Fry and Desmond MacCarthy, to describe an exhibition of French paintings organized by them at the Grafton Galleries in London in 1910. It opened to derisory criticism from the press but polarized opinions and attitudes about 'modern' art. (LEFT)

Installation shot of the Armory Show in New York in 1913. (ABOVE)

Exhibit from the International Surrealist Show in Paris in 1925. (RIGHT)

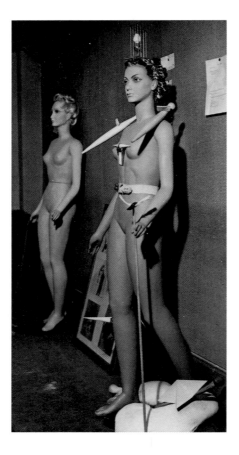

art. The most utopian moments of social and political awareness in art took place in Russia from the beginning of the revolution in 1917 to the early 1920s, only to be extinguished in the mid to late 1930s, driven underground or transmuted by Stalinist excesses. Poets, designers and artists provided agit-prop art, both fine and applied art, propaganda trains and posters and even strikingly simplified dress for the new society that was supposed to be emerging. For a while it seemed as though intellectuals could lead, or at least be part of, a genuinely populist movement. The art form that survived best was photography, with artists such as Alexander Rodchenko managing still to function under increasingly active oppression. In the 1920s, artists began to take up that which the Great War had interrupted. Some 'advanced' artists produced work that became internationally recognized and made substantial contributions to art in Europe.

An end to the fervent innovation and utopian hopes of the artistic community came about during the Spanish Civil War which broke out in 1936. Picasso's *Guernica*, painted in response to the bombing of civilians, is one of the most extraordinary paintings of the twentieth century. It put into ideological service all the sophisticated pictorial techniques of modern art. So strong was his rage and indignation at the merciless slaughter of unarmed civilians that images which Picasso had created in earlier paintings for their privately expressive or purely formal qualities were here transformed into symbols which could be understood by everyone. *Guernica* was exhibited in the Spanish pavilion at the international exposition in Paris 1937. Picasso pledged that the painting would never be seen in Spain until democracy returned; up to 1981 it was housed in New York's Museum of Modern Art and then, equally controversially, in Madrid.

Strangely and terribly, one of the biggest exhibitions of the century was held in the same year that *Guernica* was painted. The Exhibition of Degenerate Art (Entartete Kunst) held in Munich was seen by over two million people. Hitler had condemned this art as degenerate but had given a very wide definition. However, it encompassed expressionism, surrealism and abstract art – the very art which has triumphed both critically and commercially in the post-war period.

The last fifty years have seen a dramatic change in our attitude towards art and the museum and art gallery. The celebrations for the two-hundred-and-fiftieth anniversary of the Louvre in 1993 were partly an expression of national pride – and the new pyramid is testimony to this. The same feeling is echoed in different ways in every major Western and Westernizing country. One need only look at the process of expansion and rebuilding of the museum islands of Berlin in the newly reunited Germany. In contrast, Frankfurt, Germany's economic and financial centre, is an established nerve-centre of museums and galleries, from the Jewish Museum to the Museum of Architecture and the Museum of Modern Art. In the new museum age, the museum itself, its contents and art in general, have come to be seen as a pantheistic focus for a kind of faith or meditation. The inter-denominational Rothko chapel in Houston, Texas, filled with deep black and red abstract expressionist paintings by Mark Rothko, is a case in point.

This expansion of the art market has brought with it a related area of growth: the phenomenon of the art dealer. There was Lord Duveen, a flamboyant figure who brought about one-way traffic

G. KLUTIS
Everyone to the Elections of the Soviets
1930, LITHOGRAPH PRINTED IN RED WITH OFFSET LITHOGRAPH, 120 x 85.7cm (47¼ x 33¾in), New York $37,950 (£25,300). 10.III.94
(LEFT)

PABLO PICASSO
Guernica
1937, OIL ON CANVAS, 3.49 x 7.75m (11ft 5½in x 25ft 5¼in). The Prado, Madrid.
(BELOW)

in Old Masters, from Europe to America. His collaboration with the Italy-based art historian and scholar of the Renaissance, Bernard Berenson, ensured the co-operation between scholars and commerce – a relation which has been a notable feature of the art market in modern times. Duveen dealt with the art of the past. The dealer as promoter, supporter and adherent of the contemporary became a significant player in the

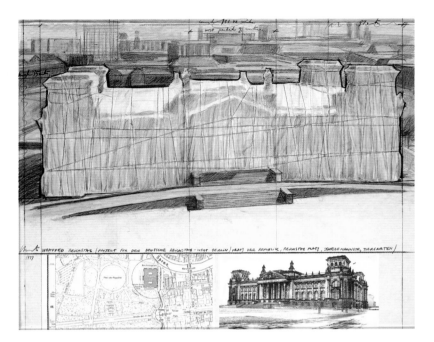

CHRISTO
Wrapped Reichstag
(Project for
Der Deutsche
Reichstag – Berlin)
SIGNED, TITLED AND DATED
1977, PENCIL, PASTEL, FABRIC
COLLAGE, STRING, MAP AND
BLACK AND WHITE
PHOTOGRAPH ON CARD,
55 x 70cm (21⅜ x 27½in)
London £32,200 ($49,900).
30.VI.94. (ABOVE)

catalogue raisonnée to the critic's review. Every respectable exhibition now produces a substantial catalogue. The publications on art and artists have multiplied almost beyond comprehension, and when we add the coverage by other media – the newspapers, film and television, photography – and the publicity generated for each show and sale, the discussion of art and artists broadens dramatically. There is a continual system of reviewing and re-viewing, of promulgation of information and reproduction of art – *Art at Auction* is itself an example of this. Newspapers assign their own art sales correspondents; the amount of information is such that the art world not only has art magazines, newsletters, sales publications and specialist guides for collectors, but since 1990 even has an international edition of *The Art Newspaper.*

The living artist has become a peripatetic creature, often engaged in amazing physical feats. James Turrell, for example, is doing nothing less than attempting to reshape a volcano in the American southwest. Christo (Christo Jachareff) is perhaps the archetypal new artist. Bulgarian-born, but a New Yorker now by way of Western Europe, notably Paris, Christo finances his work by an extraordinary means of artist as capitalist. He sells the parts of his projects – the collages, drawings and small sculptures – as stocks and shares to raise the finance for his ephemeral works. Christo wrapped several miles of Australian coastline in plastic sheeting in the 1960s, temporarily installed a 24-mile curtain of translucent white material across the landscape of northern California in the 1970s (*Running Fence*), wrapped the Pont Neuf in Paris, and has received permission to wrap the Reichstag in Berlin in 1995. The completed projects cost millions to produce but are free to the public; they involve the collaboration of hundreds of technical experts and assistants and remain in the memory through the media of film, photography, television and publication.

More and more artists are actually working with the materials of the media, with photography, television and computers. At the end of the modern period, a new visual art is emerging: it is a time-based art which depends on mechanical

market at the time of the impressionists, the post-impressionists and the cubists. In the post-war period dealers were discovering and supporting new artists and new movements – Leo Castelli and Denise Rene made their mark in the 1960s and 1970s, Mary Boon in New York and Nicholas Logsdail in London in the 1980s and 1990s. Firms have established themselves nationally and internationally, from Agnews in London to Wildenstein in Paris, probably the biggest dealers in the world. Some firms have specialized, such as the Marlborough, in international modern art.

Influential, too, but to a much lesser extent, has been the critic, perhaps the best known being Clement Greenberg, champion of the abstract expressionists. Indeed, journalistic criticism and analysis have been a pertinent aspect of the contemporary art world. The vivid analysis of the influence of the modern art gallery on contemporary artists given in Brian O'Doherty's essay, 'The Great White Space', is a supreme example. Here he suggests that much art of the post-war period was made to be shown in the large, white-walled, light-filled, pristine rooms of modern exhibition space: site-specific and sight-specific.

Art literature can be a vital part of the validating process of the product, and extends from the

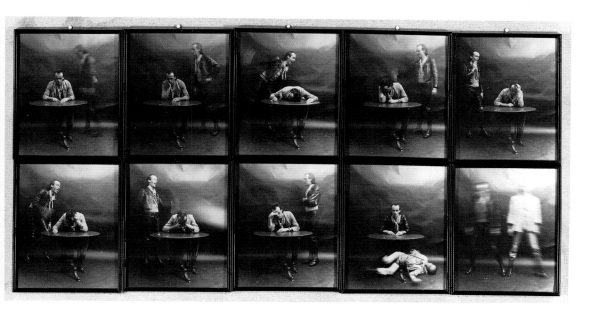

devices and sources of electric power. In tandem, reverence for the tangible evidence of the past, the material culture so carefully preserved by museums and individual collectors, has increased strikingly. The museum is resembling ever more a kind of temple where commercial and spiritual values become more closely intertwined. Visitor numbers may measure the success of a museum, as monetary value measures the success of a work of art. Art, which has always been intimately involved with religion, is simultaneously tied to the notions of power and status. This has not changed over the years.

What has changed in the twentieth century is not only the extraordinary and unprecedented possibilities for making, showing and selling art, but the accessibility to visual imagery and to verbal and written information about it. Geographically, both the making and showing of modern art has moved across the Atlantic from the Old World to the New, and is continuing to encircle the world, by moving across the Pacific to Japan and other Asian countries. Moreover, certain agreed values have changed: where there was once an understood hierarchy in art-making and appreciation, anything can now be studied, sold and collected – and intellectually and philosophically justified. There are those who would

argue that a juke box is as aesthetically significant as a painting by Balthus. The one-off might continue to succeed simply by virtue of its rarity.

Many would contend that the most singular characteristic of the last hundred years can be summed up simply with the qualifying adjective – more. There is more: more art, more materials, more media, more artists, more markets, more collectors, more museums, more galleries, more money, and more public.

Queues at the British Museum in London for the Treasures of Tutenkhamun Exhibition, held in 1972. (ABOVE)

THE AUCTION HOUSE REVISITED *by Wendell Garrett*

CONDITIONS OF SALE.

I. THAT he who bids moſt is the Buyer; but if any Diſpute ariſe, the Book or Books be put to Sale again.

II. That no Perſon advance leſs than Six-pence each Bidding; and after the Book ariſes to One Pound, no leſs than One Shilling.

III. The Books are in moſt elegant Condition, and ſuppoſed to be perfect; but if any appear otherwiſe before taken away, the Buyer is at his Choice to take or leave them.

IV. That each Perſon give in his Name, and pay Five Shillings in the Pound (if demanded) for what he buys; and that no Book be deliver'd in Time of Sale, unleſs firſt paid for.

V. The Books muſt be taken away at the Buyer's Expence, and the Money paid at the Place of Sale, within Three Days after the Sale is ended.

Any Gentleman who cannot attend the Sale, may have their Commiſſions receiv'd and faithfully executed,

By their moſt Humble Servant,

SAMUEL BAKER.

The Conditions of Sale from the catalogue of one of Samuel Baker's earliest auctions in 1764.
(ABOVE)

To the High Victorian Thomas Carlyle, 'the history of the world is but the biography of great men,' those heroes who tower above the rest and lead the way. Likewise, the history of an auction house is principally about the men whose personalities have marked a way through the economic ups and downs, the tides of taste and fashion, changing demand and scarcity, and government restrictions on free trading between countries. The story of Sotheby's and how it became the world's foremost fine art auction house is really that of two companies; one founded 250 years ago by a London bookseller, the other founded in 1883 to promote art in America. The growth, development and ultimate unification of these two companies is one of the great success stories of the art market.

Sotheby's founder, the bookseller Samuel Baker, is known to have been retailing books as early as 1734. His first documented auction was that of the valuable library of Sir John Stanley on 11 March 1744, where he appears in the catalogue as the auctioneer. Following its success, Baker embarked on a series of auctions of major private libraries and, as business prospered, he moved in 1754 into the first permanent auction room in York Street, Covent Garden.

In 1767, at the age of fifty-five, Baker brought in a young assistant, George Leigh. Leigh was a natural auctioneer who recognized the value of theatrical props and the actor's sense of timing. As a contemporary wrote of him, 'When a high priced book is balancing between £15 and £20, it is a fearful sign of its reaching an additional sum if Mr Leigh should lay down his hammer and delve into his snuff box.' Upon Baker's death in April 1778, his estate was divided between Leigh and Baker's nephew, John Sotheby and the firm's name was changed to Leigh and Sotheby. The Sotheby family was to be at its helm until 1861, but the business has borne their name ever since.

The 1840s saw the rise of two men who were to steer the company through the nineteenth century. In 1842 John Wilkinson, a shrewd and successful businessman, became a partner of the firm, now located at 13 Wellington Street, and five years later Edward Grose Hodge was brought in, primarily as a cataloguer. With the death of the last Sotheby in 1861, Wilkinson appointed Hodge as his partner and in 1864 the firm was renamed Sotheby, Wilkinson & Hodge.

Some of the company's greatest sales were conducted during this partnership and in 1868 the firm reached an unprecedented level of activity, staging as many as ninety-five sales in that year. Sotheby, Wilkinson & Hodge was undoubtedly the leading auction house in the realm of books and was making inroads into the antiques

A portrait of John Sotheby, the nephew of Sotheby's founder, Samuel Baker. (ABOVE)

years into the industrialized world power of the twentieth century. Mark Twain called it the Gilded Age and the name caught on. The decade was rich not merely in material things, but also in contributions to the mind and spirit; the writers Walt Whitman, Mark Twain and Henry James all reached maturity during this period, while work by the artists George Inness, Winslow Homer, James McNeill Whistler, Thomas Eakins and Mary Cassatt assured America a place in the history of art. In October 1883, on East 23rd Street, at Madison Square, a new organization called the American Art Association opened its doors to the public for 'the exhibition and sale of works of art and literature'.

At first dedicated exclusively to exhibitions and retail sales, providing 'a hospitable centre where American Art can, at last, after long waiting, be sure of a welcome,' the American Art Association shifted its *modus operandi* to auctions in 1885, when New York's Metropolitan Bank failed and its owner, George T. Seney, was forced to sell his extensive art collection. The auction was a triumph and others followed including the George Whitney Collection in 1885; the Mary Jane Morgan sale in 1886; and the dispersal of the contents of A. T. Stewart's mansion in 1887. Major loan exhibitions were also held at the Association, including a showing of paintings by George Inness in 1884, and in the spring of 1886, the French art dealer Paul Durand-Ruel presented the first French Impressionist exhibition ever held in the United States.

In London, the final years of the nineteenth century at Wellington Street witnessed a number of changes in both the direction of the business and in the composition of the staff. After decades of concentrating mainly on books, Sotheby's, Wilkinson & Hodge made a slow and tentative diversification into the world of fine art auctioneering. In May 1907 Edward Grose Hodge died intestate, and his son, 'young' Tom Hodge, who had joined the firm in 1878, continued to run the business single-handedly. Learned and dignified, Tom Hodge was widely respected in the trade for his knowledge of books, prints and coins. However, complications with dividing the inheritance between numerous siblings forced

market, while Christie's held undisputed sway in the field of fine arts. Often it would happen that at the auction of an important estate, Sotheby's would sell the books and Christie's the furnishings and works of art. By 1876 the economy in the United Kingdom had entered a period of recession, caused partly by cheap corn imports from the United States. Land values tumbled and countless bankruptcies followed. The shock waves reached the auction rooms, as private collections and family libraries accumulated over the generations came up for sale in increasing numbers.

It is probably not just a coincidence that during this period Sotheby's predecessor firm in New York was established. In the United States, the 1880s was a decade of transition, a volcanic era whose great achievement was the institutionalization of those turbulent forces that were transforming the isolated, rural America of the pre-war

Hodge to set about selling the business. It was bought in 1909 by Sir Montague Barlow, a barrister, with two other partners – Felix Walter Warre and Geoffrey Dudley Hobson. Warre took charge of the Antiquities and Coins department and Hobson was responsible for Works of Art – that is, ceramics, glass, arms and armour, oriental and European *objets d'art*.

Tom Hodge continued to work for the firm. Following the outbreak of war in 1914, however, the arrival of an increasing number of women on the premises in wartime conditions precipitated a crisis between Hodge and the other partners. An uncompromising Victorian who could not adapt to a changing world, Hodge left the firm at the end of 1916.

In 1917 the lease at Wellington Street expired and the partners decided to move to larger premises at Nos. 34 and 35 New Bond Street and widen their sales categories. A team of cataloguers and new experts were recruited including Charles Francis Bell, Keeper of Fine Arts at the Ashmolean Museum, Oxford, who was asked to make weekly visits and assume the responsibility of cataloguing pictures; Charles des Graz who joined the Book department, and Jim Kiddell who was recruited to the Works of Art depart-

ment. The 1920s were prosperous years for the company, during which time the turnover in the Book department remained steady and sales of works of art and pictures continued to expand. In 1924 Sotheby, Wilkinson & Hodge, which until now had been a simple partnership, became a private, unlimited company.

In New York, the American Art Association was bought in 1923 by Cortland Field Bishop, a wealthy New York collector. The prosperity of the 1920s fuelled a boom in collecting in a variety of branches of art and antiques. One new area of collecting took off with the success of the famous Girl Scout Loan Exhibition of American antique furniture in 1929, organized by a group of wealthy collectors through the American Art Association. The bubble burst, however, in October 1929 when Wall Street crashed and the subsequent Great Depression wreaked havoc on the art market. When Bishop died in 1935, the firm was in a weakened financial position and in 1937, following a dispute with Bishop's widow, the company's managers, Hiram Parke and Otto Bernet, decided to found their own company, taking with them the entire expert and managerial staff. In January 1938 Parke-Bernet Galleries Inc. held its first auction in a makeshift gallery at 742 Fifth Avenue at 57th Street. By 1939 Mrs Bishop's direction of her late husband's company brought about the demise of the American Art Association. At the same time, Parke and Bernet had so completely taken over the leadership of the industry that they were able to buy up what was left of the meagre assets and goodwill of their nearly defunct parent company and move back with their staff to the old premises.

Reverberations from the Wall Street crash were felt all over the world, and in London Sotheby's was able to survive only by a vicious retrenchment in overhead costs and a drastic reduction in staff. This distressing period in history was shared by the owners of country houses, many of whom asked the firm to sell their works of art to raise ready money. Over the next decade, Sotheby's undertook a number of pioneering sales, held on the premises, of the contents of stately houses. As well as raising additional revenue this type of auction attracted considerable

Part of the exhibition of American antique furniture in aid of the Girl Scout movement. (BELOW)

publicity. The fact was now generally recognized that London had achieved a paramount position as the world centre of the art market. But clouds were gathering over Europe and, when war broke out in 1939, a stagnant atmosphere pervaded the auction room.

The company that emerged at the end of the war, though vastly different from that founded 200 years earlier, was still relatively small and London-based. The man responsible for transforming Sotheby's into the international auction house of today was Peter Wilson, who joined the Furniture department in 1936 and was promoted to director and partner soon after the war. In 1947 Wilson travelled to New York to make the first tentative approach on behalf of Sotheby's to acquire Parke-Bernet. Temporarily defeated by the constrictive grip of the British Board of Trade and Treasury's regulations on the export of sterling to buy an overseas business, he returned to London, while Parke-Bernet moved into magnificent new premises at 980 Madison Avenue and continued in business strongly.

The 1950s saw a dramatic growth both in the volume of sales and the number of owners consigning property, putting enormous strain on the organizational and administrative resources of the London firm. The solution was to increase the autonomy of the departments, making the principal experts responsible for the success of their sales by ensuring works were catalogued to a high standard and often taking the auction themselves. Until 1964 there were eight departments: Old Master Pictures, English and Modern Pictures, Prints and Drawings, Books and Manuscripts, Silver and Jewels, Works of Art, Antiquities and Coins, and Furniture. By 1967 the departments had been divided into more specific categories and the Works of Art department, for example, became fifteen independent components.

In 1953 British trade restrictions were relaxed and Vere Pilkington, Chairman of Sotheby's, persuaded John (Jake) Carter, a celebrated figure in the world of antiquarian books, to become Sotheby's 'associate' in New York. Working from a friend's office on lower Broadway, Carter called on collectors, lawyers, bankers, dealers and museum directors to find properties which could be sent to London for auction, and solicited potential buyers in the United States for major items coming up for sale in Bond Street. He also toured the country with the English Speaking Union, generating publicity by giving lectures on Sotheby's and the international art market.

Peter Wilson, on the rostrum, selling *Goldfinder* by George Stubbs on 31 October 1973 for £225,000. (LEFT)

The breakthrough in the American market came in 1957 with the sale in London of the William Weinberg Collection of French Impressionist and Post-Impressionist paintings, which were sent from America. The avalanche of press, radio and television coverage which surrounded the sale helped to increase the flow of properties from America, and in 1958 the Goldschmidt Collection was consigned to London. The collection comprised just seven paintings, which took only twenty-one minutes to sell and broke every record in the book, with Cézanne's *Garçon au Gilet Rouge* achieving more than seven times the previous record for a modern picture at a British auction. The sale was a watershed in fine art auctioneering and a *coup de maître* for Peter Wilson, not only for the prices and promotion realized, but also because the contract that had been agreed with the Goldschmidts demonstrated a new flexibility on commission rates that was to be of great importance in the future. Sotheby's was prepared to back its judgement on values by predicting the reserve prices below which only a minuscule commission would have to be paid, but once that barrier was broken the firm stood to receive a much greater share of the proceeds than was usually the case. This acceptance of a new level of risk led to the firm's great surge forward in the following decade.

It was now clear that it was essential to have a fully-staffed office in New York. Peter Wilson's choice to head this venture fell on Peregrine Pollen, an assistant in the picture department. Pollen set up offices in the Corning Glass Building at Fifth Avenue and 55th Street in 1960 and, after an extremely successful season of sales, engaged in a campaign to acquire Parke-Bernet. The merger was consummated in 1964 and a new era was begun.

Pollen's role now was to oversee the transition of the New York office and boost its sales. With skillful management and considerable diplomatic skills, Parke-Bernet's fortunes were restored and by mid-1966 the galleries were able to announce the highest turnover in their history.

London and New York, Bond Street and Madison Avenue – the twin centres of the art market on either side of the – Atlantic had at last

become a reality. That still left vast areas of the world untapped where art was in demand. It was an adventurous time of global expansion. In the late 1960s Sotheby's opened offices in Beirut, Edinburgh, Florence, Johannesburg, Melbourne, Munich, Paris, Tokyo, Toronto and Zürich. Between 1973 and 1979 further offices were opened in Amsterdam, Brussels, Dublin, Frankfurt, Geneva, Hong Kong, Milan, Monaco, Rome and Stockholm, and in the United States in Boston, Chicago, Hawaii, Houston, Los Angeles, Palm Beach, Philadelphia and San Francisco.

During the 1960s and 1970s the art market exploded. Auctioneer John Marion in New York conducted one record-breaking sale after another. By the late 1970s the firm had outgrown the building on Madison Avenue and in September 1980 Sotheby Parke Bernet moved to new office and exhibition space in York Avenue, occupying an entire block between 71st and 72nd Streets, making it the largest auction house in the world.

In September 1983, one hundred years after the founding of the American Art Association, the company was acquired by A. Alfred Taubman, an American businessman, philanthropist, art patron and collector. A strengthened financial base, enhanced international marketing, expanding client services, and a name change to Sotheby's across all continents were the direct results of this return to private ownership.

The central theme of Sotheby's history over a quarter millennium has been one of steady development, a process which has involved decisive turning points without the violent overthrow of an existing order. Each constellation of managing partners has recognized the need to find something new and different for their own epoch. Today's firm is the product not only of global expansion, but also of the determination to find ways of conducting business beyond the restricted perimeters of the Anglo-American world, with the strength to transform coming from the will and imagination of those involved. Perhaps this transformation can be best explained by the Greek term *metanoia* – a turning round of the mind – or the Latin, *redivivus* – revived or living again. So with the prophet Ecclesiasticus, 'Let us now praise famous men,' and women.

PAUL CÉZANNE
Garçon au Gilet Rouge
1888-90, OIL ON CANVAS,
89.5 x 72.4cm (35¼ x 28½in)
One of the seven pictures in the Goldschmidt sale at Sotheby's in 1958. It sold for £220,000 – a record price for a modern picture at a British auction. Private Collection. (LEFT)

SPEARS, CANDLES AND HAMMERS *by Sandy Mallet*

SIR LAWRENCE ALMA-TADEMA
A Picture Gallery
OIL ON CANVAS, 219.7 x 166cm (86½ x 65½in). (ABOVE)

We cannot ascertain when the first sale by auction took place any more than we can pinpoint when the first ever work of art was made. However, it seems likely that the auction process would have been an integral part of the cultures of a number of early civilizations. The simple logic of the auction, with its demonstrable evenhandedness, must have appealed as clearly to the ancients as it does to us today. Moreover, the structure of the auction, requiring as it does an arbiter and an abiding code of conduct, must have proved attractive to any culture wishing to endorse a higher level of order than was allowed by other, less regulated methods of sale.

Some of the earliest recorded auctions appear in Greek literature of the fifth century BC. Herodotus describes a Babylonian village custom of disposing of maidens in marriage by delivering them to the highest bidders in an assembly held annually for the purpose (Book i: 196). Later, in Roman culture, the sale of military booty and captives in war was traditionally held by auction *sub hasta* (under the spear), the spear being the symbol of quiritarian ownership. Gibbon relates that after the murder of Pertinax, the Praetorian Guard proclaimed from their ramparts that the Roman world was to be disposed of by public auction to the highest bidder (vol. i. ch. v). Pliny the Elder also mentions in his *Natural History* that in 146 BC a valuable root from the Greek cities was auctioned to the public.

At this period the sacking of foreign cities by the Romans was usually followed by an auction of the booty. After the sack of Corinth in 146 BC, a famously high bid of 100 talents was made for a painting of Dionysus by Aristides. The picture had been used by Roman soldiers as a dice table, and the bid so astonished the Roman general Lucius Mummius that he withdrew the painting from the sale and included it among his dedications in the temples of Rome. This auction, with its great number of ancient treasures, marked the beginnings of the Roman art market, with its accompanying dealers (such as the Greek Damasippus, an early Duveen), its fakers (some who falsely aged marble), and its collectors.

It is likely to have been the Romans who introduced auctions of works of art to Northern Europe, where, by the early Middle Ages, various auction systems were developing in different countries. In France, the idea of the auctioneer as an instrument of the law became prominent after 1254, when King Saint-Louis established special officers, *sergents à verge et cheval*, to be responsible for compulsory legal sales. In 1552 French auctioneers acquired the status of state-appointed protectors of the public good, a system known as the *commissaire priseur*, which prohibited all other persons from selling goods or merchandise by public auction – a privilege still enjoyed today by French auctioneers.

During the reign of Henry VIII a similar system was developed in England. This system, where the Crown appointed special officers called *atropers* as auctioneers, lasted into the seventeenth century. One popular method by which auctions were held was by lighting an inch or half inch of candle-wick, the bidding taking place while the wick burnt down. The buyer was the last to bid before the fall of the wick. This method had gained official acceptance by the second half of the seventeenth century, and in 1698 an act of William III prescribed that the auction of all goods imported from the East Indies should be sold 'by the candle'. Samuel Pepys describes one such sale in his diary entry for 3 September 1662.

'After dinner, by water to the office, and there we met and sold the Weymouth, Successe and Fellowship Hulke. Where pleasant to see how backward men are at first to bid; and yet when the candle is going out, how they bawl and dispute afterward who bid the most first. And here I observed one man cunninger then the rest, that was sure to bid the last man and to carry it; and enquiring the reason, he told me that just as the flame goes out the smoke descends,

which is a thing I never observed before, and by that he doth know the instant to bid last which is very pretty.'

Auctions 'by the candle' persisted in parts of England right into the nineteenth century. By the 1670s, however, new methods of auctioning goods began to supercede this haphazard system, methods already in extensive use on the continent which appear to have originated among Dutch traders and businessmen.

Auctions of books and pictures had been held in Holland since the early years of the seventeenth century. In 1636, Dutch traders were the first to have introduced the concept of the buyer's

Some early art dealing taking place in the courtyard of Amsterdam's first auction house, the Oude-Zyds Heerenlogement, as depicted in an eighteenth-century engraving. (ABOVE)

The auctioneer's hammer in use at Sotheby's between 1744 and 1837. (TOP)

A book sale at Sotheby's auction room held in May 1888. (ABOVE)

premium, part of which was used as a payment to the poor. (This benevolent arrangement was soon withdrawn, however, after widespread abuse.) Records exist of some notable auctions of works of art, including the sale of seventy-eight paintings from the collection of the English Earl of Arundel held in Amsterdam in September 1684, and the sales in 1657 and 1658 of Rembrandt's paintings, drawings, prints and art collections, which had been ordered by the Amsterdam Chamber of Insolvent Estates.

These auctions were conducted by a method we would recognise today, the participants calling out higher and higher bids until one bidder emerged unchallenged. As illustrated by the Earl of Arundel's sale, respect for the Dutch art market and their auction methods was international. However, this good reputation was eventually soured by disreputable auctioneers eager to make a quick fortune. The Dutch guilds conspired to obtain a share of the great wealth being created, and they successfully influenced the state to make it obligatory for all auctions to be attended and observed by a guild notary and for all auction results to be reported to them.

The Dutch auction world's freedom from such regulation had been the root of its success, and by the beginning of the eighteenth century the profession was in sharp decline. By the time the English auction houses were established later that century, London had taken over as the centre of the north European art trade.

The earliest recorded auction sale of paintings in London was held at Somerset House in 1674. The sale of 'rare Italian pictures' was advertised in the *London Gazette* (14 - 18 May), and the paintings were to be 'sold (by way of out-cry) peece by peece to those who shall bid most'. Despite experiments with various auctioning methods such as 'mineing' – a system whereby the first person to shout 'mine' was the purchaser – by 1680 regular auctions of books and paintings were being held in London using the new continental method. Rules of payment became standardized as well.

The more enterprising auctioneers had also begun to create a standard practice. They were active in London throughout the 'season' (few sales were ever held in the summer months to judge from the surviving evidence), and in August they followed the fashionable world to Epsom and Tunbridge Wells.

The auction room satisfied two demands for social entertainment during this period: a sale of paintings was both an opportunity for fashionable display, and something of a gamble. Auctions also fulfilled the needs of those people, increasing in number, who were interested in art, offering them the opportunity to learn the names of the more famous painters, and what their paintings looked like.

During the 1680s and 1690s London auctions were held in the City inns and coffee-houses, at the Banqueting House (which, it appears, could be hired by anyone close to the King), and at the new Exchanges, which possessed large rooms let for such purposes. These remained the locations for most sales in the early eighteenth century, and only the most successful auctioneers were able to rent or buy their own premises.

The earliest examples of the standard auctioneer's tool – the hammer – appear to date from around this time, although the device is probably far more ancient in origin. Preserved at Sotheby's in London is the hammer used by Langford, Baker (the founder of the firm) and then Leigh, from whom it passed to Benjamin Wheatley, who had once served as clerk to both Leigh and Sotheby and who subsequently set up as a book auctioneer on his own in Piccadilly. Langford was active in 1710, and this is one of the few hammers which can be fairly accurately dated. This same hammer was eulogized in a poem written by Dibden in 1812, *Bibliography: A poem.*

'and down
Th' important hammer drops (this instrument
Had wielded been of old by Langford; he
With dying breath to Baker did bequeath
This sceptre of dominion, which now decks
The courteous hand of Leigh).'

Methods of catching the auctioneer's eye have become more and more sophisticated. Christopher Weston, Chairman of Phillips, has told of the time he took his first ever sale in the company's main salerooms. After the sale was over a large gentleman came up to him shaking his fists: 'You little ...,' he screamed, 'You didn't take my bid.' 'I am sorry, sir,' Weston replied, 'but you were not in the room then.' 'Don't you know that when I go out of the room, I am bidding. I've been coming here for twenty-three years – you ought to know.'

Other tales of misinterpretation abound, as do those that reveal the harsher side of auctioneering. At the beginning of the century a print seller by the name of Rimell used to attend auctions at Sotheby's when the formidable Sir Anderson Montague-Barlow was at the rostrum. Rimell suffered from sleepiness and often nodded off. It may be that Sir Montague misinterpreted the

gentle nodding, or it may be that he found such behaviour a little too impolite, but when Rimell awoke he frequently found himself the purchaser of a good number of unexpected lots.

These days auctioneers are not often so dictatorial, and a sense of humour is sometimes an important part of maintaining control. On one recent occasion during a book sale the bidder sat on a fire extinguisher, unexpectedly releasing the contents and covering the room and its occupants with white foam. The auctioneer patiently waited until the chaos had died down and addressed the culprit quite calmly, saying, 'Do I take that as a bid, sir?' Such jinks would never have been countenanced in the days of the Praetorian Guard.

The 'Art of Bidding' cartoon which appeared in *Punch* on 25 January 1933. (ABOVE)

CHRONOLOGY

SOCIAL & POLITICAL HISTORY		THE VISUAL ARTS	
1745-6	Second Jacobite Rebellion	1745-54	Zimmerman: The Wieskirche
		1749	Canaletto: *A View of St James's Park*
		1759	Wedgwood sets up in business
		1760-9	Adam: Syon House
1765	Watt develops the steam engine	1765	Reynolds: *Lady Sarah Bunbury*
1768	Cook's first voyage to Australia	1768	Royal Academy, London, founded
1776	American Declaration of Independence		
1780s	Industrial Revolution begins in Britain	1784-5	David: *Oath of the Horatii*
		1787-93	Canova: *Cupid and Psyche*
1789	French Revolution; Declaration of the Rights of Man	1789	Houdon: *Thomas Jefferson*
		1795-1827	Soane: Bank of England, London
1796	Senefelder invents lithography		
1803-15	Napoleonic Wars		
1806	Jacquard invents his mechanical loom	1808-16	Goya: *The Disasters of War*
		1812	Turner: *Snowstorm* (Hannibal)
1815	Battle of Waterloo		
		c.1817	Friedrich: *Wanderer above the Mists*
		1817	Constable: *Flatford Mill*
		1819	Géricault: *The Raft of the Medusa*
		1823-47	Smirke: British Museum, London
		1831	Delacroix: *28 July: Liberty leading the People*
1837-1901	Reign of Queen Victoria		
1839	Invention of photography	1839-52	Barry/Pugin: Houses of Parliament
		1842	Fabergé established in St Petersburg
1848	Revolutions in France, Germany, Italy and Austria	1848	Pre-Raphaelite Brotherhood formed
		1849	Courbet: *The Burial at Ornans*
1851	Great Exhibition, London	1851	Paxton: Crystal Palace, London
1853-6	Crimean War		
		1859	Ingres: *The Turkish Bath*
1861	Emancipation of serfs, Russia	1861	Morris, Marshall, Faulkner & Co founded
1861-5	American Civil War	c1861	Garnier: Opéra, Paris
		1863	Manet: *Déjeuner sur l'Herbe*
1869	Suez Canal opened; Transcontinental railroad completed in USA	c.1869	Renoir: *La Grenouillère*

LITERATURE		MUSIC	
1751-72	Diderot: *Encyclopedie ... des Sciences, des Arts et des Metiers*	1749	J.S. Bach: *The Art of the Fugue*
1759	Voltaire: *Candide*		
1762	Rousseau: *The Social Contract*		
1764	Winkelmann: *History of Art*		
1770s	Sturm und Drang (Storm and Stress) movement		
1787	Schiller: *Don Carlos*	1787	Mozart: *Don Giovanni*
1789	Blake: *Songs of Innocence*		
		1804	Beethoven: *Eroica Symphony*
1808	Goethe: *Faust*, part 1		
1812	Byron: *Childe Harold's Pilgrimage*	1815	Schubert: *Erl King*
1831	Hugo: *The Hunchback of Notre Dame*		
		1839	Berlioz: *Romeo and Juliet*
1848	Marx and Engels: *Communist Manifesto*		
1851-3	Ruskin: *Stones of Venice*		
		1853	Verdi: *La Traviata*
1859	Darwin: *The Origin of the Species ...*	1859	Wagner: *Tristan and Isolde*
1864	Verne: *Journey to the Centre of the Earth*	1864	Bruckner: *Mass No. 1 in D Minor*
		1869	Brahms: *German Requiem*

1870	Franco-Prussian War; Schliemann begins excavations in Troy		
		1872	Monet: *Impression – Sunrise*; Whistler: *Nocturne in Blue and Silver*
		1874	First Impressionist exhibition, Paris; Degas: *Ballet Rehearsal*
		1878	Muybridge: *Galloping Horse*
1880	Boer riots, South Africa	1880	Rodin: *The Gates of Hell*
		1888	van Gogh: *Night Café*
1894	Dreyfus trial, Paris	1894	Sullivan: Guaranty Building, New York
1900	World Exhibition, Paris; Boxer Rising, China	1900	Munch: *Dance of Life*
1904-5	Russo-Japanese War	1904	Cezanne: *Mont Sainte Victoire*
		1906	Matisse: *Joy of Life*; first Die Brucke exhibition
		1907	Picasso: *Les Demoiselles d'Avignon*
		1909	Birth of Futurist Movement
		1913	Kandinsky: *Composition VII*; Epstein: *Rock Drill*; Armory Show, New York
1914-18	World War I		
1917	Russian Revolution	1917	Duchamp: *Fountain*
		1919	Gropius founds the Bauhaus, Weimar
		1920	First international Dada-Fair, Berlin
1921	Foundation of Fascist Movement, Italy		
		1926	Moore: *Reclining Figure*
1929	Wall Street Crash	1929	Ernst: *Les Femmes 100 Têtes*
		1932	Hopper: *Room in New York*
1936-9	Spanish Civil War	1937	Picasso: *Guernica*
1939-45	World War II		
		1943	Mondrian: *Broadway Boogie-Woogie*; F.L. Wright: Guggenheim Museum, New York
1945	Atomic bombs: Hiroshima, Nagasaki	1949-50	Marini: *Horse and Rider*
		1950	Le Corbusier: Notre Dame du Haut, Ronchamp
		1958	Johns: *Three Flags*
		1962	Bacon: *Three Studies for a Crucifixion*
1965-75	Vietnam War		
1966	Cultural Revolution, China		
		1967	Warhol: *Marilyn*; Hockney: *Bigger Splash*
1969	First man on the moon		
		1971-7	Pompidou Centre, Paris
1985	Gorbachev to power, USSR	1985	Beuys: *Plight*
1989	Fall of Berlin Wall; student riots, Beijing		
1992	Hostilities in the Balkans		
		1993-4	Rachel Whiteread: *House*

		1870	Wagner: *The Valkyrie*
1871-2	Eliot: *Middlemarch*	**1871**	Verdi: *Aida*
		1874	Musorgsky: *Pictures at an Exhibition*
1876	Twain: *Tom Sawyer*		
1880	Zola: *Nana*; Ibsen: *Ghosts*		
1883	Nietzsche: *Thus Spoke Zarathustra*	**1883**	Dvořák: *Stabat Mater*
1891	Wilde: *The Picture of Dorian Gray*		
		1894	Debussy: *Prelude d'après-midi d'un faun*
1900	Freud: *The Interpretation of Dreams*;	**1900**	Sibelius: *Finlandia*
	Chekhov: *Uncle Vanya*; Conrad: *Lord Jim*	**1904**	Janáček: *Jenufa*; Puccini: *Madame Butterfly*
1905	Einstein: *Theory of Relativity*	**1905**	R. Strauss: *Salome*
		1907	Delius: *Brig Fair*
1909	Gertrude Stein: *Three Lives*	**1909**	Schoenberg: *Gurrelieder*
1913	D.H. Lawrence: *Sons and Lovers*; Proust:	**1913**	Stravinsky: *The Rite of Spring*
	Remembrance of Things Past		
		1914-16	Holst: *The Planets*
1917	Kafka: *The Trial*; Mann: *Man of Straw*	**1917**	Satie: *Parade*
		1919	de Falla: *The Three-Cornered Hat*
1920	Wharton: *Age of Innocence*	**1920**	Milhaud: *Le Boeuf sur le toit*
		1921	Walton: *Façade*
1926	T.E. Lawrence: *The Seven Pillars of Wisdom*		
1932	Huxley: *Brave New World*		
		1937	Shostokovich: *Symphony No. 5*
1942	T.S. Eliot: *Four Quartets*		
1945-9	Sartre: *Les Chemins de la Liberté*	**1945**	Britten: *Peter Grimes*
1949	Beauvoir: *The Second Sex*; Orwell: *1984*		
1958	Capote: *Breakfast at Tiffany's*; Pinter:	**1958**	Varèse: *Poème Electronique*
	The Caretaker		
1967	Marquez: *One Hundred Years of Solitude*		
		1969	Henze: *Sixth Symphony*
		1985	Birtwistle: *The Mask of Orpheus*
1988	Rushdie: *Satanic Verses*	**1988**	Reich: *Different Trains*
1993	Vikram Seth: *A Suitable Boy*		

II
ART
AT
AUCTION

THE FINE ARTS *by Alexander Apsis*

CHARLES LEROY
SAINT-AUBERT
**Une Brasserie au
Quartier Latin
(detail)**
SIGNED AND DATED *1884,*
OIL ON CANVAS,
182.2 x 254.3cm
(71¾ x 100⅛in)
New York $607,500
(£400,950). 26.V.94. (LEFT)

The 1993–94 season saw the continuing consolidation of the art market, following the end of the boom period of 1987–90. When the market was at its peak there was a large number of speculative investment buyers as well as collectors. In the weak market that followed, the great majority of these buyers disappeared and have not returned, allowing a growing number of private collectors to enter or re-enter the market. The 1993–94 season was one of overwhelming dominance by these collectors.

Impressionist and Modern sales in New York and London this season clearly illustrated this trend. The two highlights of the November sale in New York were Henri Matisse's La Vis and the Stanley J. Seeger Collection of works by Pablo Picasso. Strong bidding from both the museum world and private collectors pushed the Matisse to a record price for any work on paper. The Picasso sale was even more remarkable, with a large number of new private collectors actively participating, and all eighty-eight works being successfully sold. The May sales in New York continued this trend with fifty of the sixty-nine works in Part I finding buyers, one of the highest success ratios for such a sale since 1990. This sale was also notable for the $11,662,500 fetched by Gustav Klimt's Dame mit Fächer, the highest price obtained by any work of art at auction in 1994. Sales in London mirrored these results, underlining the truly international nature of this market. In June Edouard Manet's Un Bar aux Folies-Bergère and Claude Monet's Peupliers au bord de l'Epte, Effet du Soir both exceeded their estimates and confirmed that there is a strong demand for top quality works, realistically estimated.

EDGAR DEGAS
La Toilette
SIGNED, PASTEL OVER
MONOTYPE ON PAPER,
31.1 x 27cm (12¼ x 10⅝in)
New York $2,092,500
(£1,404,362). 11.V.94.
From the Estate of Wendell
Cherry (BELOW)

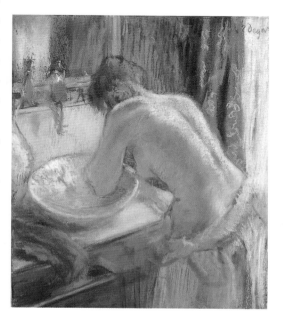

FREDERIC REMINGTON
Coming Through the Rye
BRONZE, BLACK BROWN PATINA,
ON A GREEN MARBLE BASE
height 73cm (28¾in)
New York $1,212,500
(£819,256). 2.XII.93.
From a Collection formed by
William C. Foxley (ABOVE)

One of the finest Old Master collections to have appeared on the market in the past twenty years was that of Peter Jay Sharp, which was sold in New York in January. Two of the highlights were Annibale Carracci's Boy Drinking, *which went to the Cleveland Museum of Art, and Giovanni Girolamo Savoldo's* Portrait of a Young Man with a Soprano Recorder, *which was returned to the artist's native city, Brescia, when it was purchased by Banco di Brescia. It now hangs in the Pinacoteca Civica Tosio-Martinengo and compliments their extraordinary collection of sixteenth-century Brescian paintings. The London Old Masters department also has had an extremely good year, culminating in the July sale, which contained an impressive group of Dutch and Flemish paintings. The highlight was clearly Aelbert Cuyp's* Orpheus Charming the Animals, *which sold for over ten times the pre-sale estimate. Unrecorded since 1768, this important addition to Cuyp's* oeuvre *was rediscovered by a Sotheby's expert on a routine visit.*

In Amsterdam three separate private collections of Dutch Old Master drawings were offered for sale during the season. The F.C. Butôt, H.R. Bijl and Jacobus A. Klaver collections all attracted a great deal of international attention and were resounding successes.

Thomas Gainsborough's Portrait of Georgiana, Duchess of Devonshire *was certainly the most talked about British picture sold in London this season, if not the most expensive. The painting was purchased by the present Duke of Devonshire and has now returned to Chatsworth, its original home. British pictures dating from post-1850 also performed well this season. Highlights included a triptych created for St Paul's church in Brighton by Sir Edward Coley Burne-Jones, which achieved £331,500, and* Love and Beauty, *also by Burne-Jones, which more than doubled its low estimate. In New York, Edwin Long's* Vashti *set a new record when it sold for $371,000.*

The top lot in Sotheby's sales of Nineteenth-Century European Paintings this season was Jean-Baptiste Camille Corot's Les Petits Denicheurs, *which sold for $1,212,500 in New York in February. In May, Charles Leroy Saint-Aubert's* Une Brasserie au Quartier Latin *achieved the extraordinary price of $607,500, far exceeding its pre-sale estimate of $150,000–$250,000.*

SIR EDWARD COLEY
BURNE-JONES
Love and Beauty
SIGNED *E.B.J.* AND DATED
1874, PENCIL,
89 x 118cm (35 x 46½in)
London £122,500 ($181,300).
30.III.94. (ABOVE)

The American Paintings and Sculpture department have had a particularly successful year with both the March and May sales exceeding their upper estimate ranges – the first time this has happened in over five years. In December, Sotheby's New York sold a large selection of works from the William Foxley Collection including Frederic Remington's Coming Through the Rye *which fetched $1,212,500, well above its pre-sale estimate. In May the American Impressionists were dominant, with John Singer Sargent's* Spanish Dancer *selling for a record $7,592,500.*

The most exciting event in the Contemporary art season was the sale of the works from the Mr and Mrs H. Gates Lloyd Collection at Sotheby's New York in May. The collection was particularly strong on post-World War II art with Arshille Gorky's Dark Green Painting *achieving $3,522,500 and David Smith's* Cubi V *selling for a record $4,072,500. The strength of the German Contemporary art market was demonstrated in Sotheby's London sales, with Gerhard Richter's* Seestück *selling for £309,500 and Joseph Beuys's* Stapelkopf Siegel *fetching a record price of £297,000.*

Although there were few headline-grabbing prices this season, there were many results that confirmed the strengthening foundation of the market. New collectors from Europe and North and South America were coupled with a nascent but growing interest in European paintings in Korea, Singapore, Malaysia, Thailand and Hong Kong, prompting us to hold in April our first preview exhibition in Hong Kong of Impressionist and Modern Art to be sold in London and New York. All the signs point to a slow but steady growth, and we look forward to another exciting season at Sotheby's.

ADRIAEN VAN DE VELDE
**Study of a Seated
Woman Holding
her Ankle, and Two
Separate Studies of
her Head**
RED CHALK,
15.6 x 14.5cm (6⅛ x 5¾in)
Amsterdam Dfl155,250
(£55,850:$83,450). 10.V.94.
From the Jacobus A. Klaver
Collection (ABOVE)

OLD MASTER PAINTINGS

GIOVANNI GIROLAMO SAVOLDO
Portrait of a Young Man with a Soprano Recorder
SIGNED *JOANES JERONIMUS SAVOLDIS DE / BRISIA / FACIEBAT*, OIL ON CANVAS, 74.3 x 100.3cm (29¼ x 39½in)
New York $1,542,500 (£1,028,300). 13.I.94
From the Estate of Peter Jay Sharp

Savoldo's influence on the development of naturalistic painting in Italy can be seen in this
portrait of a young man. The sitter has been momentarily interrupted in his playing by the
artist and gazes quietly and confidently at the viewer. From his clothing he is revealed as a
courtier, engaged in one of the requisite pursuits of a gentleman. (ABOVE)

ANNIBALE CARRACCI
Boy Drinking
OIL ON CANVAS,
55.9 x 43.8cm (22 x 17¼in)
New York $2,202,500
(£1,468,300). 13.I.94
From the Estate of Peter Jay Sharp

This startling image, now in the Cleveland Museum of Art, was created by Carracci during the first years of the 1580s, a most crucial period in the history of Italian painting. It probably dates to just after the artist's journey to Venice (*circa* 1581) and the subsequent founding of the Accademia dei Desiderosi in 1582 by Annibale and his brother Agostino in their cousin Ludovico's studio. The Accademia was both a workshop and a teaching institution, with emphasis on drawing on observed reality through the study of anatomy and optics, as well as literature and philosophy. The Carracci believed that only through the study of all these subjects could the artist re-'create' nature, and ultimately achieve the ideal. *Boy Drinking* is probably an exercise in the reflection of light and perspective. The artist's concern to capture a moment in time is revealed through the obvious rapidity with which he must have worked, even leaving parts of the canvas bare. (LEFT)

OSIAS BEERT THE ELDER
Still life
OIL ON PANEL, 52.5 x 73.3cm (20 ¾ x 28⅜in)
London £738,500 (1,137,300). 6.VII.94

Osias Beert was apprenticed to the Antwerp painter Andries van Baseroy in 1596 and
six years later, in 1602, was formally received as Master into the Guild of Saint Luke.
Little is known of his life, but his importance as one of the most influential artists of
the earliest generation of still life painters in Flanders has always been acknowledged.
The present, hitherto unpublished, work represents a particularly fine example of the
artist's predilection for so-called 'laden table' still lifes, which became a speciality in
Antwerp and Haarlem in the first two decades of the seventeenth century. (ABOVE)

PIETER DE WIT

Portrait of Dirck Wilre in the Castle of Elmina

SIGNED AND INSCRIBED *PR DE WIT FECIT IN'T KASTEEL ST GEORGE*, OIL ON CANVAS,
103.2 x 141.4cm (40½ x 55½in)
London £749,500 ($1,154,250). 6.VII.94
From the Collection of the Rt Hon. The Lord Harlech

Long thought to be a portrait of the Dutch admiral Michiel de Ruyter (1607–76), this painting has more recently been identified as depicting Dirck Wilre (1636–74).

Born the son of a ship-captain from Graft, Wilre is recorded as working for the Dutch West India Company on the Gold Coast (now the Republic of Ghana) a year after his arrival there in 1658. In 1662 he was briefly appointed Director-General of the North and South Coast of Africa and was re-appointed to the post from 1668 to 1674. Having survived the lethal climate for an unusually high number of years, Wilre left the Gold Coast in 1674 to return to Holland, only to be drowned at sea.

The artist's inscription at the foot of the painting identifies the interior as part of the castle of St George d'Elmina, which the Dutch captured from the Portuguese in 1637. Though nothing is known of the artist Pieter de Wit, his faithful attention to detail marks out the painting as a unique representation of the Dutch way of life in their African colonies. (ABOVE)

Orpheus Charming the Animals
SIGNED *A CUYP*, OIL ON CANVAS, 113 x 167cm (44½ x 65¾in)
London £4,181,500 ($6,439,500). 6.VII.94

This, one of Cuyp's largest and most ambitious works, was unrecorded from 1768 until its rediscovery early in 1994. The subject is taken from Ovid's *Metamorphoses,* which was popularized in the early seventeenth century by Karel van Mander's translation and commentary. It is a subject often found in Dutch paintings of the period, particularly in those of artists who specialized in depicting animals, and was also popular because of its political overtones – Orpheus was held to represent wise and peaceful government. (ABOVE)

FRANS JANSZ. POST

Brazilian Landscape with Three Figures by a Stream, Fort Frederik Hendrik on Antônio Vaz Island in the Distance

SIGNED AND DATED *F. POST 1640*, OIL ON CANVAS, 61.6 x 88.9cm (24¼ x 35in)
New York $3,577,500 (£2,396,900). 19.V.94

Frans Post left for Brazil on 25 October 1636 in the party of Prince Johan Maurits of Nassau-Siegen and landed at Recife in January 1637, remaining in the country for seven years. *Landscape with Three Figures by a Stream, Fort Frederik Hendrik in the Distance* is one of only six known surviving works painted by Post while he was in Brazil, the rest of his *oeuvre* being produced from sketches and from memory upon his return to Holland. The six Brazilian paintings (four of which are owned by the Musée du Louvre, Paris, and the fifth by the Rijksmuseum, Amsterdam) are dated from 1637 to 1640 and were part of a gift of forty-two works (including twenty-nine Post paintings) presented as a diplomatic gift to King Louis XIV of France by Prince Johan Maurits in 1679. Although the paintings were intended as topographical records of specific places – Fort Frederik Hendrik, on Antônio Vaz Island, had been newly laid out by the Prince as the new Dutch capital of Brazil – their simplicity of composition and starkness of form are striking in their boldness. The three figures in the foreground seem to be deliberately chosen and highly symbolic, representing the three races living together in Brazil at the time: an Indian, a black African and a European immigrant. (ABOVE)

FRANÇOIS-XAVIER FABRE

A View of Florence from the North Bank of the Arno looking East

SIGNED *F.X. FABRE. / 1813*, OIL ON CANVAS, 95.9 x 134.6cm (37¾ x 53in) London £309,500 ($476,650). 6.VII.94

In 1787 Fabre won the *Prix de Rome* and moved to Italy, where he remained, living principally in Florence, until 1826. While there he painted surprisingly few views of the city, concentrating mainly on portraiture. The first building seen here on the north bank of the river is the watermill, la Mulina della Vagaloggia, which was built in the fourteenth century and demolished in 1854 to make way for the new Lungarno Vespucci. Beyond is the Palazzo della Signoria and to the left the dome of the Duomo. (LEFT)

ABRAHAM STORCK

Admiralty Sailing in Formation on the Ij, with Amsterdam Beyond

SIGNED *A STORCK*, OIL ON PAPER LAID DOWN ON PANEL, 23 x 34cm (9 x 13⅜in) Amsterdam Dfl322,000 (£114,200:$170,370). 16.XI.93 From the F.C. Butôt Collection

This fine painting, dating from the 1690s, shows *boeier* and *bezan* yachts, each flying the Admiralty flag, sailing in formation. Such displays were arranged on the occasion of state visits, so that the Dutch Navy could impress eminent visitors with their handling skills at close quarters. The small cannon being fired by the vessel in the left foreground is giving a signal to the participating yachts. (RIGHT)

GERARD VAN SPAENDONCK
Still Life
SIGNED AND DATED *G. VAN SPAENDONCK 1787*, OIL ON CANVAS, 100 x 81.6cm (39⅜ x 32⅛in)
New York $1,047,500 (£701,800). 19.V.94
From the Estate of Wendell Cherry

The Salon of 1787 included two paintings by van Spaendonck – one painted for Louis XVI in 1785 and now at Fontainebleau, and the present still life, which belonged at the time to Louis' brother, the Comte d'Arthois. The correspondent to the *Mercure de France*, in reviewing the exhibition, wrote that the Comte d'Arthois' painting was in no way inferior to that of the King and he placed van Spaendonck 'beside the celebrated Van Huysum'. (ABOVE)

OLD MASTER DRAWINGS

ADRIAEN PIETERSZ, VAN DE VENNE
To Each His Own Pastime
SIGNED *ADR V VENNE*, RED CHALK, 35.2 x 44.9cm (13⅞ x 17¹¹⁄₁₆in)
Amsterdam DFL209,300 (£74,200:$110,750). 17.XI.93
From the H.R. Bijl Collection

Van de Venne made his reputation in seventeenth-century
Holland through his illustrations to the popular moralizing
publications of Jacob Cats. He also produced a number of
independent drawings and paintings in a similar vein,
including the present work. *To Each His Own Pastime*
operates on at least three levels: aesthetic, humourous and
allegorical. It is a highly-skilled drawing which conveys
drama and subtlety of composition and texture. The
humorous element is provided by the faintly ridiculous pose
of the gentleman and by the elegant couple's attempts to
play shuttlecock in a domestic interior. On a symbolic level,
van de Venne's opinion of the motto is made clear by his
inclusion of the time honoured *vanitas* symbols of discarded
playing cards and drinking vessels, and by the figure of
death peeping out from behind the curtain. (LEFT)

BALDASSARE FRANCESCHINI,
CALLED IL VOLTERRANO
La Burla del Vino
RED CHALK AND RED WASH,
24.2 x 36.7cm (9½ x 14⅝in)
London £91,700 ($141,200). 4.VII.94

This previously unknown drawing
is a preparatory study for
Volterrano's famous painting *La
Burla del Vino*, now in the Palazzo
Pitti, Florence. The painting was
executed *circa* 1640 for Francesco
Parrocchiani, who was in the
service of Lorenzo de'Medici. The
drawing focuses on the priest,
Arlotto Mainardi, a comic
character belonging to the Tuscan
tradition of burlesque humour,
who appears on the right of the
work, carrying a jug of wine.
(RIGHT)

GERARD TER BORCH THE
YOUNGER

A Milk Market in a Town Square
16 x 20.1cm (6⅜ x 7¹⁵⁄₁₆in)
Amsterdam DFl276,000
(£99,300:$148,400). 10.V.94
From the Jacobus A. Klaver
Collection

This highly atmospheric drawing of a marketplace is probably the finest of the very small number of ter Borch's drawings which did not pass to the Rijksmuseum, Amsterdam, with the rest of the artist's studio estate in the late nineteenth century. It was probably executed not long after ter Borch's apprenticeship with Pieter Molijn in 1634. (LEFT)

CLAUDE GELLÉE, CALLED CLAUDE
LORRAIN

Apollo as a Herdsman, Playing a Pipe, Mercury in the Background
GREY WASH HEIGHTENED WITH WHITE AND PEN AND
BROWN INK, 19.4 x 27.1cm (7⅝ x 10¹¹⁄₁₆in)
New York $101,500 (£67,650). 12.I.94

The subject of this drawing is taken from Ovid's *Metamorphoses*, Book i. Apollo is sent by Zeus to serve Admetus, King of Pherae. While Apollo sits attending the King's herds and piping his divine music, the mischievous Mercury steals the cattle behind him. (RIGHT)

BRITISH PICTURES 1500–1850

THOMAS GAINSBOROUGH
Portrait of Georgiana, Duchess of Devonshire
OIL ON CANVAS, 127 x 101.5cm (50 x 40in)
London £265,500 ($416,800). 13.VII.94
From the Estate of Mabel Satterlee Ingalls

On 6 May 1876 the sale of this portrait was described in the Art Sales column of *The Times*: 'All the world had come to see a beautiful Duchess created by Gainsborough, and, so far as we could observe, they all came, saw, and were conquered by the fascinating beauty.' At that sale the work fetched an astonishing 10,000 guineas – a record price at auction for any picture – and, as the correspondent wrote, 'the whole affair was, of its kind, one of the most exciting ever witnessed'. The sitter was the eldest daughter of John, 1st Earl Spencer and his wife Georgiana Poyntz. At the age of seventeen, she married William, 5th Duke of Devonshire, and became the leader of fashionable society in London. Widely regarded as one of the most beautiful and gifted women of her generation, she was a great favourite of both Gainsborough and Reynolds, for whom she sat on a number of occasions. This portrait, dated *circa* 1785–88, was bought at Sotheby's London in July by the present Duke of Devonshire, and is now on display in the public rooms at Chatsworth. (RIGHT)

The Presentation of a Pineapple to Charles II

ENGLISH SCHOOL, *c.*1677, OIL ON CANVAS, 103 x 118cm (40½ x 46½in)
London £463,500 ($686,000). 13.IV.94
From the Collection of the Rt Hon. the Lord Harlech

By tradition, this celebrated image shows John Rose, the Royal Gardener, presenting the first pineapple raised in England to Charles II. Judging from the age of the monarch and the date of his costume, the picture was probably painted *circa* 1677 and is a rare example of the King in ordinary day dress. It is extremely likely that the man holding the pineapple is John Rose, but although the fruit was certainly known in England by Charles II's reign, having been imported from the West Indies and later from Holland, none was grown in this country until the end of the century. A smaller version of this early conversation piece was formerly in the collection of Horace Walpole. (ABOVE)

BEN MARSHALL

Portrait of a Sportsman Carrying a Gun, with a Pointer in a Landscape

SIGNED AND DATED *B. MARSHALL PT. 1799*, OIL ON CANVAS, 68.5 x 89cm (27 x 35in) London £276,500 ($409,200). 10 XI.93 From the Estate of the late Mrs Norma Moller

Ben Marshall (1768–1835) was a pupil of the portrait painter Lemuel Francis Abbott, but having found 'many a man who will pay me fifty guineas for painting his horse, who thinks ten guineas too much for painting his wife', he decided to concentrate on sporting pictures. (LEFT)

SIR EDWIN HENRY LANDSEER, R.A.

Poachers Deerstalking

OIL ON CANVAS, 150.8 x 66cm (20 x 26in) New York $222,500 (£146,850). 3.VI.94

Landseer (1802–73) made his first visit to the Scottish Highlands in 1824, and its scenery, along with the excitement of hunting, exercised a strong influence on his work for many years. As Queen Victoria's favourite painter, he moved in the highest social circles from an early age, and was often invited on more lawful deerstalking expeditions than that depicted in the present work. (RIGHT)

HENRY WALTON AND SAWREY GILPIN
Portrait of Richard Bendyshe
INSCRIBED *RICHARD BEYNDYSHE / FIGURE PAINTED BY WALTON / DOG BY GILPIN*, OIL ON CANVAS,
74 x 62cm (29 x 24½in)
London £98,300 ($145,500). 13.IV.94

The sitter in this portrait was the second son of Ralph and Mary Bendyshe.
In 1783 he married Jane, daughter of John Jervis of Darlaston, Staffordshire,
by whom he had four sons. In 1777 he inherited Barrington Hall, near
Cambridge, from his uncle, also Richard Bendyshe, who never married. (BELOW)

ARTHUR DEVIS
Portrait of Frederick Montagu
SIGNED *A DEVIS FE 1749*, OIL ON CANVAS, 160 x 41cm (23¾ x 16in)
London £95,000 ($140,600). 10.XI.93

Frederick Montagu was the son of Charles Montagu of
Papplewick Hall and his wife Anne Colladon. He was
educated at Eton and Trinity College, Cambridge, and
from an early age showed literary and theatrical interests.
At the age of sixteen he took part in a performance of
Joseph Addison's celebrated tragedy *Cato*, which covers
the last phase of the life of Marcus Cato, the Republican
who killed himself rather than surrender to Caesar. The
performance took place at Leicester House, home of
Frederick, Prince of Wales, who was a friend of the
family. In this portrait Devis depicted the young
Montagu dressed for his role. (ABOVE)

BRITISH WATERCOLOURS

JOSEPH MALLORD
WILLIAM TURNER

Beach Scene on the South Coast

WATERCOLOUR OVER PENCIL,
29 x 43cm (11½ x 17in)
London £89,500 ($132,450).
14.IV.94

In this work, dating from
the mid 1820s, Turner
holds together the
complicated arrangement
of figures in the
foreground by using
broad plains of colour to
make up the sky and
beach. Research suggests
that the distant tower on
the headland is St
Leonard's Church,
Folkstone, making the
viewpoint East Wear
Bay, between Folkstone
and Dover. (LEFT)

JOHN CONSTABLE

A Ploughman near East Bergholt Overlooking the Stour Estuary

WATERCOLOUR OVER PENCIL ON LAID PAPER, 19.5 x 30.5cm
(7¾ x 12in)
London £95.000 ($140,600). 11.XI.93

This recently discovered work shows a small
coombe to the west of East Bergholt looking
south-east to the Stour estuary. It is one of
only three known watercolours dating from
1805, an important year in Constable's career
as a painter, which 'marks the start of a sudden
and dramatic development in Constable's
understanding and management of the art of
landscape'. (Ian Fleming-Williams, *Constable
and his Drawings*, 1991.) (RIGHT)

THOMAS GIRTIN

Berry Pomeroy Castle, Devon

SIGNED *GIRTIN*, WATERCOLOUR OVER PENCIL ON LAID PAPER, LAID ON CONTEMPORARY
WASHLINE MOUNT, 27.5 x 39cm (10¾ x 15¼in)
London £63,100 ($99,050). 14.VII.94

During the summer of 1797 Girtin travelled to the south-west of England.
The watercolours he made during that expedition are characterized by a
brighter palette and more vigorous drawing style than is associated with
his earlier tours. These characteristics are exemplified in this recently
discovered work, which dates from 1797 or 1798. (ABOVE)

THOMAS GAINSBOROUGH

Study of Mallows

PENCIL ON LAID PAPER, 19 x 15cm (7½ x 5⅜in)
London £25,300 ($37,444). 14.IV.94
From the Cornish Torbock Collection

This delicate drawing is Gainsborough's only known detailed plant
drawing. Dating from the late 1750s it is probably a page from the
artist's sketchbook and is perhaps a study for the foreground detail
of an eventual landscape. (LEFT)

BRITISH PICTURES FROM 1850

FREDERIC, LORD LEIGHTON
Greek Girls picking up Pebbles by the Sea
OIL ON CANVAS, 84 x 129.5cm (33 x 51in)
London £1,304,620 ($881,500). 30.III.94

Greek Girls picking up Pebbles by the Sea, first exhibited in 1871, represents the culmination of Leighton's move towards a type of subjectless classicism. Instead of taking a mythological or historical theme, the artist has simply arranged four elegant female figures across the composition. By concentrating on the abstract rhythm of shapes and colours to produce a harmonious overall pattern in this painting, rather than adhering to a logical scheme of perspective, Leighton achieved one of the most sublime expressions of the principles of the Aesthetic Movement. (ABOVE)

SIR EDWARD COLEY BURNE-JONES

Triptych: The Adoration of the Kings; the Annunciation

THREE PANELS, EACH OIL ON CANVAS, CENTRE PANEL108 x 156cm
(42½ x 61½in), SIDE PANELS EACH 108 x 77.35cm (42½ x 29in)
London £331,500 ($487,305). 3.XI.93
From the Property of the Parochial Council of St.Paul's, Brighton

During the early years of Burne-Jones's professional career much of his time was spent creating decorative furnishings for churches. He was in touch with the various architects of the day who were interpreting and adapting medieval prototypes in their construction and restoration of ecclesiastical buildings, and was conversant with the contemporary debate about appropriate styles of church decoration. The culmination of Burne-Jones's work as a designer of church furnishings, as well as one of the masterpieces of his career as a painter of religious subjects, is the present altarpiece, painted in 1861 for St Paul's church in Brighton. (ABOVE)

MODERN BRITISH PAINTINGS

WALTER RICHARD SICKERT
A Beribboned Washstand
SIGNED, OIL ON CANVAS, 56 x 46cm (22 x 18in)
London £155,500 ($239,470). 22.VI.94
From the Collection of Sir Tristan Antico, Sydney, Australia

The Beribboned Washstand belongs to the first major group of *intimiste* interiors of
Sickert's career and is one of his first known nudes. It was painted during his second
period in Venice in 1903–04, during which he largely forsook the landscape subjects
which had dominated his earlier visit of 1900–01. (ABOVE)

JACK BUTLER YEATS
The Great Tent has Collapsed
SIGNED, OIL ON CANVAS, 61 x 91.5cm (24 x 36in)
London £106,000 ($157,940). 24.XI.93

Painted in 1947, *The Great Tent has Collapsed*
was the first work produced by the artist after
the death of his wife, Cottie, in April of that
year. In *Jack B. Yeats: a Biography* Hilary Pyle
sees the painting as an expression of Yeats's
grief, describing it graphically: 'It is a day of
gale, and the great tent has collapsed, still
flapping in the wind. The crowd is scurrying
away in the background; but the ringmaster,
bareheaded…steps out of the light-coloured
remains of the big top and walks forward…
to meet the blowing storm.' (LEFT)

EDWARD BURRA
Dockside Café, Marseilles
SIGNED AND DATED *1929 AUG*, TEMPERA ON CANVAS, 48 x 67.5cm
(19¼ x 26½in)
London £111,500 ($171,700). 22.VI.94

Dockside Café, Marseilles dates from Burra's visit to the
ports of the South of France in September 1927 with
William Chappell, a friend from Chelsea polytechnic.
It is the first of a series of dockside bar scenes painted
between then and 1931, which take their subject from
direct experience rather than romantic vision. (RIGHT)

NINETEENTH–CENTURY EUROPEAN PAINTINGS

ALFRED DE DREUX
The Mounts of Abd el Kader
SIGNED AND DATED *58*, OIL ON CANVAS, 86.5 x 112.5cm (34 x 44 1/4 in)
London £463,500 ($685,980). 17.XI.93

From an early age De Dreux specialised in horse portraits and riding subjects, counting among his many patrons the Duc de Chartres, the Duc d'Orléans and Napoleon III. It was through his work for the Duc d'Orléans that he came to paint this equestrian portrait, depicting the mounts of the exiled Abd el Kader, the former leader of the Algerian forces in the war with the French. De Dreux won many prizes during his illustrious career and was at the height of his powers in the 1850s, having been made a *Chevalier* of the *Légion d'Honneur* in 1857. (ABOVE)

FERDINAND GEORG WALDMÜLLER
Die Blüthezeit (Blossom Time)
SIGNED AND DATED *1851*, OIL ON PANEL 85.1 x 64.8cm (33½ x 25½in)
New York $629,500 (£415,500). 26.V.94

Prof. Dr Rupert Feuchtmüller describes this painting as 'a characteristic "generation" subject, in which
a lively game played by children (the butterfly chase) represents the longing of youth as contrasted
with the contemplation (woman) and resignation (man) of old age. The positive title of the painting,
Blossom Time (poppies and meadow flowers bound into wreaths), refers to Waldmüller's main
principle of seeing and capturing in his art the liveliness and spring-like qualities of nature.' (ABOVE)

JEAN-BAPTISTE CAMILLE COROT
Les Petits Denicheurs
SIGNED TWICE, OIL ON CANVAS , 71.8 x 100.6 cm (28¼ x 39⅜in)
New York $1,212,500 (£819,250). 16.II.94

Painted at the end of his career (*circa* 1872–73), *Les Petits Denicheurs* is an example of Corot's later romantic landscapes. The viewer is invited into an enchanted world of youthful pleasures, hazy light and calm lakes bordered by verdant forests. (ABOVE)

FRANZ VON DEFREGGER
Wallfahrer
SIGNED AND DATED *1901*, OIL ON CANVAS,
136.5 x 178.5 cm (53¾ x 70⅛in)
Münich DM634,400 (£249,750:$372,150) 7.XII.93

A pupil of Karl Piloty, Franz von Defregger
rejected his teacher's predilection for historical
paintings, preferring to depict scenes of Tyrolean
rural life, such as this work. (LEFT)

JULIEN DUPRÉ
Le Regain (The Second Crop)
SIGNED, OIL ON CANVAS,
100 x 127.5 cm (9⅜ x 50⅜in)
New York $398,500
(£263,000). 26.V.94

Like his predecessor
Jean-François Millet,
Dupré was inspired to
portray the traditions
of rustic life in the late
nineteenth century,
producing a nostalgic
record of a way of life,
which both artists
rightly believed would
soon pass away. (RIGHT)

FILIPPO PALIZZI

Scavi di Pompei

SIGNED AND DATED *1870*, OIL ON CANVAS, 118 x 85cm (46½ x 33½in)
Milan L204,700,000. (£127,450:$193,100) 9.VI.94
From the Collection of the Ferruzzi Group

The rediscovery of Pompeii in 1748 caused immense excitement. This was
heightened when the systematic excavation of sculpture, paintings, mosaics
and other works of art, smothered under lava and ashes from the volcano
Vesuvius in August AD79, began in the Roman city in 1763. (RIGHT)

JEAN-LOUIS ERNEST MEISSONIER

The Battle of Friedland, 1807

SIGNED AND DATED *1888*, WATERCOLOUR ON PAPER, 144.8 x 252.7cm (57 x 99½in)
New York, $321,500 (£211,500). 13.X.93
From the Forbes Magazine Collection, New York

In the 1870s Meissonier began planning a cycle of five paintings to celebrate the
important events in the life of Napoleon I. Only two of these were completed:
one on the 1807 Battle of Friedland, and one on Napoleon's 1814 defeat. The
present work is a watercolour repeating Meissonier's amazingly detailed oil
painting, now in The Metropolitan Museum of Art. (BELOW)

Eugène Delacroix
Two Morrocans Seated in the Countryside
SIGNED, WATERCOLOUR,
22.4 x 28.5 cm (9 x 11¼in)
London £243,500,($370,100) 15.VI.94
From the Michel Bivort Collection, France

From January to May 1832 Delacroix visited Morocco with the Comte de Mornay's diplomatic mission sent by Louis-Philippe. Here the artist was greatly impressed by the North African light and the Moroccan people. During his stay he executed seven sketchbooks, three of which are now in the Louvre Museum. He kept these sketchbooks until his death, using them regularly as references for his compositions. This highly finished watercolour dates from between 1833 and Delacroix's 1844 exhibition in Marseille. (LEFT)

Giovanni Fattori
Sosta di Cavalleria
SIGNED, WATERCOLOUR,
35 x 47.5 cm (13¾ x 18¾in)
London £205,000 ($311,600) 15.VI.94

Giovanni Fattori was one of the leading members of the Macchiaioli, a group of artists working mainly in Florence, who were influenced by Corot and Courbet. In 1861 Fattori won a prize with his *Battle of Magenta,* which he followed with other military subjects, including the present work. (LEFT)

IMPRESSIONIST AND MODERN ART

EDOUARD MANET
Un Bar aux Folies-Bergère
OIL ON CANVAS, 47 x 56cm (18½ x 22in)
London £4,401,500 ($6,822,300). 28.VI.94
From a descendant of Franz Koenigs

This first realization of Manet's *Bar aux Folies-Bergère* was painted in the summer of 1881, a year before
the final version (p.40). The artist made various sketches of the Folies-Bergère, a variety theatre opened in
1869, which he used when painting this spontaneous rendering of a man's conversation with a barmaid
against a background of spectators reflected in the mirror behind. (ABOVE)

PIERRE-AUGUSTE RENOIR

Les Laveuses

SIGNED, OIL ON CANVAS, 65.4 x 54.6cm (25¾ x 21½in)
New York $4,952,500 (£3,346,300). 3.XI.93
From the Josephine Bay Paul and C. Michael Paul Foundations

Despite being crippled with arthritis towards the end of his life, Renoir painted ceaselessly and produced some of his greatest works. *Les Laveuses* was one of two canvases of washerwomen executed around 1912, which reveal the artist's concern with the integration of the female figure and the landscape, and show a return to a more classical manner of painting. (ABOVE)

CAMILLE PISSARRO
Route, Soleil d'Hiver et Neige
SIGNED, OIL ON CANVAS, 46 x 54.9cm (18⅛ x 21⅝in)
New York $2,202,500 (£1,488,200). 3.XI.93
From the Estate of Mrs Lucy Smith Battson

Pissarro moved to Louveciennes in 1869 and painted extensively there in the following three years, only interrupted by his exile in London during the Franco-Prussian War. The works from this period show a natural shift to a more suburban imagery, and often use the same basic format: a road receding into the distance, cutting a diagonal across the picture space, seen under different atmospheric conditions at all times of the year. (ABOVE)

EDOUARD VUILLARD
Sous le Portique
SIGNED, OIL ON BOARD, 61 x 48.5cm (23⅞ x 18⅞in)
London £463,500 ($690,600). 30.XI.93
From the Pierre Berès Collection

Painted in the summer of 1899 or 1900 in the garden of a rented house in L'Etang-la-Ville, *Sous le Portique* is a fusion of an intimate interior and the exterior landscape. Vuillard makes an 'interior' space using the structural frame of the portico and the lattice fence. The two seated ladies and young man sitting opposite are depicted in the shadows of the arbour taking afternoon tea. From this shaded vantage point, the figures are silhouetted against the lush, sunlit garden beyond. (ABOVE)

CLAUDE MONET

Peupliers au bord de l'Epte, Effet du Soir

SIGNED AND DATED *91*, OIL ON CANVAS, 100 x 65cm (39⅜ x 25½in) London £4,841,500 ($7,504,300). 28.VI.94

Early in 1891 Monet found a row of poplars lining the river Epte, two miles above Giverny. The trees were due to be cut down, so the artist bargained with their owner, delaying their fate until he had painted them. The *Poplars* series was begun in the summer of 1891. Monet worked from a flat-bottomed boat, giving him a viewpoint just above the waterline with the trees towering above him and the foreground entirely taken up by reflections. As with his other series, Monet worked on several canvases at once in order to capture the light of a particular time of day. Sometimes the effect lasted for just seven minutes, after which he would turn to the next canvas. (RIGHT)

GUSTAV KLIMT
Dame mit Fächer
OIL ON CANVAS, 100 x 100.3cm (39⅜ x 39½in)
New York $11,662,500 (£7,827,200). 11.V.94
From the Estate of Wendell Cherry

From the mid-1890s Klimt began a series of portraits of Viennese *grandes dames,* which demonstrated his ability to create iconic images that maintained a likeness to the sitter. *Dame mit Fächer* is dated to *circa* 1917–18, and shows an unidentified woman wearing a Chinese robe, holding a Japanese fan and standing against an embroidery or wall-hanging. The phoenix in the upper left corner is the emblem of the Chinese Empress, while lotus flowers signify purity in Buddhist art, giving the work a symbolic dimension. (ABOVE)

PABLO PICASSO
**Tête d'Homme
à la Pipe**
SIGNED, CHARCOAL
ON LAID PAPER,
61.9 x 47.6cm (24⅜ x 18¾in)
New York $1,597,500
(£1,079,400). 4.XI.93
From the Stanley J. Seeger
Collection

Executed in the summer
of 1912, *Tête d'Homme
à la Pipe* shows Picasso
already moving away
from the restrictions of
analytical Cubism. The
clearly defined outlines
of each plane and the
distinction between the
man and his surrounding
space suggest the artist
began from a naturalistic
line drawing. Picasso's
earlier works in this form
show no hint of emotion
but as Jean S. Boggs has
observed, 'humour for
the first time appears in
his work…in the hat, the
moustache, the mouth
and even in the mockery
of the analytical Cubist
eyes' (Boggs, *Picasso and
Man,* 1964, p.72). (RIGHT)

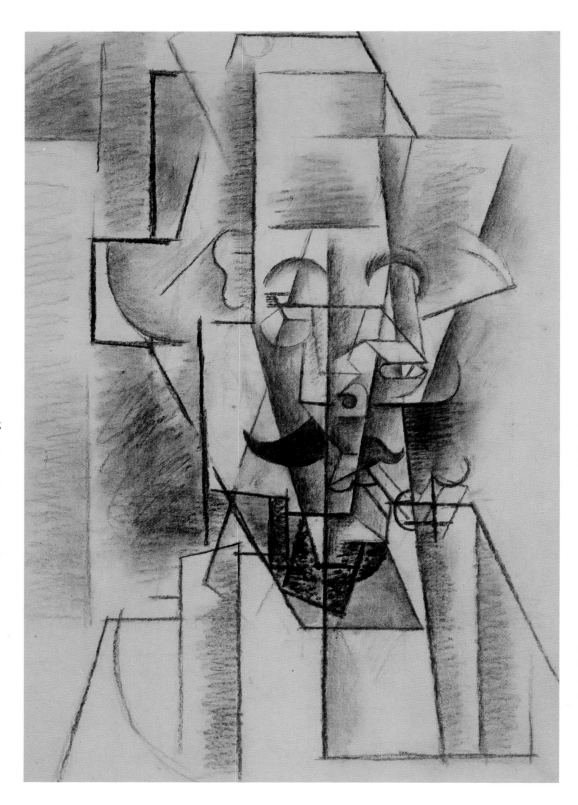

PABLO PICASSO

Femme et Enfants au Bord de la Mer
SIGNED, OIL ON CANVAS, 81 x 100cm (31⅞ x 39⅜in)
New York $4,402,500 (£2,974,600). 4.XI.93
From the Stanley J. Seeger Collection

Picasso spent the summers of 1930 and 1931 in the South of France at Cannes and Juan-les-Pins. On returning to Paris he began to paint women and children frolicking on the beach, including *Baigneuses, Le Sauvetage* and the present work, all dating from November 1932. These works are related to the beach scenes from previous summers in Dinard, but in this later series the figures are rendered with more fluid and organic contours. *Le Sauvetage* depicts the rescue of a swooning or drowning woman and this tragic element profoundly affects the mood of *Femme et Enfants au Bord de la Mer.* In spite of its apparently innocuous title, the present work is characterized by extreme contrasts – light-hearted activities and tragic events, downward swooping and upward reaching movements, none of which is clarified by the superimposition of a sequence of strongly coloured, irregularly shaped planes. (ABOVE)

PABLO PICASSO

Compotier avec Grappe de Raisin

SIGNED, PAPER COLLAGE, GOUACHE, CHARCOAL AND CRAYON ON PAPER, 48 x 42.5cm (18⅞ x 16¾in)

London £815,500 ($1,264,000). 28.VI.94

Formerly in the Collection of Darius Milhaud

Having seen Braque's *Compotier et Verre* in the summer of 1912, Picasso began to experiment in the medium of collage that autumn, and continued to produce many such examples throughout the 1910s and 1920s. *Compotier avec Grappe de Raisin*, executed in Paris in the spring of 1914, belongs to the most prolific phase of Picasso's activity in the medium and exhibits many of the characteristics of his *papiers-collés* of this period, such as pointillist stippling, a heightened and more lively use of colour, and a *trompe-l'oeil* effect, in this case produced by the introduction of a strip of wallpaper border, which casts a 'shadow' on the surrounding background. (ABOVE)

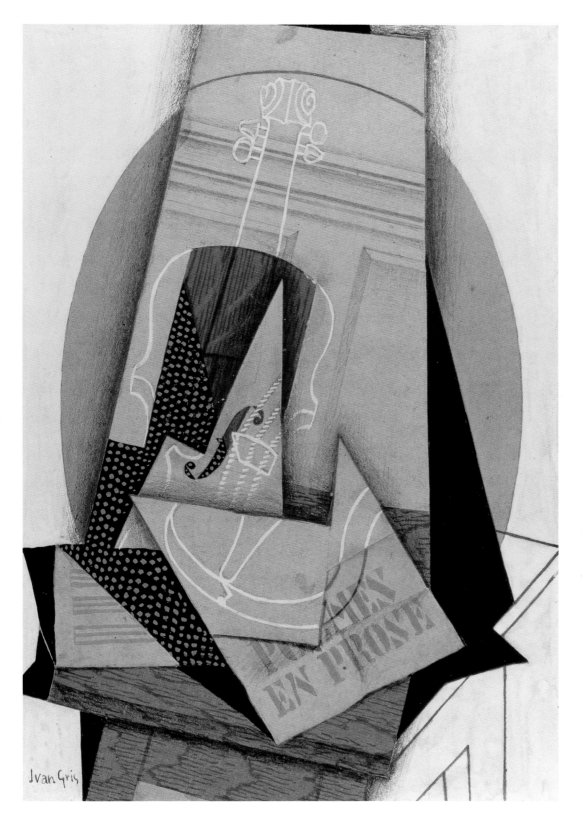

JUAN GRIS
Composition au Violon
SIGNED, COLLAGE, GOUACHE
AND PENCIL,
28 x 19.4cm (11 x 7⅝in)
London £463,500 ($690,60).
30.XI.93
From the Pierre Berès
Collection

Among Gris's circle of
friends in Paris during
World War I was the
poet Pierre Reverdy,
whose *Poèmes en Prose*
was published in 1915.
The first three copies of
this book had original
covers by Gris, of which
the present copy is the
second in the series. It is
possible that this is the
only book left with its
original cover intact. In
Composition au Violon
Gris applies layers of
solid planes of colour on
a white gouache ground.
The tabletop and violin
are defined using 'fake
wood' wallpaper, while a
pointillist black ground
indicates shadow. The
fragmented form of the
violin is shown in white,
and the leg and right
corner of the table are
finished in bold black
outline. (LEFT)

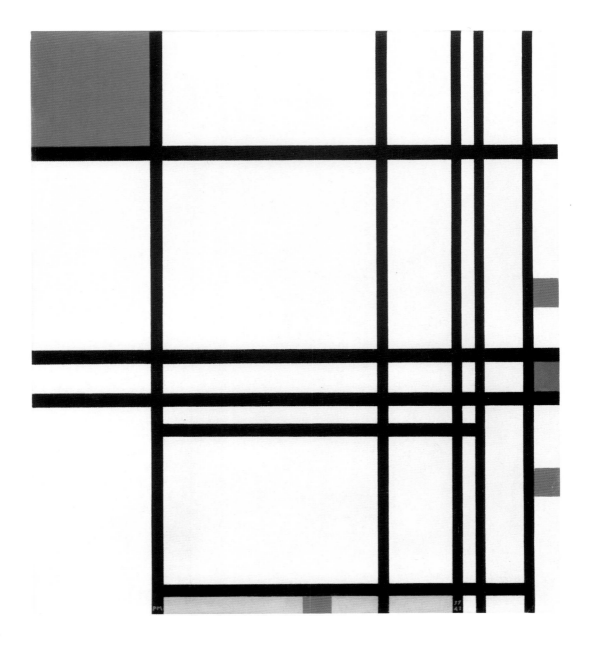

PIET MONDRIAN
Composition No.8
SIGNED WITH INITIALS AND DATED *39–42*, OIL ON CANVAS, 74.9 x 67.9cm (29½ x 26¾in)
New York $5,612,500 (£3,766,800). 11.V.94
From the Collection of Mr and Mrs H. Gates Lloyd

With the clouds of war gathering over Europe, Mondrian left Paris for London on 21 September 1938. The situation in London soon deteriorated, however, and as bombs began to fall the artist accepted an invitation to New York, arriving on 3 October 1940. *Composition No.8* dates from 1939–42 and is one of fifteen abstractions shown at Mondrian's first one-man exhibition at the Valentine Gallery, New York, at the beginning of 1942, where it was bought by Mr and Mrs H. Gates Lloyd. (ABOVE)

HENRI MATISSE
La Vis
GOUACHE ON PAPER, CUT AND PASTED, 174.9 x 81.9cm
(68⅞ x 32¼in)
New York $13,752,500 (£9,292,200). 3.XI.93

When Matisse created *La Vis* in 1951 he was no longer
working in two of the media that had characterized his
work up to this point – his last sculpture was executed
in 1950 and his last oil dates from the following year.
Yet Matisse, who had been a semi-invalid since 1941,
was no less active than before, and his paper cut-outs
represent the culmination and synthesis of his career,
combining, as they do, the expressive elements of
sculpture, drawing and painting. In *La Vis (The Wine
Press)* Matisse flattens the carved forms of the press,
creating jagged profiles that unify the top and bottom
halves of the composition. The richness of nature and
the satisfaction of a good harvest are suggested by the
two large organic forms over the geometric planes, the
two blue butterfly shapes halfway up the composition,
and the bottom row of purple angular shapes. (LEFT)

CONTEMPORARY ART

ARSHILE GORKY
Dark Green Painting
1948, SIGNED, OIL ON CANVAS, 111.1 x 141cm (43¾ x 55½in)
New York $3,522,500 (£2,332,800). 4.V.94
From the Collection of Mr and Mrs H. Gates Lloyd

Dark Green Painting was the last major painting Gorky produced before his suicide in July 1948. As with much of his *oeuvre,* nature, and in particular the landscape and farm life of his native Armenia and later in Virginia, was the inspiration behind the forms and colour of this work. (ABOVE)

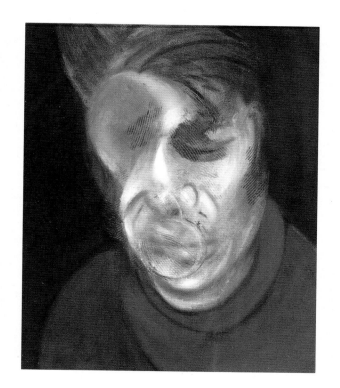
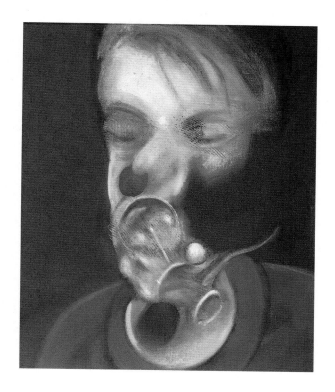

FRANCIS BACON
Self Portrait – Diptych
SIGNED AND DATED *1977*, OIL ON CANVAS, each canvas 35.5 x 30.5cm (14 x 12in)
London £353,500 ($523,200). 2.XII.93

Bacon's predilection for series was, as he once told David Sylvester, 'Partly because I see every image all the time in a shifting way and almost in shifting sequences.' His *Self Portrait – Diptych* of 1977 simultaneously draws and repels. The top of the head is cut off in both panels, as if the viewer were too near, yet the artist's eyes are closed, denying that nearness. The very work is a contradiction. Why should an artist who so often professed his self hate, produce so many self portraits? The answer perhaps lies in another conversation with David Sylvester: 'I loathe my own face…One of the nicest things that Cocteau said was "Each day in the mirror I watch death at work." This is what one does oneself.' (ABOVE)

JOSEPH BEUYS
Stapelkopf Siegel
SIGNED AND DATED *52,* ASSEMBLAGE WITH CARDBOARD, FAT, GOUACHE, PENCIL, HOUSE PAINT,
PENCIL LEADS AND GLASS IN ARTIST'S FRAME, 78 x 52cm (30¾ x 20½in)
London £298,500 (£462,675). 29.VI.94

Stapelkopf is a deeply evocative work. Its layering of fat, card and paint calls to mind
the sedimentation of earth, while the space between the collage and the glass suggests
the echoes of memory. The scratches in the glass and the cool colouring surrounding
the earthy, organic tones in the centre of the piece evoke the remains of ancient life,
as if preserved in ice. The signs of past life come to the fore through movement in the
scratchings and the markings which are so reminiscent of fingerprints. (ABOVE)

GERHARD RICHTER
Seestück (Leicht Bewölkt)
SIGNED AND DATED 69, OIL ON CANVAS, 200 x 200cm (78¾ x 78¾in)
London £309,500 ($458,050). 2.XII.93

In the late 1960s Richter moved away from subjects taken from newspaper cuttings to the painting of landscapes. Between 1969 and 1970 he produced a series of seascapes, which, though their origins (like much of his earlier work) lay in photographs, show a distinct shift towards classical painting. Richter's seascapes share an affinity with Monet's landscapes, with the artist exploring the variations of mood and atmospheric changes on the sea, as some of the titles of this series exemplify: *Seapiece (Contre Jour), Seapiece (Cloudy), Seapiece (Morning Mood)* and this work – *Seapiece (Slightly Cloudy).* (ABOVE)

LUCIAN FREUD
The Painter's Room
OIL ON CANVAS, 62.2 x 76.2cm (24½ x 30in)
London £507,500 ($786,600). 29.VI.94

Painted in 1943, shortly after Freud moved to a flat of his own, *The Painter's Room*
was the artist's largest picture to that date. A nearby junk shop provided him with the
battered sofa depicted in the painting, while the zebra was modelled from a stuffed
zebra's head then in the artist's possession. *The Painter's Room* has made some critics
suspect Freud of an early alignment with the Surrealists. The artist denies this,
however, and it is true that in the 1940s the number of stuffed trophies on English
walls would have made this effigy look less incongruous then it seems now. (ABOVE)

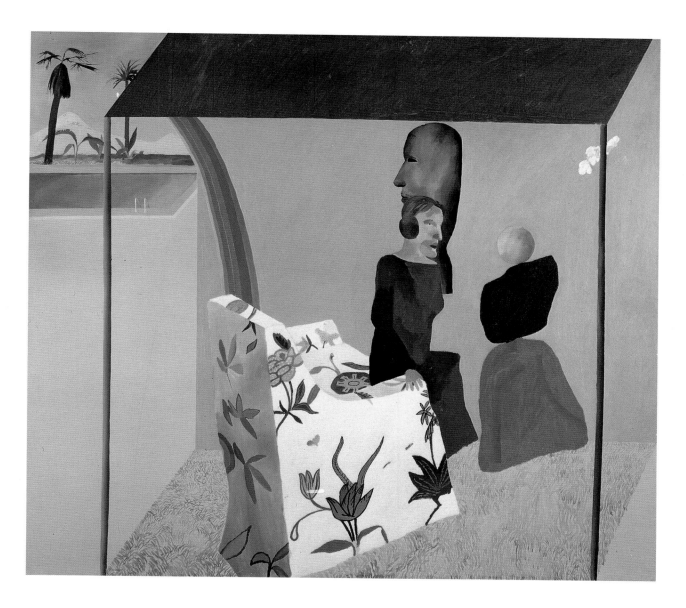

DAVID HOCKNEY

California Art Collector

1964, ACRYLIC ON CANVAS, 152.4 x 182.9cm (60 x 72in)
New York $1,020,000 (£689,200). 10.XI.93

California Art Collector was Hockney's second painting during his first stay in Los
Angeles in 1964 and his earliest major composition to incorporate the dramatic
impact that his new surroundings had on his subject matter, materials and technique.
In this work Hockney began to use acrylic paint, depicted his first swimming pool
and synthesized his initial impressions of the affluence and glamour of Beverly Hills.
The picture is not of a specific person but is a composite, generalized portrait of the
collectors Hockney visited during that revelatory trip. (ABOVE)

DAVID SMITH
Cubi V
SIGNED, TITLED AND DATED *JUNE 16, 1963*, POLISHED STAINLESS STEEL,
243.8 x 185.4 x 55.9cm (96 x 73 x 22in)
New York $4,072,500 (£2,697,000). 4.V.94
From the Collection of Mr and Mrs H. Gates Lloyd

Cubi V is one of the twenty-eight Cubi sculptures made by Smith between 1961 and
his death in 1965. The series represents the highpoint of the artist's career, showing
him drawing on Cubism, Constructivism, Surrealism and Expressionism to create his
own sculptural form. The three-dimensional geometric volumes of stainless steel
show a Cubist influence in their dynamic balance, yet their brilliantly polished
surfaces reflect the light to give a seemingly weightless quality to the sculptures. The
series is acknowledged as a masterpiece of American art. (ABOVE)

ALEXANDER CALDER

Constellation

SIGNED WITH INITIALS AND DATED *60*
PAINTED METAL STANDING MOBILE, overall 442cm (14ft 6in)
New York $1,817,500 (£1,228,000). 10.XI.93
From the Collection of the late Vera Neumann

This sculpture was acquired directly from the artist by the artist, designer and
entrepreneur Vera Neumann. The prominent red disc is a reference to her affinity
for solar motifs in her designs and prints. (ABOVE)

AMERICAN FOLK ART

EDWARD HICKS
Peaceable Kingdom of the Branch
OIL ON WOOD PANEL, 85.4 x 125.7cm (33⅜ x 49½ in)
New York $486,500 (£330,950). 24.X.93
From the Estate of Eugene Sussel

Edward Hicks was born in Pennsylvania in 1780. He was originally trained as a carriage and fancy sign painter, evidence of which can be seen in the lettering around this version of *The Peaceable Kingdom*. Hicks turned to easel painting on becoming a Quaker and during the early 1830s developed a format for his *Peaceable Kingdoms* based on the prophecy of Isaiah 11: 6–9. This composition shows a Delaware River landscape in the background with a flag on the stern of the ship in the harbour proclaiming 'Peace on Earth'. On the left is a small vignette of William Penn's Treaty with the Indians, another frequent theme in Hicks's paintings. (ABOVE)

ATTRIBUTED TO REUBEN MOULTHROP

A pair of portraits of Mr and Mrs James Blakeslee Reynolds
of West Haven, Connecticut

OIL ON CANVAS, 114.3 x 91.4cm (45 x 36in)
New York $745,000 (£500,000). 29.I.94
From the Bertram K. Little and Nina Fletcher Little Collection

Reuben Moulthrop (1763–1814) was best known as a modeller in wax, although in
1793 he advertised portrait and miniature painting. Variation in style and scarcity of
pictures create uncertainty in attributing much of his work, but it is likely that he
painted these portraits of James Blakeslee Reynolds, said to have been a farmer, and
his wife Mary (Kimberly) Thomas around 1788, shortly after their marriage. (ABOVE)

AMERICAN PAINTINGS

JOHN SINGER SARGENT
Spanish Dancer
OIL ON CANVAS, 222.9 x 151.1cm (87¾ x 59½in)
New York $7,592,500 (£5,011,050). 25.V.94
From the Estate of Wendell Cherry

Painted in Paris between September
1880 and the spring of 1881, one year
after the artist's first trip to Spain,
Spanish Dancer clearly reveals Sargent's
knowledge of the works of Velázquez
and Manet's Spanish scenes. Shortly
after its completion the work somehow
came into the possession of Sargent's
temporary maid, who in turn gave the
painting to a former employer, an art
collector who lived outside Paris. It is
obvious that *Spanish Dancer* must have
disappeared without Sargent knowing,
for in 1897 he wrote in response to a
request for authentication from the
owner: 'It is a painting which was done
quite a number of years ago and which
I had lost sight of. I would be curious
to know by what circumstances it came
to be in your possession, and by the
way I would congratulate you for it.
If it is not too great an imposition I
would be pleased if you could tell me
something about it. I would even dare
to ask you to be good enough to let
me know in the event you might be
tempted to part with it.' (RIGHT)

JOHN SINGER SARGENT
A Parisian Beggar Girl
SIGNED *JOHN S. SARGENT* AND DEDICATED
À MON AMIE EDELFELDT, OIL ON CANVAS,
64.1 x 45.1cm (25¼ x 17¾in)
New York $827,500 (£546,150). 25.V.94

The *Beggar Girl* is dated to 1880, just after Sargent's return from a trip to southern Spain and Tangier in the winter of 1879–80, and is dedicated to Albert Gustaf Edelfeldt (1854–1905), a Finnish artist who studied and was working in Paris at the same time as Sargent. The monochromatic palette of the painting links it directly to the aesthetic concerns being championed by Sargent's contemporary, Whistler, who espoused working within a single prevailing colour harmony. In the *Beggar Girl* Sargent builds his image through the interaction of silver and white tones, accented with dashes of pink, peach and black, which provide counterpoints to the limited tonal variations within the painting. (LEFT)

RICHARD EDWARD MILLER
Spring (The Open Window)
SIGNED *MILLER*, OIL ON CANVAS,
148.6 x 114.3cm (58½ x 45in)
New York $662,500 (£437,250). 25.V.94

Spring was painted in France, most
probably in the Breton village of St-
Jean-du-Doigt, where Miller and his
family summered between 1912 and
1914. The work shows the artist's
wife, Harriet Adams, quietly sewing
by an open window. The bird cage
on the floor is a motif often found in
paintings of women done at this time,
and is simultaneously suggestive of
the pleasures of, and restrictions on,
women of the leisured class. (LEFT)

DANIEL GARBER
Mending
SIGNED *DANIEL GARBER*, OIL ON CANVAS,
116.8 x 106.7cm (46 x 42in)
New York $398,500 (£263,000). 25.V.94
From the Estate of Caroline L. Morris

Daniel Garber (1880–1958) is best
known for his idyllic, lyrical paintings
of the Bucks County countryside of
Pennsylvania. His deliberate technique
with its intricately woven brushwork
has often been compared to tapestry
work. As a young man Garber earned
his living as an illustrator and portrait
painter. His skill as the latter is shown
in *Mending,* dating from the summer
of 1918. It is thought that the sitter is
the artist's daughter, Tanis. (RIGHT)

ALBERT BIERSTADT
Kern's River Valley, California
SIGNED, OIL ON CANVAS,
90.2 x 132.1cm (35½ x 52in)
New York $1,157,500
(£782,100). 2.XII.93

Albert Bierstadt was born in Germany in 1830, but emigrated with his family to America when he was two years old. He joined a surveying expedition to the largely unexplored West in 1859. On his return he set to work in his studio, depicting the stately mountains and dramatic waterfalls of the Far West and producing paintings which captured the imaginations of the American and European public. (LEFT)

THEODORE ROBINSON
The Gossips
SIGNED *TH. ROBINSON* AND DATED *1891*,
OIL ON CANVAS, 46.4 x 58.4cm (18¼ x 23in)
New York $1,102,500 (£727,650). 25.V.94

Theodore Robinson was one of the pioneers of American Impressionism. While visiting Giverny in 1888, his exposure to and subsequent friendship with the reclusive Claude Monet left a lasting imprint on his development as a painter. In this work Robinson depicts peasant women going about their everyday chores – a prevalent theme in nineteenth-century Barbizon paintings. (RIGHT)

LATIN AMERICAN PAINTINGS

JOSÉ CAMPECHE
Dama a Caballo
OIL ON PANEL, 41.8 x 33.3cm
(16⁷⁄₁₆ x 13⅛in)
New York $288,500
(£193,300). 17.V.94

José Campeche was the
mulatto son of a freed
black slave. He found
acceptance among the
society beauties of San
Juan by creating a type
of feminine equestrian
portrait. This is the third
known example of *Lady
on Horseback.* (RIGHT)

DIEGO RIVERA
Naturaleza Muerta con Flores
SIGNED AND DATED *MARS, 1916*, OIL ON CANVAS, 81.3 x 65.7cm (32 x 25⅞in)
New York $387,500 (£261,800). 22.XI.93
From the Josephine Bay Paul and C. Michael Paul Foundations

Born in Guanajuato in Mexico, Rivera had been in Europe for nine years when he painted this still life. He had become familiar with the advanced techniques of modern European art and was just hitting his stride as one of the most daring and experimental painters of the Parisian wartime avant-garde. The entire composition is set against a stark black ground that exists in another dimension and thrusts the subject, the vase with flowers, into an abstract and spatial realm. (ABOVE)

MATTA
Inscape (Psychological Morphology No.104)
SIGNED AND DATED *39*, OIL ON CANVAS, 73 x 92.4cm (28¾ x 36⅜in)
New York $552,500 (£370,175). 17.V.94

In his *Psychological Morphologies* Matta created a realm which reached beyond the waking state and the dream world of the Surrealists. To enter this space-time the artist placed small quantities of paint along the edge of a palette knife and then made automatic gestures on the canvas, so that the colours were juxtaposed and mixed in unpredictable ways. The different elements in the composition represent biomorphic forms which are undergoing continuous metamorphoses. (RIGHT)

LEONORA CARRINGTON
Le Grand Adieu
SIGNED AND DATED *1958*, OIL ON CANVAS, 50.5 x 100.3cm (19⅞ x 39½in)
New York $244,500 (£163,800). 17.V.94

When Carrington moved to Mexico in 1942 she discovered a country rich in magic and 'primitive' religion and, like many artists who chose to live there, she became deeply influenced by the lore of Latin America. (ABOVE)

CANADIAN ART

ALEXANDER COLVILLE, R.C.A.
Ocean Limited, 1962
SIGNED AND DATED, OIL AND SYNTHETIC RESIN ON BOARD, 68.5 x 119.3cm (27 x 47in)
Toronto CN$148,500 (£73,000:$105,000). 11.V.94.

Ocean Limited depicts the track where the main train, which runs between Montreal
and Halifax, passes through Sackville – the artist's home town. From the right the
high speed locomotive crosses the Tantramar marshes, whose flat monotony provides
an endless horizon of dried up grass and winter sky. In contrast to the train, an old
man walks slowly in the opposite direction, wrapped up in thought. Colville's work
verges on a non-commital lack of emphasis, but its precise definition and the
purposeful focus on the individual and objects create an atmosphere of significance
that makes this work a direct social comment on his provincial environment. (ABOVE)

AUSTRALIAN ART

BRETT WHITELEY
Lavender Bay
SIGNED, OIL ON BOARD, 205 x 76.5cm (80¾ x 30⅛in)
Melbourne A$90,500 (£40,750:$62,000). 19.IV.94

Like his acknowledged artistic influences – Verlaine,
Rimbaud and Francis Bacon – Whiteley embarked
upon an elaborate course of self-destruction as if this
was the natural way to achieve the ultimate freedom in
self-expression. Having travelled in Europe, America
and Asia during the 1960s, he settled in Lavender Bay,
Sydney, where he produced paintings of the harbour,
including the present work of around 1974. (LEFT)

PRINTS

REMBRANDT HARMENSZ. VAN RIJN

Christ Healing the Sick; The Hundred Guilder Print

ETCHING, DRYPOINT AND BURIN, THE SECOND STATE OF TWO, ON JAPAN PAPER, 28.2 x 39.2cm (11⅛ x 15⅞in)
London £221,500 ($343,300). 28.VI.94

Christ Healing the Sick, a print which demonstrates the full range of Rembrandt's technique as
an etcher, has always been keenly sought after in fine, early impressions. According to an old
legend, the artist himself bought back a fine impression for one hundred guilders, hence its
second title. This exceptionally harmonious example on a warm-toned Japan paper, giving an
effect of evening, is notable for the carefully manipulated area of surface tone on the garment of
Christ. Rembrandt used this subtle technique to envelope Him in soft shadow. Treasured by
generations of distinguished collectors, the sheet is in almost flawless condition. (ABOVE)

Veduta della Piazza di Monte Cavallo

GIOVANNI BATTISTA PIRANESI

Vedute della Piazza di Monte Cavallo

FROM A COLLECTION OF 33 ETCHINGS
ENTITLED *VEDUTE DI ROMA,* FIRST STATES,
each sheet *c.*52 x 71.3cm (20½ x 28⅛in)
New York $56,350 (£37,550) for the
collection. 12.V.94

Piranesi worked on his series of
etchings, the *Views of Rome,* at
intervals from the 1740s until
his death in 1778. He issued
them as individual plates as well
as in collections, often with prints
from other series. The present
group closely corresponds to the
early sets of *Le Magnificenza di
Roma,* 1751. (ABOVE)

HENRI FANTIN-LATOUR

Bouquet de Roses

1879, LITHOGRAPH, SECOND (FINAL) STATE,
41.5 x 35.5cm (16¼ x 14in)
London £25,875 ($38,300). 2.XII.93
From the Henri Vever Collection

Fantin-Latour has always been
particularly admired for his
painted still-lifes, especially
those of flowers. However,
Bouquet de Roses is the only
time the artist used the
subject for a lithograph,
hence this print is highly
sought-after, not only for
its immense beauty and
delicacy, but also because
of its rarity. (LEFT)

HENRI DE TOULOUSE-LAUTREC
La Clownesse au Moulin Rouge
1897, LITHOGRAPH PRINTED IN COLOURS, sheet 40.9 x 32cm (16⅛ x 12⅜in)
New York $354,500 (£239,500). 18.XI.93

Toulouse-Lautrec produced several portraits of Cha-u-kao, a dancer and clown at the Moulin Rouge and Nouveau Cirque, whose curious stage name is derived from a phonetic transcription of *chahut-chaos,* a riotous dance not dissimilar to the cancan. Here she is shown arm in arm with the model Gabrielle-la-Danseuse. In the background appears the bearded profile of the novelist and dramatist Tristan Bernard, while the slightly blowzy figure by his side could be the Irish singer May Belfort. (ABOVE)

PABLO PICASSO

La Minotauromachie

1935, ETCHING WITH SCRAPER WORK AND BURIN ENGRAVING, SEVENTH (FINAL) STATE, SIGNED AND INSCRIBED
DERNIÈRE ÉPREUVE D'ÉTAT PARIS LE 3 JANVIER DE L'AN DE GRACE MCMXXXVI, 49.7 x 69.4cm (19½ x 27¼in)
London £507,500 ($786,600). 28.VI.94
From the Collection of the late Miss Helen Shipway

La Minotauromachie, one of the most important prints of the twentieth century,
was held in high regard by Picasso himself who often presented it to his friends and
colleagues, including Man Ray, Paul Éluard, Igor Stravinsky and Mme Apollinaire.
One of the reasons for this is the powerful iconography which closely relates to one
of the most traumatic periods in Picasso's life. In 1934, Picasso's mistress, Marie-
Thérèse Walter was pregnant and this could no longer be kept secret from his wife,
Olga, who subsequently left Picasso taking their son, Paulo. In *La Minotauromachie,*
Picasso depicts himself as the Minotaur, half beast, half man, who is seen shielding
his eyes against the light of the candle, which signifies the annunciation of the child's
birth. The central figure, lying on the horse's back dressed as a *torera,* represents his
mistress, and the horse has been interpreted as symbolizing Olga. (ABOVE)

EDWARD HOPPER

Night on the El Train

1918, ETCHING, 18.9 x 20.1cm (7½ x 7⅞in)
New York $52,900 (£35,250). 12.V.94

This rare print is accompanied by a note from Hopper's wife briefly explaining it:
'[the elevated trains] ran along level with the second story of houses. At night, with
their interiors illuminated, they made interesting subjects. The Museum of Modern
Art owns a Hopper canvas of this subject, the dark outside of the house and view of
figures inside of a lit room. It's called *Night Windows*'. (ABOVE)

GEORGES BRAQUE

Etude de Nu

1907–08, ETCHING, SIGNED AND INSCRIBED *H.C.,* ON RIVES PAPER, 27.8 x 19.7cm (11 x 7⅞in)
Los Angeles $36,800 (£24,500). 23.III.94

Braque executed this etching shortly after seeing Picasso's *Les Demoiselles d'Avignon*
for the first time and meeting its artist. At first Braque was shocked by the painting's
wilful ugliness, but his work soon began to move in a parallel manner to Picasso's and
the artists started to collaborate on the development of Cubism. (LEFT)

JASPER JOHNS
Savarin
LITHOGRAPH PRINTED IN COLOURS, SIGNED, DATED *77* AND INSCRIBED *PRINTERS' PROOF 2/2*,
sheet 105.7 x 87cm (41⅝ x 34¼in)
New York $68,500 (£45,200). 14.V.94
From the Thomas and Nancy Driscoll Collection of Contemporary Prints from Universal Limited Art Editions

In 1960 Johns cast a Savarin coffee can in bronze, painted it, and titled the replica *Painted Bronze.* Since then, the Savarin can has become a Johnsian trademark. Between 1977 and 1978 he created over a dozen Savarin images– delicate monotypes, a series of lithographs, and a poster for his retrospective at the San Francisco Museum of Art (1978). It was at this exhibition that Thomas Driscoll first became interested in contemporary art. (ABOVE)

PHOTOGRAPHS

JULIA MARGARET CAMERON
Mrs Herbert Duckworth (née Julia Jackson)
*c.*1867, ALBUMEN PRINT, MATTED, 33.7 x 25.8cm (13¼ x 10⅜in)
London £19,550 ($29,300). 13.V.94

Julia Margaret Cameron was born in Calcutta in 1815. At the age of forty-eight she
was given her first camera by her daughter and quickly developed into an outstanding
amateur photographer. Between 1863 and her return to India in 1875 she produced
acclaimed portraits of such Victorian celebrities as Tennyson, Darwin, Newman and
Carlyle. Julia Duckworth sat for numerous portraits for her aunt, Julia Margaret
Cameron, several of which are among her most successful works. This print is from
the subject's personal collection, and is a previously unrecorded portrait. (ABOVE)

EDWARD S. CURTIS
Photogravure from
The North American Indian
A SERIES OF 20 TEXT VOLUMES AND 20 PORTFOLIOS
PICTURING AND DESCRIBING THE INDIANS OF THE UNITED
STATES AND ALASKA, SIGNED AND DATED *1907–30,*
PRINTED ON JAPANESE TISSUE,
New York $662,500 (£435,850) for the set. 7.X.93

From 1896 Edward S. Curtis devoted his career
to the enormous enterprise of recording North
American Indian tribes and their way of life,
which was to vanish almost completely during
his study. Funded by J Pierpont Morgan and
with the enthusiastic support of Theodore
Roosevelt, Curtis published twenty volumes
between 1907 and 1930, which combined
poignant and beautiful photographs with an
informative text. In contrast to many earlier
American photographers, who portrayed the
Indians as warriors, Curtis stressed their
peaceful culture. (BELOW)

DIANE ARBUS
Identical Twins, Roselle, N.J.
TITLED AND DATED *1967,* GELATIN SILVER PRINT, MATTED,
39.1 x 37.1cm (15⅜ x 14⅝in)
New York $70,700 (£47,450). 23.IV.94
From The Museum of Modern Art

Diane Arbus was born in New York City in 1923. She
began working as a fashion photographer, but rebelled
against convention, seeking to depict people 'without
their masks'. She achieved fame in the 1960s with her
stark portraits of unusual people which were widely
published in *Esquire* and *Harper's Bazaar.* This portrait
of identical twins Cathleen (left) and Colleen was
included in *New Photography USA* (1969–71), a
travelling exhibition organized by The Museum of
Modern Art. (ABOVE)

LITERARY PROPERTY *by Stephen Roe*

Literary Property has always been one of the lynch-pins of Sotheby's auctions. The company first traded as a book auction house, and on 11 March 1994 we celebrated our 250th anniversary with, among many other festivities, a book sale, our auctioneer Roger Griffiths resplendent in a specially commissioned, eighteenth-century-style waistcoat. At 250 years old, Sotheby's surely ranks as one of the oldest book sellers in the world; books have been sold here since before the establishment of the British Museum and before the founding of the United States.

Although enormous sales of books were held by our eighteenth-century predecessors, I believe they would be surprised by the vast range of material now sold under the Literary Property umbrella: books in most Western and Classical languages, from the dawn of printing in the late fifteenth century to publications of the 1990s, encompassing the sciences, literature and art; bindings; maps and atlases; playing cards, ephemera, handbills, all examples of the printer's art; archives, manuscripts, autograph letters and music, both printed and manuscript; Western medieval and Oriental manuscripts and miniatures. It is astonishing in its multifariousness and diversity.

Just as Samuel Baker's first auction contained the library of the Rt Hon. Sir John Stanley, Bart., so Sotheby's has always paid special attention to single owner sales. There were several of great interest during this season, notably the auction of incunabula (books printed before 1501) from the library of Joachim, Prinz zu Fürstenberg. This contained over 300 books – a further 91 had been sold privately through Sotheby's to Baden-Württemberg – and thus formed one of the largest sales of such early books since at least World War II. This magnificent collection contained many items which had been bought by the prince's ancestors in the fifteenth and sixteenth centuries and were in a sense not yet second hand. Their rarity and condition attracted

CONRADUS PFETTISHEIM
Geschichte Peter
Hagenbachs und
der Burgunder
Kriege (detail)
1477, CHANCERY FOLIO,
10 LEAVES
London £177,500 ($273,350).
1.VII.94
From the Court Library at
Donaueschingen (LEFT)

From a collection of
manuscript verse
belonging to the
Duke of Ormonde,
including many
occasional poems
presented to him
*c.*1640S–1680S, NEARLY
SEVENTY POEMS OF DIFFERENT
KINDS, WRITTEN OVER A PERIOD
ON SEPARATE SHEETS, NOW
BOUND TOGETHER
London £19,550 ($30,500).
19.VII.94 (ABOVE)

HENRI MATISSE
Jazz
1947, SIGNED, 20 PLATES
COLOURED BY POCHOIR AFTER
COLLAGES AND CUT-PAPER
DESIGNS BY MATISSE, WOOD-
ENGRAVED COVER DESIGN AND
TEXT IN FACSIMILE FROM THE
AUTHOR'S HAND, 42.5 x 32.5cm
(16¾ x 12⅜in)
London £71,900 ($111,450).
28.VI.94 (ABOVE)

Machzor
SEPTEMBER 1485–21 AUGUST
1486, FOLIO
London £133,500 ($200,250).
6.XII.93
From the library of the late
Salman Schocken (BELOW)

many buyers from German-speaking lands and around the world to make this one of the most successful sales in recent years. Notable among major items in the sale were the blockbook Ars moriendi *and the* Blood-letting Calendar for Vienna, 1462, *each of which achieved £221,500.*

Other single-owner collections of importance included natural history books sold on behalf of the Glenbow Museum Library, Calgary, Canada. This attractive sale contained many beautiful colour-plate books, with John Gould's A Monograph on the Trochilidae, or Family of Hummingbirds, *realizing $85,000. A collection of scientific books from the library of Robert S. Dunham was a great success, with prices paid for works by Newton, Copernicus and Galileo way above expectations – a first edition of Newton's* Principia *reached the heights of $211,500, more than double its top estimate. Five thousand pamphlets and manuscripts from the Fairfax Library, including several early 'newsbook' volumes (in effect the first English newspapers), were sold in over 500 lots, realizing nearly £400,000, while the papers of James Butler, the first Duke of Ormonde (like Fairfax a key player in the English Civil War), achieved in excess of £120,000. In the world of modern books, an anonymous private collection of* livres d'artistes *sold extremely well in June, highlights being Chagall's* Daphnis and Chloé *(£122,500) and Matisse's* Jazz *(£71,900).*

The field of printed and manuscript Judaica has seen two immensely important sales this year. Hebrew books from the library of the late Salman Schocken achieved £1.1 million in December, while in June, the fifth and perhaps final auction of Hebrew and Samaritan manuscripts from the library of the late David Solomon Sassoon realized £2.3 million.

Highlights from our sales of Western manuscripts and miniatures have included a probable autograph manuscript of Savonarola's sermons of 1490–91. Savonarola was one of the great Christian orators of the Middle Ages and his stature was reconfirmed when this volume made an astonishing £210,500, more than ten times its estimate.

The Oriental manuscripts and miniatures market was strengthened by a group of fifty-six exceptional Indian miniature paintings of the Mughal and Rajasthani Schools from the Collection of the British Rail Pension Fund, which were all sold when auctioned in April, achieving £497,855.

Another feature of the work of the Literary Property departments today that would surprise Samuel Baker is the extent of research carried out by our experts. This season we gave the first detailed description of one of the most exciting discoveries in English music this century, the autograph manuscript of twenty-one keyboard works of Henry Purcell, which realized £276,500. Undoubtedly, Simon Maguire's description of the manuscript will enter the Purcell bibliography.

The Purcell manuscript naturally attracted a great deal of worldwide attention in the press, but rarity and high prices are not the only criteria to interest the media. The market for English Literature and History continued its revival and provided material to fill hundreds of newspaper column inches. Long, questing articles were written about Graham Greene's sex-life on the basis of the revelations in his letters to his mistress Catherine Walston (£5,720). Much was made in the press of the sale of the copy of the privately printed edition of the Tale of Peter Rabbit, signed by Beatrix Potter, which netted £62,000, underlying the incipient strength of the children's books market. Headlines were made by the extraordinary price of $101,500 paid for the first edition of A Christmas Carol, inscribed by Dickens to his sister Letitia on the friday before Christmas, 1843.

The market for atlases, travel, and natural history documents was a little less buoyant than in previous years, despite some major successes. Good prices were paid for beautiful books such as the Bleau Atlas Major (£118,100), Thomas and William Daniell's Oriental Scenery (£95,000) and Redouté's Les Liliacées ($332,500).

The area which is undoubtedly going from strength to strength is Printed and Manuscript Americana. George Washington surpassed Abraham Lincoln as the dominant figure in the field this season, with an unpublished draft of a letter to Henry Knox, expressing the first president's reluctance to assume the mantle of office, realizing $635,000, while Washington's signed copy of Thomas Jefferson's Notes on the State of Virginia achieved an astonishing $145,000. The market for Lincoln was also strong: an oval salt print portrait photograph, described as 'the most famous signed photograph' of the president, made $112,500, the highest price paid for any historical signed photograph. Manuscripts relating to the more recent history of the United States also performed well. A Japanese map of Pearl Harbor showing the damage inflicted by their airforce was sold for $312,000. This material is all a long way from what Samuel Baker was selling in 1744. I wonder what our successors will be auctioneering in 2244, early CD-ROMs?

ABRAHAM LINCOLN
Portrait photograph
SIGNED AND DATED *FOR MRS LUCY G SPEED, FROM WHOSE PIOUS HAND I AC- / CEPTED THE PRESENT OF AN OXFORD BIBLE TWENTY YEARS AGO. / WASHINGTON, D.C. OCTOBER 3, 1861. A. LINCOLN,* oval, 29.3 x 24.2cm (11½ x 9½in)
New York $178,500 (£120,600). 1.XI.93
From the J. B. Speed Art Museum, sold for the Benefit of the Art Acquisition Fund of the Museum (ABOVE)

PRINTED BOOKS & AUTOGRAPH MANUSCRIPTS

JOHANNES DE TURRECREMATA
Meditationes seu contemplationes devotissimae
MAINZ, 3 SEPTEMBER 1479, FIRST EDITION
WITH METALCUTS, chancery folio
London £111,500 ($171,700). 1.VII.94
From the Court Library at Donaueschingen

Cardinal Turrecremata's *Meditationes* was first printed in Rome in 1467 in an edition which contained woodcuts, making it one of the earliest Italian illustrated books. The present edition was printed by Johann Numeister, who used metalcuts which, though based on the original woodcuts, are artistically superior. (RIGHT)

Ars moriendi

SOUTH GERMANY, *c.*1475, BLOCKBOOK, chancery 8vo
London £221,500 ($341,100). 1.VII.94
From the Court Library at Donaueschingen

The *Ars moriendi* presents in eleven scenes, with facing text, a battle between devils and angels for the soul of a man on his deathbed. The dying man is tempted by False Religion, Despair, Impatience, Vainglory or Idleness, and Avarice, each of which is countered by angelic counsels. The final scene shows a successful death – the soul of the man, received by angels as a lit candle, is placed in his hands, under the protection of the crucified Christ and the Virgin. (LEFT)

Blood-Letting Calendar for Vienna, 1462

VIENNA, [1461], chancery broadsheet (top half shown)
London £221,500 ($341,100). 1.VII.94
From the Court Library at Donaueschingen

Blood-letting calendars were a guide to one of the most fundamental beliefs of ancient and medieval medicine: that there are good and ill-favoured days for letting blood, taking medicines and subjecting oneself to purgatives. The present calendar is the earliest known piece of printing produced in Vienna and the two woodcuts are the earliest known examples of illustrations which are printed integrally with the type. (RIGHT)

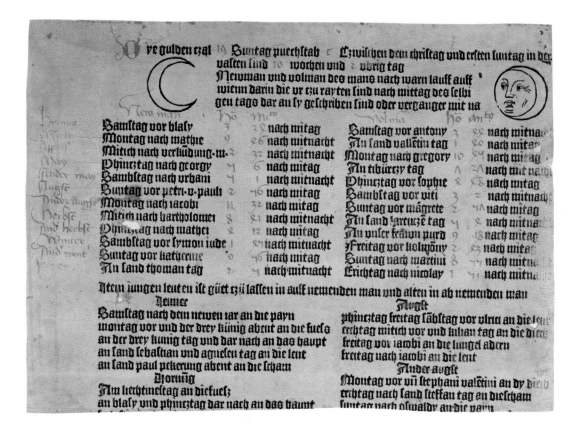

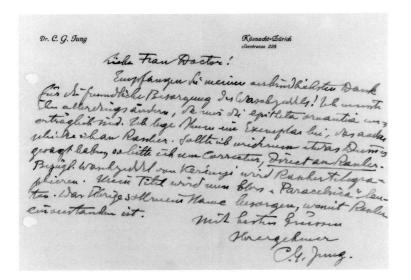

C.G. JUNG

Series of over eighty autograph and typed letters to his pupil Dr Jolande Jacobi

20 NOVEMBER 1928 TO 30 JANUARY 1961, *c*.120 PAGES, folio and 8vo
London £29,900 ($45,150). 26.V.94

Jolande Jacobi was a Hungarian analyst practising in Vienna, from where she escaped, with Jung's help, and settled in Zürich. She was the author of *The Psychology of C.G. Jung*, the standard handbook to the elements of Jung's psychological theories. Many of the letters in the present series relate to Dr Jacobi's attempts to present Jung's theories to a wider public, in which Jung replies to her queries or comments on drafts. (LEFT)

NAPOLEON I

Group of fifty letters

SIGNED, 17 JANUARY TO 10 MARCH 1813,
22.9 x 16.8cm (9 x 7⅜in)
New York $40,250 (£26,550). 10.VI.94

Following his disastrous invasion of Russia and retreat from Moscow in the winter of 1812, Napoleon rushed to Paris to raise new levies, stem the rising panic in the city, and belie rumours of his death. These letters were written to his Minister of War, H.J.G. Clarke, Duc de Feltre at the beginning of 1813, and show the emperor ordering supplies, designating the movement of his troops and providing battle instructions. (RIGHT)

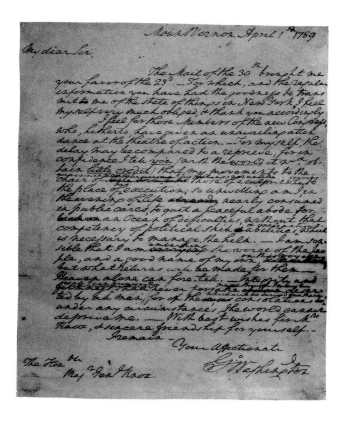

GEORGE WASHINGTON
Autograph letter
SIGNED, MOUNT VERNON, 1 APRIL 1789, 1 page, 23.3 x 19cm
(9⅛ x 7½in) New York $635,000 ($429,054). 1.XI.93

This is a newly discovered first draft of Washington's
famous letter to his close friend Henry Knox, in which
the former expressed his doubts and reluctance on the
eve of assuming the office of First President of the
United States. Washington's military fame, lack of
personal ambition, and steadfast determination not to
profit from public service, made him the unanimous
choice of his compatriots to be the nation's first chief
executive. He was himself ambivalent about the office,
however, telling Knox that 'my movements to the
chair of government will be accompanied by feelings
not unlike those of a culprit who is going to the place
of his execution.' (LEFT)

MITSUO FUCHIDA
Post-Battle Damage Assessment Report Map
of Pearl Harbor
DECEMBER 1941, PEN AND WATERCOLOUR ON LIGHT WOVE PAPER,
80.7 x 60.2cm (31¾ x 23⅝in)
New York $321,500 (£212,900). 3.V.94

This map was prepared by Commander Mitsuo
Fuchida, who led the Japanese air attack on Pearl
Harbor on 7 December 1941, for a briefing with
Emperor Hirohito on 27 December 1941. Despite
the devastation shown by the map, the surprise aerial
attack on Pearl Harbor did not accomplish the
Japanese goal of eliminating the United States naval
presence from the Pacific. While three battleships
were sunk and five others severely damaged, only the
Oklahoma and the *Arizona* did not return to active
service. Moreover, 'the date which will live in infamy'
galvanized the American public and effectively ended
the movement for neutrality and isolationism. (RIGHT)

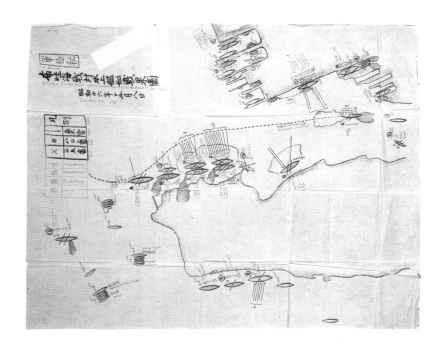

WILLIAM SHAKESPEARE
The Tragedy of Hamlet, Prince of Denmarke
FOURTH 4TO EDITION, BOUND IN CONTEMPORARY VELLUM
London £150,000 ($225,000). 13.XII.93

The text of this edition is roughly the same as that of
the Second Quarto of 1604, which most critics have
agreed is by far the most authentic form of the play,
the First or 'Bad' Quarto of 1603 being only about half
the length of later editions. The fourth edition dates
from between 1619 and 1630 and is one of the rarest
Hamlet quartos, with only another twenty copies
recorded. When it came to auction this was the only
known copy in private hands, and the first copy to
appear at auction in seventy-five years. (RIGHT)

CHARLES DICKENS
A Christmas Carol
CHAPMAN & HALL, 1843, INSCRIBED BY DICKENS TO HIS SISTER LETITIA, 8vo
New York $101,500 (£67,650). 10.XII.93

Dickens wrote three Christmas books, *The Christmas Carol* (1843), *The Chimes*
(1844) and *Cricket on the Hearth* (1845), all of which were hugely successful. This
first edition of *A Christmas Carol* was inscribed by Dickens to his sister Letitia on the
Friday before Christmas 1843. (LEFT)

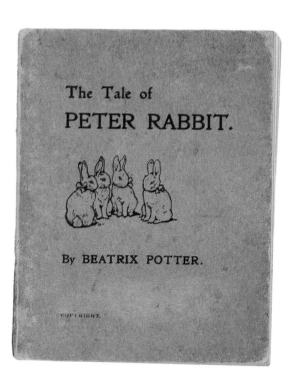

RAOUL DUFY AND ALPHONSE DAUDET
Tartarin de Tarascon
PARIS, SCRIPTA ET PICTA, 1937, 141 LITHOGRAPHS
PRINTED IN COLOUR, COVERS WITH COLOURED
MOROCCO ONLAYS TOOLED IN GILT, 4to
London £25,300 ($39,200). 28.VI.94

That Dufy fully understood the need for a
balance between text and illustrations in
the *livre d'artiste* can be seen in his colour
lithographs for this edition of Daudet's
Tartarin de Tarascon. The author is best
known for his series of short stories about
Provençal life, which were first written for
Le Figaro. Daudet continued the charming
extravaganza *Tartarin de Tarascon* (1872)
in *Tartarin sur les Alpes* (1885) and *Port
Tarascon* (1890). (BELOW)

BEATRIX POTTER
The Tale of Peter Rabbit
[1901], FIRST EDITION, FIRST ISSUE,
INSCRIBED BY THE AUTHOR, COLOUR
FRONTISPIECE AND BLACK AND WHITE
ILLUSTRATIONS
London £62,000 ($93,620). 19.V.94

Beatrix Potter first created Peter
Rabbit in a picture letter sent to
Noel Moore, dated 4 September
1893. A few years later she wrote
and asked Noel whether she could
borrow the letter in order to turn
it into a book. After being rejected
by at least six publishers she had
the book printed privately, giving
the first 250 copies to her friends
and relations. (LEFT)

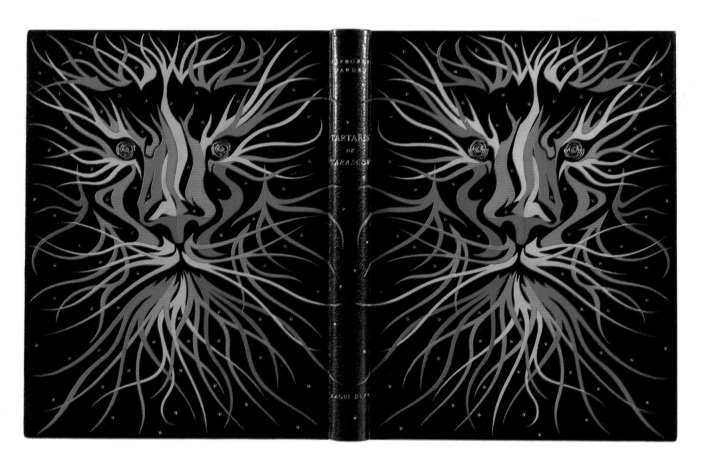

JOHN GOULD
The Birds of Asia
LONDON, 1850–1883, SEVEN VOLUMES, FIRST EDITION, folio
New York $74,000 (£49,650). 23.IV.94
From the Glenbow Museum

Isabella Tree has called *The Birds of Asia* Gould's 'most demanding preoccupation ... a publication begun in 1849 and destined to run for thirty-four years at the rate of roughly one part (containing seventeen plates) a year. Although, as Gould confessed, many species that appeared in *Birds of Europe* and *Century* would also appear in the work on Asia, the seven-volume, 530-plate publication would represent the conquest – in the style of an ornithological Marco Polo – of the largest continent in the world.' (ABOVE)

PIERRE JOSEPH REDOUTÉ
Les Liliacées
BY A.P. DE CANDOLLE AND OTHERS, PARIS, 1802–16, EIGHT VOLUMES, FIRST EDITION,
folio 54.7 x 36cm (21½ x 14¼in)
New York $332,500 (£221,650). 13.I.94
From the Estate of Peter Jay Sharp

Les Liliacées (The Lilies and Related Plants) was first produced under the patronage of the Empress Josephine of France, for whom Redouté worked as botanical artist at Malmaison. The plates were executed by means of stipple engraving (using etched dots) and the printing in colours was usually done from a single plate, the various colours being applied by a rag-stump before every impression. The prints were then finished by hand. (ABOVE)

HANS JOACHIM HENNEBERGER
Ein Thüer Vögel Fisch und Bluomen Buoch
WIESENSTEIG, 1673, c.28.5 x 18cm (11¼ x 7in)
London £91,700 ($136,600). 7.XII.93

Henneberger was an artist working in Wiesensteig, Germany, in the second half of the seventeenth century. His natural history book's 210 pages of watercolour drawings vividly depict hundreds of different species, including mythical beasts, mammals, birds, fish and aquatic creatures, insects, floral displays in vases, composite flowers and fruit. (ABOVE)

JOHANNES BLAEU
Atlas Major
AMSTERDAM, 1662–65, ELEVEN VOLUMES, LATIN TEXT, folio
London £118,100 ($175,950). 7.XII.93

The son of a Dutch mapmaker, mathematician and astronomer who specialized in globes, Johannes Blaeu is renowned for his *Atlas Major*. Its 593 engraved maps, plans, views and plates are contained in eleven volumes, titled: Northern Europe (which includes fourteen plans and plates illustrating Tycho Brahe's observatory on Ven in Öresund); Northern and Eastern Europe and Greece; Germany; Netherlands; England and Wales; Scotland and Ireland; France and Switzerland; Italy; Spain, Portugal and Africa; Asia; and America. (ABOVE)

MUSIC MANUSCRIPTS

HENRY PURCELL

Autograph working manuscript of twenty-one harpsichord pieces
*c.*1692–95, 85 PAGES WITH SEVENTEEN WORKS BY GIOVANNI BATTISTA DRAGHI, oblong 4to
London £276,500 ($417,500). 26.V.94

Henry Purcell is the most important British composer between the beginning of the
seventeenth century and the end of the nineteenth century. The present manuscript
is the only autograph source of Purcell's harpsichord music. Moreover it is a
composing score: the other major Purcell autograph sources (including the three
'Great Score Books', the partial autograph of the *Fairy Queen* and the 'Guildhall
Song Book') are for the most part his fair copies rather than working manuscripts.
Indeed, with its five previously unknown works, unrecorded arrangements of his
music for the theatre, and new texts of known works, this manuscript is the greatest
discovery in British music for many years. (ABOVE)

MODEST MUSORGSKY

A cabinet-style photograph

ST PETERSBURG, 1876, SIGNED AND INSCRIBED ON VERSO WITH AN AUTOGRAPH MUSICAL
QUOTATION FROM THE OPERA *SOROCHINSKY FAIR*, 17 x 11.2cm (6⅝ x 4⅜in)
London £29,900 ($44,550). 2.XII.93

Musorgsky is thought by many to have been the most talented of the
school of Russian nationalist composers, which included Rimsky-
Korsakov and Dargomizhsky. Autograph material by Musorgsky is
extremely rare and even unsigned photographs are difficult to obtain.
This cabinet-style photograph of 1876 is signed twice by Musorgsky
and is inscribed with a musical quotation from his opera *Sorochinsky
Fair*, a work then in the earliest stages of composition, which
remained unfinished at his death in 1881. (ABOVE)

GUSTAV MAHLER

Autograph sketchleaf for the choral section of the final movement of the Second Symphony ('Resurrection')

HAMBURG, *c*.1893, 1 PAGE, large folio
London £25,300 ($37,700). 2.XII.93

Mahler's Second Symphony took a relatively long time to evolve. An
early conception of the work was as a symphonic poem, *Todtenfeier*
(1888), which eventually became the first movement of the symphony.
The remaining three movements were largely composed in 1894, with
the first performance of three movements taking place in March 1895
and the entire work being given at the end of that year. The gigantic
finale was Mahler's largest score to date. This early sketchleaf contains
the memorable, hushed first entry of the chorus. (ABOVE)

WESTERN MANUSCRIPTS

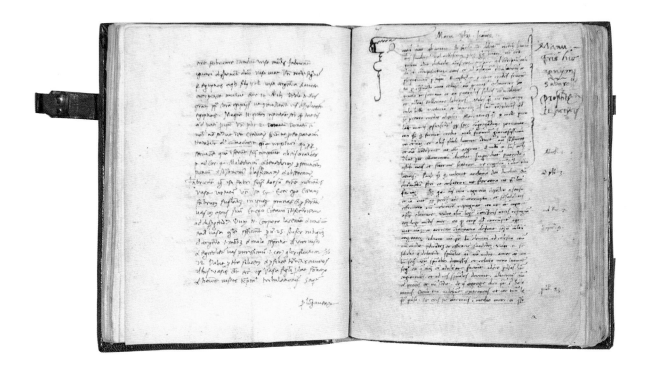

GIROLAMO SAVONAROLA

Sermones XVIII super Epistolam Johannis Primam and other texts

FLORENCE, *c.*1490–98, MANUSCRIPT ON PAPER, CONTEMPORARY GILT BINDING, 14.3 x 10.2cm (5⅝ x 4in)
London £210,500 ($315,750). 6.XII.93
From the Collection of the late Philip Robinson

This remarkable volume is a partly autograph work by the great preacher and martyr Savonarola (1452–98). Sixty-one leaves of the book are in his own handwriting. In 1491 he became the prior of San Marco in Florence, from whence his astonishing oratory, visions, prophesies, and absolute belief in reform and liberty brought him fame throughout Europe. He was regarded by thousands as a living saint, but his enemies trumped charges against him, making him the scapegoat of all the troubles of Renaissance Florence. He was arrested in April 1498, tortured, and burned at the stake the following month. The manuscript, like others written by Savonarola himself, passed into the hands of his close friend Girolamo Benivieni (1453–1542). (ABOVE)

VEGETIUS PUBLIUS RENATUS
Mulomedicina
NAPLES, *c.*1475–80, IN LATIN, ILLUMINATED MANUSCRIPT ON VELLUM, 27.5 x 19cm (10¹³⁄₁₆ x 7½in)
London £111,500 ($171,700). 21.VI.94

The *Mulomedicina* is the most important surviving classical text on horse medicine. This copy
was illuminated for Ferrante I of Aragon, king of Naples (1458–94), one of the supreme royal
bibliophiles and collectors of the Renaissance, and is signed by the royal scribe Pietro Ippolita
da Luna. It was afterwards acquired by Lorenzo de'Medici (1449–92), ruler of Florence, and
was brought to England in the early nineteenth century. (ABOVE)

CONRAD WAGNER
The Visitation
AUGSBURG, *c.*1485–89, HISTORIATED INITIAL ON AN ILLUMINATED
LEAF FROM THE MISSAL OF JOHANNES VON GILTLINGEN, IN LATIN,
ON VELLUM, 34.6 x 25.5cm (13⅝ x 10in)
London £25,300 ($38,950). 21.VI.94

This is a hitherto unrecorded leaf from an exceptionally
well-documented illuminated manuscript. The Missal
of Abbot Johannes von Giltlingen is recorded in the
late fifteenth-century chronicle of Augsburg, describing
the making of the book in 1485–89 by Wagner, an
illuminator, illustrator and binder, from Ellingen who
died in 1496. (BELOW)

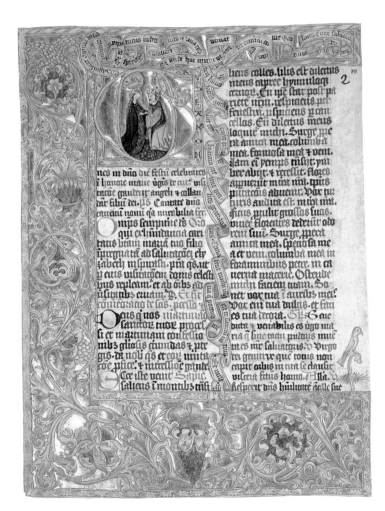

SEXTUS JULIUS FRONTINUS
Les Stratagèmes
WEST CENTRAL FRANCE, LATE FIFTEENTH CENTURY, IN FRENCH,
ILLUMINATED MANUSCRIPT ON VELLUM, 32.6 x 23cm (12¹³⁄₁₆ x 9in)
London £22,425 ($33,650). 6.XII.93

This is a French translation of the *Strategemata* of
Frontinus (died AD103), Roman governor of Britain
and a friend of the poet and epigrammatist, Martial.
Frontinus's book became very popular towards the
end of the Middle Ages as a model for chivalry and
knightly conduct. This, the third of four illuminated
miniatures, depicts an army of knights riding up to a
besieged city with soldiers looking over its ramparts,
and is now in the National Library of Wales. (ABOVE)

Bible, the Pentateuch, Haftarot, and five scrolls, with the Targum Onkelos and the commentary of Rashi

NORTHERN FRANCE, MID TO LATE THIRTEENTH CENTURY, IN HEBREW, MANUSCRIPT ON VELLUM, 19.6 x 15cm (7¾ x 5⅞in)
London £331,500 ($510,500). 21.VI.94
From the Library of the late David Solomon Sassoon

This manuscript contains around 150 drawings, of which all but about thirty are partially or entirely formed of micrographic writing. These form a vast and rare anthology of Jewish pictorial art from an age which usually forbade book illustration unless concealed within micrographic texts. It was one of seventy-six manuscripts from the supreme library of David Solomon Sassoon (1880–1942), sold in London in June 1994. (BELOW)

Haggadah, with the commentaries of Moses, Alshekh and Ephraim ben Aaron of Lenczycz

AMSTERDAM, 1796, IN HEBREW, ILLUMINATED MANUSCRIPT ON VELLUM, 30.4 x 19.7cm (11¹⁵⁄₁₆ x 7¾in)
London £161,000 ($247,950). 21.VI.94
From the Library of the late David Solomon Sassoon

The *Haggadah* is the narration of the story of Exodus as recited at the Seder service at Passover. The custom of illustrating *Haggadot* began in the late Middle Ages and developed over the centuries. By the seventeenth century illuminated *Haggadah* manuscripts were the most richly-decorated of all Hebrew texts, and even after printed copies became easily available they were often made for wedding presents or luxury use. The present copy, with sixty-seven illustrations and a folding map, was the final manuscript in the Sassoon library, acquired in 1940. (ABOVE)

ORIENTAL MANUSCRIPTS

A Deccani Qur'an
GOLCONDA, c.1560-1600, ARABIC MANUSCRIPT ON GOLD-SPRINKLED PAPER,
COPIED BY ABD AL-QADIR AL-HUSAINI, 43.7 x 28.1cm (17⅛ x 11in)
London £172,500 ($259,720). 27.IV.94

The Persian scribe Abd al-Qadir al-Husaini was a native of Shiraz, but moved to
Golconda in the Deccan, where, by 1562, he was employed at the court of the Qutb
Shah Sultans. This magnificent Qur'an, with thirty-four double pages of fine
illumination, was almost certainly a royal commission. In 1687 the Mughal Emperor
Aurangzeb captured Golconda and probably took the treasures of the royal library
back to Delhi, hence, on the flyleaves of the manuscript, the series of seal impressions
dating from 1703 of the Mughal Royal library. (ABOVE)

GOVARDHAN
A Portrait of Dara Shikoh
MUGHAL, *c.*1635, GOUACHE WITH GOLD, OVAL,
INSCRIBED *AMAL-I GOVARDHAN* (WORK OF
GOVARDHAN), 18.3 x 9.9cm (7⁷⁄₁₆ x 3⁷⁄₈in)
London £41,000 ($60,400). 22.X.93

Dara Shikoh (1615–59) was the eldest
son of Shah Jahan and heir apparent to
the Mughal throne. As the emperor's
favoured son he was able to indulge his
passion for literature and painting as
well as fulfilling his court duties. Had
he lived to assume the Mughal throne
there can be little doubt that he would
have become a great patron of the arts
and that the course of Mughal painting
would have been different. Govardhan
was the son of a court artist. He built
his reputation through his portraits and
seems to have had a special relationship
with Dara Shikoh, producing some of
the most significant portraits of the
prince. (RIGHT)

A Chinese Qur'an section
YUNNAN, A.D.1470, ARABIC MANUSCRIPT ON THICK PAPER, COPIED BY
SHAMS AL-DIN IBN TAJ AL-DIN, 25.1 x 17.4cm (9⅞ x 6⅞in)
London £34,500 ($53,650). 22.X.93

Yunnan is the south-western province of China, a
seemingly unlikely area for Qur'anic production in the
fifteenth century, but, due to the lasting effects of
Mongol trade routes, Yunnan had a strong Muslim
population during the Ming dynasty. The fact that this
Qur'an section is signed, dated and gives the location of
its production makes it extremely rare. (LEFT)

ATTRIBUTED TO EITHER KUSHALA OR GAUDHU
An illustration to the *Gita Govinda* poem
KANGRA, *c.*1780, BLUE INNER BORDER, 24.8 x 14.6cm (9¾ x 5¾in)
New York $40,250 (£27,195). 1.XII.93

The *Gita Govinda* or *Song of the Herdsman* was an ecstatic celebration of the romance of the divine lovers Radha and Krishna, culminating in lyrical descriptions of their lovemaking. Illustrations of the song were customarily produced at important Pahari weddings, and this illustration is thought to be part of a series produced in anticipation of Raja Sansar Chand's marriage to the daughter of Kishan Singh of Suket in 1781. On the left, Krishna adorns Radha with jewellery after a night of passion, represented to the right where they make love on a bed of leaves within the forest. Radha is also seen with a confidante, in the middle distance on a hillock, where she relates her experiences. (ABOVE)

An Unlikely Love
MANKOT, *c.*1730, RED BORDER, folio 28.6 x 21.3cm (11¼ x 8⅜in)
New York $31,625 (£20,875). 4.VI.94

In this illustration to the *Bhagavata Purana* Krishna encounters Kubja, a woman famed for her unguents of sandalwood paste and vermillion, 'whose eyes were beautiful but whose back was curved as lightening.' Krishna's beauty and loving glances captivated Kubja who offered her unguents to him. Pleased by her devotion, Krishna thereupon placed his left foot on her toes, with his right hand lifted her body up by the chin and made it straight and supple. (RIGHT)

A Portrait of a Persian warrior

MUGHAL, c.1615–20, GOUACHE WITH GOLD MOUNTED ON COTTON-BACKED ALBUM PAGE WITH BORDERS OF COLOURED PAPER, 16.5 x 9.5cm (6½ x 3⅜in)
London £29,900 ($44,551). 26.IV.94
From the Collection of the British Rail Pension Fund

This warrior's distinctive turban tells us that he is a Persian noble visitor to the Mughal court. He could have been one of the Persian ambassadors who are known to have visited the Mughal court in 1612, 1615, 1616 and 1620 to try and resolve the battles between the Mughals and Iranians for the fort at Qandahar. These missions for peace were not successful and Qandahar finally fell to the Iranians in 1622.

(RIGHT)

Three elephants running through a village, escorted by crowds and followed by Maharana Sangram Singh

UDAIPUR, c.1720, RED BORDER WITH BLACK RULE, 44.5 x 87.5cm (17½ x 34⅜in)
London £18,400 ($27,400). 26.IV.94
From the Collection of the British Rail Pension Fund

Udaipur was the capital city of Mewar and was ruled by the Maharanas, the premier rulers of Rajasthan, who were legendarily descended from the sun and the moon. The Maharanas' year was punctuated with festivals, entertainments and seasonal hunts which, from the reign of Amar Singh (1698–1710), were recorded in ever larger and more detailed paintings. The elephants depicted in this work are probably on their way to the *Chaughan* or sports arena to participate in some special event. (ABOVE)

THE DECORATIVE ARTS *by Robert Woolley*

When Sotheby's moved to New Bond Street in 1917 we were still primarily an auctioneer of books and literary property, also dealing in other small items such as prints, coins and ceramics. However, the move to bigger premises made it possible for larger works, such as furniture, to be shown in the galleries, opening the way for Sotheby's to expand in both the nature and quantity of items sold. A process of diversification and specialization began – from one Works of Art Department in the 1920s, which handled furniture, tapestries, carpets, needlework, porcelain, pottery, glass and bronzes, we now hold sales in more than twenty different categories under the decorative arts umbrella in our offices worldwide.

The twentieth century has witnessed a huge growth of interest in, and appreciation of, art from non-Western cultures, with many collectors and museums now devoted solely to Asian, Islamic or Tribal art. Perhaps the first indication of the strength of this new market was the astronomical rise in prices of early Chinese porcelain, beginning in the 1950s. In 1973 we set up an office and saleroom in Hong Kong, an innovation which led to the sale there and in London of the Chow Collection of Ming and Qing Porcelain for almost £9 million. Today, Sotheby's Asian network has expanded to include offices in Japan, Taiwan, Singapore and South Korea. This season's series of sales in Hong Kong saw solid results achieved in the Chinese ceramics and jewellery categories and a record-breaking sale of Chinese snuff bottles. In Taiwan our sale of modern Chinese art in April was an outstanding success, bringing NT$45.9 million. A separate sale of Chinese paintings from the Dingyuanzhai Collection made nearly three times the pre-sale high estimate. During Asian Arts Week in New York our Chinese works of art auction, one of the strongest in years, included an Imperial *zitan* long table, which sold for $354,500, a record for Chinese furniture, while in the London auction, a terracotta troop of musicians on horseback, the only such equestrian orchestra known to exist, sold for £331,500.

An Attic black-figure 'Tyrrhenian' neck-amphora (detail)
height 47.2cm (18⅝in)
London £122,500 ($2182,500).
9.XII.93
From the Hirschmann
Collection (LEFT)

Peachbloom-glazed vase
MARK AND PERIOD OF KANGXI,
height 19.7cm (7¾in)
New York $288,500
(£190,400). 1.VI.94 (ABOVE)

A Louis XVI
ormolu-mounted
lacquer *secrétaire
à abattant*
SIGNED *I DUBOIS, JME*
*c.*1770–75, PARIS,
height 156cm (5ft 1½in)
New York $745,000
(£506,800). 20.XI.93 (ABOVE)

In a sense, the Decorative Arts at Sotheby's are now the foundation upon which everything else is built. There will always be sales of glass, porcelain and furniture, for while a million-dollar painting on the wall is not a necessity, a chair to sit on is, so it might as well be an antique one! Both French and English furniture have sold well this season, with single-owner collections adding lustre to sales full of works of the finest quality. In London the celebrated Moller Collection of English Furniture brought £4,845,900, well above the estimate. In New York we sold property from the estate of Wendell Cherry, including a Louis XIV ormolu-mounted ebony and Boulle marquetry bureau plat, cartonnier and clock ($2,202,500) and a George II giltwood chandelier, commissioned for St Giles's House in Dorset ($827,500).

Our predecessor firm in New York, the American Art Association, had an excellent record in the promotion of both fine and decorative American art. This commitment was continued by Parke-Bernet and then Sotheby's in New York, and has paid off in dividends. As well as the first sale of the legendary Little Collection, this season has seen the Fendelman Folk Art Collection and property from the Estate of Wilbur Ross Hubbard of Chestertown, Maryland, at auction. Our series of Americana sales in January brought $6.9 million and showed signs of renewed enthusiasm from private collectors and dealers. There was strength at the top-end of the market and an improvement in the market for mid-range property. A record for an American dressing table was set when the Nicholas Biddle Family Chippendale carved mahogany lowboy brought $387,500.

The sales in London of two exceptional collections of antiquities helped to make this one of the best seasons in the department's history. The Greek Vases from the Hirschmann Collection and the Benzian Collection of Ancient and

Islamic Glass were both of a quality rarely seen at auction. The latter included works that spanned some 3,000 years and achieved £1.4 million.

European works of art brought to auction this year have also been of exceptional quality. In New York a Florentine bronze group depicting Hercules wrestling with Achelous in the form of a bull, from the estate of Wendell Cherry, achieved $1,817,500, while European bronzes and statues from the Peter Jay Sharp Collection made a total of $1,663,600.

Nineteenth-century sculpture sales were dominated this season by the Joey and Toby Tanenbaum Collection sold in New York in May. Bidders from across the globe paid record prices for works by many sculptors including $343,500 for Jean-Baptiste Clésinger's Perseus and Andromeda *and $189,500 for Louis-Ernest Barrias's* Oath of Spartacus.

Sotheby's pioneered sales in art nouveau and art deco works when we opened an auction room in Belgravia, London, in 1971. The market grew rapidly, prompting a move to Bond Street and similar sales to be started in New York. This season saw the auction in New York of a collection of glass and jewellery from the 1920s and 1930s, formed by the restaurateur Michael Chow. The sale included works by glass artist Maurice Marinot and jewellery by Georges and Jean Fouquet, Raymond Templier and Jean Desprès. In London, highlights from the sales in applied arts included a washstand from the blue bedroom at Hous'hill by Charles Rennie Mackintosh, which achieved £243,500.

A Wedgwood fairyland lustre 'Ghostly Wood' ginger jar and cover
DESIGNED BY DAISY MAKEIG-JONES, 1920s,
height 33cm (13in)
London £14,950 ($22,575).
5.X.93 (BELOW)

Although we have been selling ceramics for longer than we have most other decorative arts, our reputation in this field was largely built by Jim Kiddell, who in fifty-eight years at Sotheby's became renowned for his expertise. He would, no doubt, have been delighted by the sale in New York in October 1993 of a private collection of English pottery, which was 93% sold, making $1,752,683, or, indeed, Sotheby's first sale devoted entirely to porcelain from the Meissen factory, held in London, which was 92% sold, bringing £685,111.

When Jim Kiddell joined Sotheby's in 1921, few of the pieces on the following pages would have been sold through the auction house, and many were not even thought of as works of art. Recognition of the decorative arts is one of the most important developments in the art market this century.

A bronze figure of Mercury
ATTRIBUTED TO BARTHÉLÉMY PRIEUR, C.1570–80, FRENCH
height 47cm (18½in)
New York $112,500 (£75,000).
13.I.94 (ABOVE)

ISLAMIC AND INDIAN ART

An Ottoman painted wood interior
DAMASCUS, EIGHTEENTH-CENTURY
London £144,500 ($215,305). 21.X. 93

This is a typical interior from a wealthy bourgeois house in Damascus of about AD1750. The merchant classes of Syria were exceedingly prosperous during the eighteenth century, thanks to the country's important trading cities, such as Aleppo, which lay on the main caravan routes between Asia and Europe. Tradesmen from all over Europe and especially from England and Italy, established 'factories', or warehouses, throughout the region. Although the stylistic features of this room and antechamber reflect contemporary Turkish fashions, in particular textiles, the rococo frames show the influence of European taste. This is not surprising, for English clocks, Venetian mirrors and French furniture can still be found in private houses in Aleppo and Damascus, where they have been preserved since their arrival two, and in some cases three, centuries ago. (ABOVE AND LEFT)

An Ottoman copper-gilt helmet

TURKEY, SIXTEENTH CENTURY, diameter 29cm (11½in)
London £106,000 ($157,950). 21.X.93

This ornate helmet, with its twenty-two flaring facets alternately engraved with flowering lotuses on a stippled ground, similarly decorated conical finial, and spiked turban knop, is incised with the emblem of the Ottoman Court Arsenal at Hagia Irene. Probably an officer's helmet, the use of soft copper (as opposed to the usual steel) and gilding suggest that it was designed for the parade ground and not the battlefield. (LEFT)

A Kashan lustre pottery bowl

PERSIA, EARLY THIRTEENTH CENTURY,
diameter 15.2cm (6in)
London £41,100 ($62,050). 28.IV.94

In the early Islamic period Kashan was an important Sassanid town on the north-south caravan route through Persia. Famous as a centre for calligraphers, administrators, scholars and craftsmen of all kinds, it was particularly renowned for its glazed pottery. In fact, in Persian the term 'kashi' came to denote glazed faience of all kinds including tiles and pottery. This unique bowl depicts a camel with a heart-shaped saddle kneeling beside a bearded camel driver. (ABOVE)

An early Tibetan portrait
THIRTEENTH CENTURY, 47 x 36.2cm (18½ x 14¼in)
New York $68,500 (£46,300). 1.XII.93

This portrait is believed to show the Lama Taglung Thangpa Chenpo, founder of the Taglung monastery, seated on a lotus throne set within a mountainous cavern. The hierarch is wearing red monastic robes, covered by a voluminous cape. Lions crouch at the base of the throne, while lion-griffins and other mythical beasts decorate its back. The surround depicts prominent members of the Kagyu lineage and Buddhist divinities within multi-coloured rocky niches. (LEFT)

A Tibetan gilt-bronze figure of Buddha
PROBABLY FIFTEENTH CENTURY, 43.8cm (17¼in)
New York $74,000 (£50,000). 1.XII.93

This serene figure of Buddha is seated in *dhyanasana*, his face downcast in a meditative expression. His left hand rests upon his knee, while his right is raised in *abhaya mudra*. This unusual posture represents a sign of compassion and protection from the Buddha. The fine patchwork robe he wears is inlaid with silver beading, a form of decoration which is also rare in Tibetan buddhas of this period. (ABOVE)

An Orissan grey schist relief
POSSIBLY KONARAK, THIRTEENTH CENTURY, 98.5cm (38¾in)
London £27,600 ($41,676). 28.IV.94

This sculpture probably depicts the personified planet Sukra. Prior to its purchase by a Devon dealer some years ago, it adorned a local garden, where the sculpture's importance, if ever known, had long been forgotten. It almost certainly comes from the same workshop as a series of Konarak sculptures in the British Museum, from the Stuart-Bridge and Church missionary society collections. The present relief is now in the collection of the Museum of Fine Arts, Boston. (ABOVE)

ORIENTAL CARPETS AND RUGS

A Mughal voided velvet and gilt metal thread floorspread
FIRST HALF OF SEVENTEENTH CENTURY,
240 x 165cm (7ft 11in x 5ft 5in)
London £51,000 ($77,000). 27.IV.94

Throughout the sixteenth and seventeenth centuries the decorative arts of the Safavid court found great favour with the Mughal emperors, and Persian craftsmen came to India to work for the Mughal court. A more purely Mughal aesthetic developed in the seventeenth century, however, as naturalistic flowering plant motifs became the dominant theme. This style, indebted to European herbals circulating at the start of the century, reached its zenith under Shah Jahan (1627–58), from whose reign appear to date the sumptuous gold and silver ground textiles, with their woven or embroidered flowering plants. The present highly rare floorspread exemplifies Mughal design of this period. A central medallion, outlined by an acanthus decoration with quarter medallions at each corner, echoes sixteenth-century Persian carpets, while the naturalistic, symmetrical arrangement of leafy spiral tendrils and blossoms are in the pure Mughal manner. (LEFT)

A Saryk Turkmen tent-door rug

TURKMENISTAN, EIGHTEENTH OR NINETEENTH CENTURY, 180 x 130cm (5ft 11in x 4ft 3in)
New York $57,500 (£38,600). 16.XII.93
From the Collection of Dr and Mrs Jon Thompson

The large numbers of dark brown or purple Saryk door rugs produced at the turn of this century give a false impression that older examples are common too. In fact they are extremely rare. The principal clues to the age of the present example are the clear, bright red colour of the ground and the use of unusual motifs, lost from the vocabulary of later pieces. (BELOW)

A Turkish carpet fragment

SIXTEENTH OR SEVENTEENTH CENTURY, 277 x 107cm (9ft 1in x 3ft 6in)
New York $54,625 (£36,600). 16.XII.93
From the Collection of Dr and Mrs Jon Thompson

The ascending arabesque lattice design of this striking fragment is a typical textile pattern. The overall accuracy of its workmanship suggests that the design was either drawn by a textile designer for the people who made it, or copied directly from a sixteenth-century brocade or velvet. Its size and quality intimate that it was produced for a wealthy patron. (LEFT)

An Azerbaijani arabesque carpet fragment
SEVENTEENTH OR EIGHTEENTH CENTURY, 248 x 184cm (8ft 2in x 6ft 1in)
London £36,700 ($55,400). 27.IV.94

The first half of the eighteenth century was a period of great turmoil in Persia, with the warrior Nadir Shah defeating the Safavids and subjugating Azerbaijan, Georgia and most of Armenia. The effects of the inevitable migration of craftsmen and designs which followed can be seen in the design of this magnificent fragment. Its structure is clearly related to seventeenth-century Persian 'Strapwork' and compartment 'Vase' carpets, while its design forms a link between these and the nineteenth-century carpets of North West Persia. (ABOVE)

An Imperial Chinese dragon carpet
LATE SEVENTEENTH OR EARLY EIGHTEENTH CENTURY, 447 x 315cm (14ft 8in x 10ft 4 in)
New York $68,500 (£45,065). 22.IX.93

This is one of a rare group of early Chinese carpets and fragments to survive. A dragon with five claws was officially the symbol of the emperor in the Ming and Ch'ing periods, which suggests that this carpet was a production of the imperial court workshops. This theory is strengthened by the large scale of the carpet, its design, structure and colour. From the highly animated, almost comical expression on the dragons' faces, the present carpet can be dated to the late Ming or early Ch'ing period. (ABOVE)

CHINESE ART

GIUSEPPE CASTIGLIONE KNOWN AS LANG SHINING
Two Deer in Autumn Grove
SIGNED, INK AND COLOUR ON SILK, 72.1 x 30.8cm (28⅜ x 12⅛ in)
New York $354,500 (£237,919). 29.XI.93

This painting comes from a Scottish private collection,
where it was stored in a trunk together with a label
stating that it had been taken from the Summer Palace
– a series of buildings in Peking which were destroyed
in 1860. Lang Shining was the adopted Chinese name
of the Jesuit missionary Giuseppe Castiglione, who
lived in China from 1716. He gained entrance to an
Imperial court fascinated by Western decorative arts
and the use of perspective in painting and engraving.
He became friends with Prince Bao, who later reigned
as the Qianlong emperor. This relationship granted
Lang an honoured place among the court painters and
thus provided the Jesuit mission with access to the
throne. Lang's unique style is a true blending of
Chinese and Western technique. (RIGHT)

Xie Yuan
Peach Blossoms
Song dynasty, handscroll, ink and colour on silk,
painting 25.8 x 64cm (10⅛ x 25⅛in)
Taipei NT$16,550,000 (£415,500:$622,500). 10.IV.94

This delicate handscroll appears to be the only surviving work of the artist Xie Yuan, who is not recorded in any of the standard texts on Chinese painters. According to James Cahill, he was 'probably an academician in the Song period.' (*An Index of Early Chinese Painters and Paintings,* 1980.) (ABOVE)

Xu Beihong
Galloping Horses
Signed *Beihong* and dated *ren wu,* 1942, spring, 95 x 180.4cm (37⅛ x 71in)
Hong Kong HK$3,320,000 (£287,450:$430,600). 28.X.93

As a child Xu Beihong (1895–1953) studied Chinese classics, poetry and painting with his father. After a short trip to Japan, Xu travelled to Paris in 1919 to attend l'École Nationale des Beaux-Arts. On his return to China in 1927 he accepted a professorship at the National Central University in Nanjing. In 1946 he was appointed President of the National Academy of Art in Beijing. (BELOW)

A blue and white dragon jar

YUAN DYNASTY, MID-FOURTEENTH CENTURY, width 34.6cm (13⅝in)
Hong Kong HK$7,720,000 (£668,400:$1,001,300). 26.X.93

The magnificent dragon depicted on this extremely
rare jar is painted in deep blue with scales carefully
rendered in reverse. The beast glares from beneath
bushy eyebrows, its massive jaws wide open revealing
jagged teeth. Its great movement and expressiveness
reflects the most mature painting style of Yuan blue
and white. (BELOW)

A group of nine painted pottery equestrian figures of musicians

TANG DYNASTY, heights 45cm to 48.5cm (17¾in to 19in)
London £331,500 ($500,550). 7.VI.94

This superbly modelled group of nine individual musicians
seated astride their mounts comprises (from the left): a male
panpipe player; a female drummer; a male flautist; a female
flautist, playing a vertical flute; a female *qin* player (a *qin* is
a Chinese stringed instrument); a male musician with hands
raised as if to hold his, now lost, instrument; a male lutenist;
a male *sheng* player (a *sheng* is a Chinese wind instrument);
and a female musician with hands raised as if to play a, now
lost, wind instrument. This is the only known orchestra of
equestrian musicians of this large size, impressive modelling,
fine detail and attractive colouring. Indeed, it is extremely
rare to find even a single figure of this type. (ABOVE)

A large and finely enamelled *doucai* vase

QIANLONG SEAL MARK AND PERIOD, height 54cm (21¼in)
New York $497,500 (£328,350). 1.VI.94

This vase was bought by Mr William O. Goodman, a prominent Chicago businessman, in about 1895 and remained in the family until Sotheby's sale in June 1994. The Goodman Collection of Chinese porcelain and other works of art furnished the family's fashionable southside mansion on 5026 Greenwood Avenue in Chicago and later at 1355 Astor Street. Much of the collection was donated to the Art Institute of Chicago, where the family also funded the building of the Goodman Theatre in 1925. In 1939 seventy-two pieces of porcelain from the collection were included in an exhibition at the Art Institute of Chicago. (RIGHT)

A gilt-bronze figure of a Dharmapala
FIFTEENTH CENTURY, height 105cm (41¼in)
New York $310,500 (£208,400). 29.XI.93

Dharmapala are Buddhist protector deities symbolizing
the wrath and ferocity of Vairooana, and are identified
by a triple head with a third eye on the forehead and
six arms. Altogether there are ten Dharmapala and the
present one may represent Yamantaka, who is often
characterized by a wheel, which usually appears on
his breast. Dharmapala were rarely depicted as three
dimensional sculptures and it is even more rare to find
a gilt-bronze figure supported on such an elaborate
pedestal. In fact, no other comparable piece appears
to be recorded. (RIGHT)

A carved Imperial *zitan* long table
EARLY EIGHTEENTH CENTURY, height 90.2cm (35½in)
New York $354,500 (£234,000). 1.VI.94

This remarkable table is one of a pair, the other being
in the Art Institute of Chicago, and was sold with
other Imperial furnishings by palace eunuchs early in
this century. Unlike most Qing furniture designs, the
exquisite carving is not constrained in a rigid pattern,
but is naturalistic. Gnarled flowering prunus branches
cling to the multi-levelled uneven surface in a style
characteristic of carving from the early eighteenth
century. (LEFT)

A carved cinnabar lacquer box and cover

MING DYNASTY, MARK AND PERIOD OF YONGLE (1403–24), diameter 23.8cm (9⅜in)
Hong Kong HK$2,220,000 (£192,200:$287,950). 3.V.94

Several lacquer boxes of this type are recorded in Peking. All are
carved with different but closely related scenes of scholars in
garden settings, surrounded by pavilions and trees and with a
lake in the background. Around the sides of both box and cover
are flower scrolls, and the bases are inscribed with reign marks,
in this case the six-character Yongle mark. (RIGHT)

An enamelled carved glass snuff bottle

FROM THE 'GRUYUE XUAN' KILNS, 1780–1830
Hong Kong HK$790,000 (£68,400:$102,450). 28.X.93
From the Collection of Eric Young

Eric Young's acquisition of an extensive snuff bottle collection was a late obsession,
reflecting the same delight in beauty and detail which already informed his other
passion – the collecting, breeding and showing of rare orchids – on which he was a
world authority. The present work shows a brightly-coloured phoenix standing on a
light green rock. Pink flowering peonies grow to either side of the bird and the sky is
filled with a ribbon of multi-coloured clouds and a red sun. (LEFT)

A jadeite and diamond ring

c.1950, the stone approx. 2.4 x 1.2 x 1.3cm (1⁵⁄₁₆ x ½ x ½in)
Hong Kong HK$5,960,000 (£516,000:$773,000). 27.X.93

Jadeite is the type of jade used for jewellery and is prized for its brilliant emerald-
green colour and translucency. This magnificent ring is mounted and set with
numerous small round diamonds. (LEFT)

KOREAN ART

KIM WHANKI
Untitled
SIGNED *WHANKI* AND DATED 57, OIL ON COMPOSITION
BOARD, 52.7 x 33.7cm (20¾ x13¼in)
New York $129,000 (£85,140). 2.VI.94

The years of 1955–59 in Paris were a
particularly productive period for Kim
Whanki. There he further explored his
interest in Korean-inspired themes and
motifs, prominent among which are the
moon, birds, flowers and ceramics. In
this painting, the flask form represented
is undoubtedly inspired by the Korean
ceramics of the Choson period. (BELOW)

Blue and white square vase
CHOSON DYNASTY, EIGHTEENTH CENTURY, height
16.2cm (6⅜in)
New York $107,000 (£71,812). 3.XII.93

This square-sectioned vase is supported on
four feet with a shaped barbed apron which
gives the impression that it has a stand. The
flat sides and rounded angled shoulders are
painted in underglaze-cobalt with bamboo,
chrysanthemums, branches and auspicious
emblems. The tapering neck is undecorated
and rises to a square-lipped mouth. (LEFT)

JAPANESE ART

EARLY UKIYO-E SCHOOL
A six-fold gold screen depicting dancers
EARLY SEVENTEENTH CENTURY, INK, COLOUR AND *GOFUN* ON GOLD LEAF PAPER GROUND,
each panel 76 x 43cm (30 x 17in)
London £1,057,500 ($1,607,400). 16.VI.94

Depicted on this screen are the dancers of the popular *Onna Kabuki* or *Kabuki* theatre,
performed only by women, which superseded the *Okuni Kabuki*, an outlandish theatre
of music and dance founded by Okuni, a shrine maiden from Izumo province. She
came to Kyoto in around 1603 and performed in the river bed of the Kamo River to
the acclaim of the newly-emerging merchant class and other commoners. (ABOVE)

Maeda Seison
Manazuru no oki
<small>Signed and sealed *Seison*, ink and colour on paper
57.8 x 83.2cm (22¾ x 32¾in)
New York $321,500 (£212,200). 2.VI.94</small>

Maeda Seison studied *yamatoe*, a uniquely Japanese style of painting established in the twelfth century, and was known as a collector of twelfth-century *mushae* or paintings depicting battle scenes. The influence of these two interests is evident in this painting, which depicts a famous battle off the Manazuru coast. (RIGHT)

A map of Nagasaki
<small>SEVENTEENTH CENTURY, INK AND COLOUR ON PAPER, 200 x 68cm (78¾ x 26¾in)
Amsterdam DFl132,250 (£47,401:$69,973). 27.X.93</small>

This map depicts a historical event which took place on 5 July 1647. On that day two Portuguese galleys, the *Santo Andre* and the *Santo Joao,* appeared in the harbour of Nagasaki, sent by the king of Portugal. The main charge of the legation aboard was to restore trade relations between Portugal and Japan, which at the time were dominated by the Dutch and Chinese. The shogun was informed of the arrival of the ships, but while awaiting his reply the Japanese blocked the harbour with a pontoon bridge. The answer was negative and the ships left the harbour on 6 September. (ABOVE)

Arita blue and white porcelain vase

LATE SEVENTEENTH CENTURY, height 31.1cm (12¼in)
New York $35.650 (£23,529). 2.VI.94
From the Jacksonville Art Museum

Each of the four slightly flattened sides of this vase are decorated
with a different rectangular panel. The side shown illustrates a
stand of bamboo, while the others depict a plum tree, a pine tree
and a landscape. All of the panels are set against a background of
grapeleaves on stylized waves. (RIGHT)

SAKAIDA KAKIEMON

A pair of models of boys seated on *go* boards

LATE SEVENTEENTH CENTURY,
height 27cm (10⅝in)
London £87,300 ($129,200).
12.XI.93

Go is a game first played
in China 3,000 years ago
and now Japan's national
game. The board's 400
squares begin empty and
are gradually filled up
with rounded stones, as
the players win territory
and capture enemy
armies by surrounding
areas of the board with
'men'. (LEFT)

SUZUKI CHOKICHI CALLED 'KAKO'
Inlaid bronze vase
STAMPED *KAKO* AND WITH THE KIRITSU KOSHO DOUBLE MOUNTAIN MARK,
LATE NINETEENTH CENTURY, height 26.7cm (10½in)
New York $46,000 (£30,875). 3.XII.93

The surface of this vase is modelled to resemble basketweave, and is
decorated with insects among
autumnal plants in gilt and copper, an enamelled moth and a stylized butterfly border. (ABOVE)

KOMA KANSAI
A five-case silver ground inro
SIGNED *KANSAI SAKU*, NINETEENTH CENTURY, 9.2cm (3⅝in)
London £18,400 ($27,960). 16.VI.94

This silver inro, or seal case, is boldly decorated
with a snake attacking a toad. The snake is
winding around the squatting toad, who is
biting the tail of its adversary. (RIGHT)

ANONYMOUS
Netsuke of a foreigner and *shishi*
IVORY, EIGHTEENTH CENTURY,
height 15.2cm (6in)
New York $79,500 (£53,350). 3.XII.93

The *shishi,* a mythological lion-
dog, stands on the shoulders
of the foreigner, who grimaces
under the weight. The man is
boldly carved with long locks
and a curling beard. His robe is
decorated with a dragon among
clouds and he clutches a fly
whisk in his left hand. (ABOVE)

TRIBAL ART

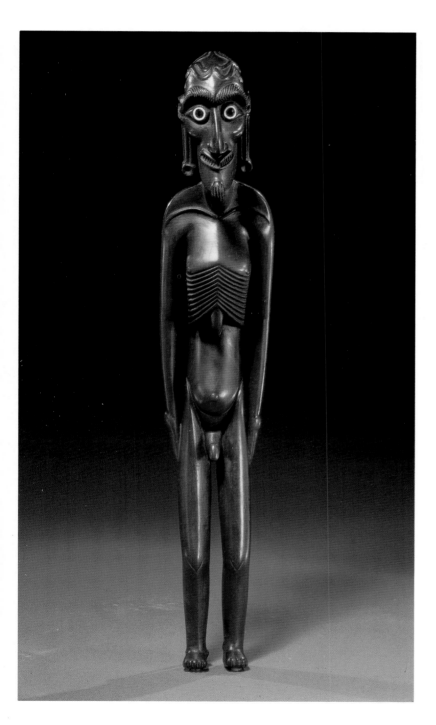

An Easter Island male figure
Height 42.9cm (16⅞in)
New York $244,500 (£166,300). 9.XI.93

G. Foster, who was Captain Cook's naturalist on his
second trip with the *Resolution,* was the first European
to report the existence of wooden statues on Easter
Island. Among these were 'several human figures,
made of narrow pieces of wood about eighteen inches
to two feet long and wrought in a much neater
proportionate manner than we could have expected
after seeing the rude sculpture of the statues. They
were made to represent persons of both sexes. The
wood of which they were made was finely polished,
close-grained, and dark brown.' (LEFT)

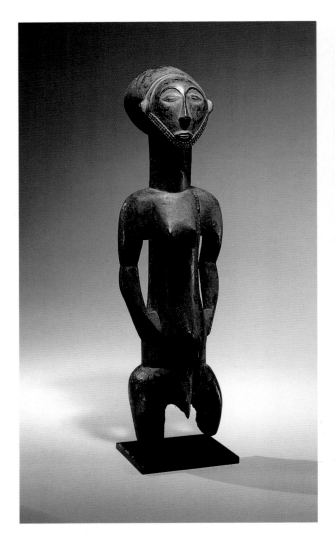

A Hemba male ancestor figure
Height 66.5cm (26⅛in)
London £23,000 ($35,650). 27.VI.94

'Amongst the Hemba the ancestor was venerated by its clan, the cult of the ancient dominating the values of the society. The figure expresses the dependence of the world of the living on that of the dead and is thus a funerary and religious symbol and indicates the ownership of land and the possession of social authority.' (F. Neyt in S. Vogel, *For Spirits and Kings, African Art from the Paul and Ruth Tishman Collection*, 1981.) (ABOVE)

A Yoruba female figure
Height 83.8cm (33in)
New York $76,750 (£52,200). 9.XI.93

This splendid female figure is typical of other shrine figures from the Yoruba town of Ilobu in Western Nigeria and is probably by the hand of an unknown, yet recognizable, carver. The coiffure of the figure has been painted repeatedly with indigo dye, suggesting a possible association with the shrine for the god Erinle. Erinle was a hunter who was deified after defending Ilobu on numerous occasions. (ABOVE)

A Lega magical figure

Height 32cm (12½in)
London £56,500 ($84,200).
29.XI.93
From the Michel Gaud
Collection

This extremely rare
magical figure probably
depicts *kimatwematiwe,*
or Mr Many Head, an
exemplary character who
was used to emphasize
the quality of equity
based on wisdom and
knowledge. (LEFT)

PRE- COLUMBIAN ART

A Chimú gold and silver ceremonial tumi

c.AD850–1050, MIDDLE SICÁN, height 35.6cm (14in)
New York $167,500 (£113,175). 22.XI.93

The Sicán kingdom flowered briefly, but dramatically, on the north coast of Peru. Not only did its political and economic influence extend into Ecuador and as far south as Pachacamac, but also its craftsmen were renowned for their intricate metal and gold work. This tumi depicts the Sicán Lord – one of the principal figures of Middle Sicán iconography – who has been variously identified as Naymlap, the legendary founder of the Lambayeque dynasty, and as the moon personified. (LEFT)

A Mayan carved cache vessel

c.AD250–450, EARLY CLASSIC, 27.3 x 45.1cm (10¾ x 17¾in)
New York $178,500 (£119,600). 17.V.94
From the Wally and Brenda Zollman Collection

This terracotta vessel is intricately carved with the principal gods of the Mayan world and calendric dates. The carvings emphasize the laws of Mayan dynastic accession rituals, through reference to the divine ancestors – Gods GI-III – of the Palenque Triad. The front panel includes one of the earliest full-figure representations of God K (on the left, distinguished by his curling serpent foot), also known as God GII, who approved the legitimacy of rulership. (ABOVE)

AMERICAN INDIAN ART

An Eskimo wood ceremonial mask
Height 87cm (34¼in)
New York $189,500 (£127,200). 4.XII.93

Alaskan Eskimos living on treeless tundra created highly imaginative masks from wood that drifted down the rivers to the sea. The masks were used in ceremonies to disguise or transform a dancer, but they also had a deep symbolic significance, as visual reproductions of a shaman's visions. This mask was likely to have been worn in a winter ceremony in Hooper Bay around 1916, to flatter animal spirits and secure a good harvest for the coming season. The thin elliptical strip of wood that surrounds the mask represents the edge of the sky. Its basic form is that of a kayak – the bow at the bottom, the stern at the top – and the bottom face represents the spirit of a seal. The Yup'ik relied heavily on the seal as a source of food and clothing, and hunted it from kayaks among the spring ice floes. Salmon, an equally important food source, are prominently represented by a carved wooden salmon on each side of the top face, a death's head whose meaning is unknown. (RIGHT)

A Western Great Lakes red catlinite effigy pipehead

PROBABLY OTTAWA OR OJIBWA, FROM MANITOULIN ISLAND, length 19.1cm (7½in)
New York $96,000 (£64,430). 4.XII.93

While researching his book *Wanderings of an Artist Among the
Indians of North America* Paul Kane sketched two effigy pipes
related to this one during his visit in 1845 to Manitowaning on
Manitoulin Island. One with a similar standing nude figure is
identified as the work of 'Awbonwaishkum', the Ottawa chief.
In his text Kane referred to the chief's carving of pipes, and it is
possible that he may have been the maker of the present example,
although there is no existing documentation to verify this. (ABOVE)

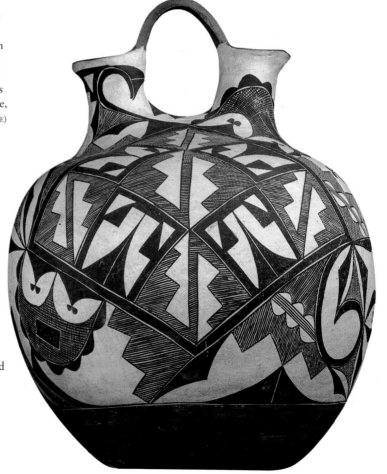

An Acoma polychrome jar

Height 59.7cm (23½in) diameter 45.7cm (18in)
New York $36,800 (£24,288). 24.V.94

The rounded body of this monumental polychrome jar is painted
in black over a greyish-white slip. Its bold geometric pattern is
composed of two diamond medallions, each enclosing hatched
and solid, serrated and curvilinear elements, forming a positive
and 'negative' design. These medallions are flanked by pairs of
finely-crosshatched scalloped foliate motifs, alternating with
spiralling 'birds' and other typical stylized elements. A strap
handle, painted in red, runs between the twin necks. (RIGHT)

ANTIQUITIES

A Roman colourless glass bowl engraved with four male figures
COLOGNE, SECOND HALF OF FOURTH CENTURY AD, diameter 10.1cm (4in)
London £91,700 ($142,150). 7.VII.94
From the Benzian Collection

The Benzian Collection of ancient and Islamic glass was formed over the last quarter-
century and included works from Persia to Western Europe, covering a span of almost
3,000 years. Most of the vessels in the collection were from Roman times such as this
blown shallow bowl, engraved with four identical male figures wearing knee-length
jerkins and holding bunches of grapes. Each figure is contained within a medallion
and between each medallion is a façade. (ABOVE)

A fragmentary Egyptian diorite head of King Apries
TWENTY-SIXTH DYNASTY, REIGN OF APRIES, 589–570 BC, height 30.3cm (11⅞in)
New York $200,500 (£132,330). 8.VI.94

King Apries, referred to in the Bible as Hophra, staged ambitious military campaigns in Palestine, Phoenicia, and against the Greek colonies of Northern Africa, none of which ultimately ended in success. His internal administration was more successful, however, and his reign was one of great prosperity for Egypt, recalling the 'Restoration' under his great-grandfather and founder of the Saitic Dynasty, Psamtik I. Many monuments of Apries were deliberately destroyed after his defeat in 570BC by Amasis, the usurper who became his successor. (ABOVE)

An Egyptian limestone round-topped stele of Neb-seni and Mut
EARLY EIGHTEENTH DYNASTY, REIGN OF HATSHEPSUT / TUTHMOSIS III, 1490–1436BC, height 37.8cm (14⅞in)
New York $217,000 (£145,637). 14.XII.93
This stele shows Neb-seni and his wife Mut seated on a lion-legged chair before a
table laden with offerings to the god Osiris, Lord of Abydos. Their eldest son, at
right, offers a libation, while their four daughters and two younger sons are depicted
below, making offerings of their own. Osiris, god of the dead and of resurrection,
was the consort of Isis, father of Horus, and brother of Seth and Nephthys, and his
worship formed one of the great cults of ancient Egypt. (ABOVE)

A Caeretan hydria
ATTRIBUTED TO THE EAGLE PAINTER, LATE SIXTH CENTURY BC, height 40cm (15¾in)
London £2,201,500 ($3,280,235). 9.XII.93
From the Hirschmann Collection

This hydria depicts a bearded and naked Hero holding a *harpe* (sickle-shaped sword) in his outstretched left hand, a stone in his upraised right hand, battling with a giant sea monster, the Ketos. There are various schools of thought as to the hero's identity, although it remains unknown. Jaap M. Hemelrijk suggests that 'The picture may... refer to a now nameless myth, lost from tradition, but preserved here, telling how the city nymph of Phocaea was nearly eaten by a monster, but was changed just in time into a *phoke* [seal], when, happily, the great hero arrived to rescue her. The *harpe* is probably meant for cutting out the monster's tongue.' (Jaap M. Hemelrijk, *Caeretan Hydriae*, Mainz, 1984.) (ABOVE)

EUROPEAN WORKS OF ART

A bronze aquamanile
NUREMBERG, c.1400, height 33cm (13in)
London £199,500 ($309,225). 7.VII.94

This vessel in the shape of a lion is
filled through the beast's head.
The handle is formed by a dragon
gripping the lion's neck and water
is poured through the spout in its
chest. The Nuremberg attribution
is based on a similar work in the
Bayerisches Nationalmuseum in
Munich, while the lion's mane
has been compared to the hair on
a bronze relief of a Fountain Mask
of a Youth, *circa* 1400, in the
Germanisches Nationalmuseum,
Nuremberg. (LEFT)

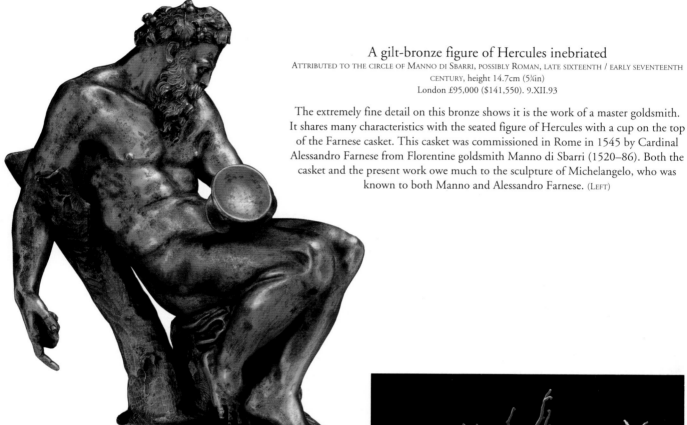

A gilt-bronze figure of Hercules inebriated

ATTRIBUTED TO THE CIRCLE OF MANNO DI SBARRI, POSSIBLY ROMAN, LATE SIXTEENTH / EARLY SEVENTEENTH CENTURY, height 14.7cm (5⅞in)
London £95,000 ($141,550). 9.XII.93

The extremely fine detail on this bronze shows it is the work of a master goldsmith. It shares many characteristics with the seated figure of Hercules with a cup on the top of the Farnese casket. This casket was commissioned in Rome in 1545 by Cardinal Alessandro Farnese from Florentine goldsmith Manno di Sbarri (1520–86). Both the casket and the present work owe much to the sculpture of Michelangelo, who was known to both Manno and Alessandro Farnese. (LEFT)

A Trapani 'fantastic' seascape

SICILY, MID SEVENTEENTH CENTURY, height 38cm (15in)
London £49,900 ($77,345). 7.VII.94
From the Collection of the Prince de Ligne

The Sicilian port of Trapani gave its name to the work of a guild of coral workers established there in 1628. After the repression of the Sicilian insurrection in 1672, however, the coral workers were dispersed around the Mediterranean. This seascape is from a collection of Trapani almost certainly initiated by Prince Claude-Lamoral Ier de Ligne, a soldier and diplomat who was appointed Viceroy of Sicily in 1669. (RIGHT)

A Roman patinated terracotta bust of the angel of the Habakkuk Group

ATTRIBUTED TO GIANLORENZO BERNINI, *c.*1655, height 23.5cm (9¼in)
New York $365,500 (£243,650). 13.I.94
From the Estate of Peter Jay Sharp

In 1652 Pope Alexander VII commissioned Bernini to restore his family chapel in S. Maria del Popolo. The sculptor directed the work and himself produced two marble statues – *Daniel* and *Habakkuk and the Angel.* The present bust is a preparatory study for the latter group. When Daniel is thrown into the lion's den by the Persian King Darius, an angel instructs Habakkuk to take him food. The prophet is lifted by the hair and carried by the angel to the lion's den, thereby giving Daniel a sign that God has not forsaken him. (BELOW)

BARTOLOMEO CAVACEPPI
A Roman white marble bust of the Emperor Caracalla

SECOND HALF OF THE EIGHTEENTH CENTURY, SIGNED, height 71.1cm (28in)
New York $96,000 (£63,360). 6.VI.94

The emergence of the neo-classical movement in the eighteenth century created a great demand for complete statues after antique prototypes found in Italy. Sculptures like the present marble bust were produced for English aristocrats on the Grand Tour, both by Italian sculptors such as Cavaceppi and Piranesi and by English sculptors working in Italy such as Wilton. Cavaceppi worked almost exclusively on restorations and this bust of the ruthless Emperor Caracalla is one of his few original sculptures. (ABOVE)

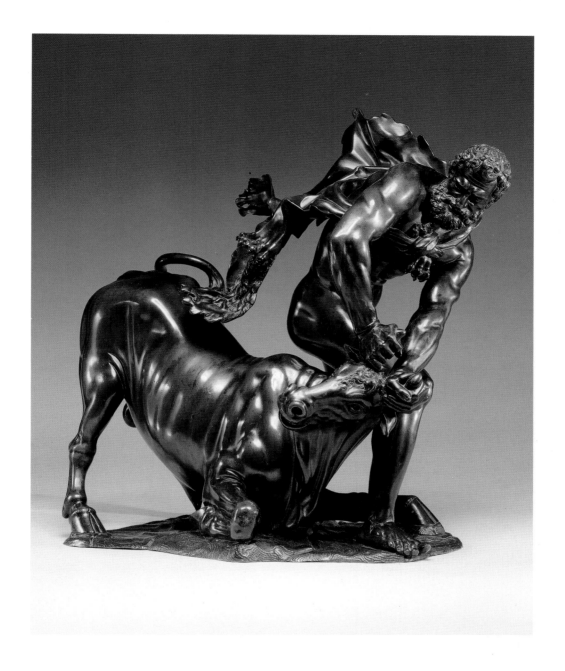

A Florentine bronze group depicting Hercules wrestling with Achelous in the form of a bull

ATTRIBUTED TO FERDINANDO TACCA, SECOND HALF OF THE SEVENTEENTH CENTURY, height 58.4cm (23in)
New York $1,817,500 (£1,199,550). 20.V.94
From the Estate of Wendell Cherry

This bronze group is described in the 1713 inventory of the collections of Louis XIV. It depicts part of the story of Hercules and his love for Deianeira. Achelous, a river god, was a rival for Deianeira's affections. During a fight between the two suitors, Achelous transformed himself into a bull. Hercules overcame him and while grasping his horns snapped one off. The horn was later offered to Ceres as the horn of plenty, the cornucopia. (ABOVE)

NINETEENTH-CENTURY SCULPTURE

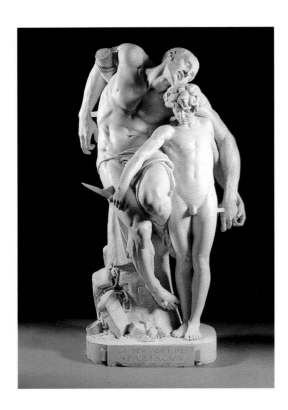

JEAN-BAPTISTE CLÉSINGER
Perseus and Andromeda
INSCRIBED AND DATED *J. CLESINGER 1875*, MARBLE, height 156.2cm (61½in)
New York $343,500 (£226,700). 26.V.94
From the Collection of Joey and Toby Tanenbaum

Peter Fusco writes on the effect of, and inspiration behind, Clésinger's work: 'His sculpture, whether through naturalistic or decorative devices, tends to provoke the senses, most frequently by being blatantly erotic. Like many of the artists of the period, his conscious models were the antique and Michelangelo; at the same time he must be credited as one of the initiators of the rococo revival in mid-nineteenth-century sculpture.' (*The Romantics to Rodin,* Los Angeles County Museum, 1980.) (BELOW)

LOUIS-ERNEST BARRIAS
The Oath of Spartacus
INSCRIBED AND DATED *E.BARRIAS 1876*, MARBLE,
height 210.8cm (83in)
New York $189,500 (£125,050). 26.V.94
From the Collection of Joey and Toby Tanenbaum

In 1858 Barrias entered the École des Beaux-Arts as a student of François Jouffroy and in 1865 he won the *Prix de Rome*. During his third year in Rome in 1869 he executed the plaster *Enfance de Spartacus* depicting the young Spartacus, a Thracian slave sold in the first century BC, holding the hand of an older, dying slave and making an oath of emancipation. Conceived in the last years of the Second Empire, this group took on a patriotic significance and evoked the ideals of freedom and of a united France. The plaster was well received and Barrias executed it three times in marble under the title *The Oath of Spartacus*. The present marble is likely to be the second version. (ABOVE)

ANTONIO FRILLI
Nude Reclining in a Hammock
INSCRIBED *A. FRILLI FIRENZE*, WHITE MARBLE, length 188cm (74in)
New York $354,500 (£239,500). 16.II.94

Antonio Frilli is first recorded as exhibiting at the 1883 *Espozione Nazionale di Roma*. Although he executed sculpture in both marble and bronze, his works are rare. *Nude Reclining in a Hammock* was purchased at the International Exhibition at St Louis in 1904 by the theatrical entrepreneur, William Goldman. The sculpture remained in Goldman's garden until 1932 when he went to manage the Jules Mastbaum Theatre in Philadelphia. Goldman had the piece installed in the theatre, complementing the vast art collection of the theatre's founder, which was already *in situ*. (BELOW)

PROSPER D'EPINAY
Ceinture d'Orée (detail)
INSCRIBED *P.D'EPINAY*, WHITE MARBLE, figure 177cm (69½in)
London £129,100 ($194,950). 20.V.94

When exhibited at the Salon of 1874 *Ceinture d'Orée* was unacclaimed by establishment critics. Undeterred, the artist entered it in the English section of the 1878 International Exhibition and was awarded the *Légion d'Honneur* as an English artist. The work's title refers to the fact that the belt was originally gilded. (ABOVE)

HENRI-MICHEL-ANTOINE CHAPU
The effigy of Victoire Auguste Antoinette de Saxe-Coburg-Gotha (detail)
INSCRIBED AND DATED *1881–1883*, WHITE MARBLE, length 229cm (90in)
London £78,500 ($116,965). 9.XII.93

Victoire was a much-loved cousin of Queen Victoria and Prince Albert, and wife of the Duc de Nemours, second son of Louis Philippe, King of France. In 1848 the French monarchy was overthrown and the royal family was exiled in England. The duchess died at Claremont in Surrey in 1857, aged only thirty-five, and was buried in the nearby church of St Charles Borromeo, where her husband had this effigy erected for her. (RIGHT)

ENGLISH FURNITURE

One of a pair of George II mahogany commodes
ATTRIBUTED TO WILLIAM VILE AND JOHN COBB, *c.*1758, height 100cm (36½in)
London £991,500 ($1,467,400). 18.XI.93
From the Moller Collection

These commodes are recorded in an inventory made at Hampden House, Buckinghamshire, in 1886, and were almost certainly supplied to Robert Trevor, 1st Viscount Hampden, soon after he inherited the house in 1754. Although Hampden was a senior public figure, diplomat and government minister, his greatest love was the arts – he was a fellow of both The Royal Society and The Society of Antiquaries, wrote Latin poetry and formed a famous collection of prints and drawings. His passion for architecture led him to embark upon an extensive programme of alterations as soon as Hampden House came into his possession, and he created a sumptuous suite of interiors in the rococo style, then at the height of fashion. It must have been at this point that Hampden commissioned the commodes, whose exquisitely carved decoration and sinuous form would so perfectly have complemented their surroundings. In keeping with their function, the commodes would have almost certainly been placed in the State Bedroom, which was decorated with a striking Chinese wallpaper and also contained a splendid four-poster bed with matching hangings. (ABOVE)

A Chinese-export gilt-decorated black lacquer secretaire bookcase
c.1740, height 244cm (96in)
New York $200,500 (£132,800). 16.X.93

This magnificent cabinet is identical in almost every detail of its form and decoration to the Flight cabinet, one of the best documented examples of Chinese export furniture in existence. The latter was made in Peking and delivered to Thomas Flight on 13 September 1740. Without doubt the Flight cabinet and the present piece came from one workshop, and it is likely that the two cabinets were produced at the same time. Throughout the eighteenth century the taste for Chinese furniture was well established in Europe, with the three major consumers of export wares – Britain, Holland and Portugal – all competing fiercely for trade concessions. The major manufacturing centre for export furniture was at Canton in the more accessible southern part of the country, and thus, this cabinet, with its indirectly documented provenance, represents a considerable rarity. (ABOVE)

A gilt-decorated black-japanned gentleman's clothes press
ATTRIBUTED TO GILES GRENDEY, c.1740, height 183cm (6ft)
New York $145,500 (£96,357). 16.X.93

Giles Grendey is thought to have labelled those pieces of his furniture which were made for the Portuguese and Spanish markets, or which were to be sold ready-made from his shop. He is best known for his japanned works, including a labelled suite he produced for the Duke of Infantado's palace at Lazcano. The present clothes press shares many characteristics with the furniture at Lazcano, such as the double serpentine shape to the panelled doors and the portrayal of Oriental figures against feathery trees, floral festoons, and leafy scrolls inhabited by birds in the ornamentation. (ABOVE)

A pair of George II mahogany cypher-back armchairs

*c.*1755, THE SPLATS CARVED WITH THE INITIALS *JC*
London £444,500 ($689,000) for the set of six. 8.VII.94
From Tonbridge School, Kent

These remarkable chairs formed part of the historic furnishings of
Tonbridge School, Kent, originally founded in the reign of Edward
VI and one of the oldest and most prestigious public schools in
England. They were commissioned by the Rev. James Cawthorne,
poet, scholar and Headmaster of Tonbridge from 1743 until 1761.
On Cawthorne's death, the chairs were presented to the school by
his sister, and remained *in situ* for almost 250 years. (RIGHT)

One of a pair of George III carved mahogany library armchairs

ATTRIBUTED TO WILLIAM VILE, *c.*1760
London £463,500 ($718,400). 8.VII.94

These armchairs form part of a suite originally commissioned by the
4th Earl of Shaftesbury for St Giles's House, Dorset, and are likely to
have been purchased by Lord Shaftesbury following his marriage in
1759, when the house was redecorated in the fashionable rococo style
recently introduced from the continent. The armchairs were evidently
produced by a leading London furniture maker, and have at various
times been attributed to Thomas Chippendale and his contemporary
William Hallett Senior. However, their date and stylistic qualities
suggest that they are most likely to have been made by Hallet's pupil
and protégé, William Vile. (LEFT)

A George II giltwood twelve-light chandelier
ATTRIBUTED TO MATTHIAS LOCK IN ASSOCIATION WITH HENRY
FLITCROFT, c.1740, height 112cm (44in)
New York $827,500 (£546,150). 20.V.94

Like the armchairs opposite, this chandelier originally
came from St Giles's House, Dorset, and dates from
the lifetime of the 4th Earl of Shaftesbury's first wife,
Lady Susannah Noel, who shared her husband's love of
the arts and was one of only four women to subscribe
to Thomas Chippendale's *Director*. Work began at St
Giles's House in 1740–41 on a magnificent new State
Dining Room in the fashionable Palladian style, and it
was for this interior that the chandelier was produced.
The Dining Room was designed by the architect Henry
Flitcroft, who probably shared responsibility for the
chandelier with the celebrated furniture maker and
carver Matthias Lock. (LEFT)

One of a pair of George II giltwood console tables
ATTRIBUTED TO HENRY
FLITCROFT, c.1740,
height 85.5cm (33⅝in)
London £232,500 ($344,100).
18.XI.93
From the Moller Collection

These superb giltwood
tables epitomize the
exuberant sculptural
style of the Palladian
period. The design is
governed by the theme
of the Four Elements,
with flowers and fruit
symbolizing earth, eagles
(as attributes of Jupiter)
evoking air and fire, and
dolphins representing
water. (RIGHT)

CONTINENTAL FURNITURE

A Louis XIV ormolu-mounted ebony and Boulle marquetry bureau plat, cartonnier and clock

ATTRIBUTED TO ANDRÉ-CHARLES BOULLE, THE CLOCK ATTRIBUTED TO CLAUDE MARTINOT,
c.1715, overall height 2.52m (8ft 3in)
New York $2,202,500 (£1,453,650). 20.V.94
From the Estate of Wendell Cherry

This work belonged to Louis-Charles de Machault (1667–1750), an influential and prosperous member of Paris society. Upon his death it descended to his son, Jean-Baptiste de Machault d'Arnouville, who was close to both Louis XV and Mme de Pompadour and rose to become Controller General of Finances before falling out of favour. The desk and clock have, since 1720, been continually inventoried and described as the work of André-Charles Boulle, leaving little doubt that they were indeed delivered from his workshops in the Louvre. Members of the Martinot family of clock-makers were also lodged in the Louvre and were known to provide Boulle with movements for his clock cases. (BELOW)

One of a pair of Louis XIV ormolu-mounted ebony and Boulle
marquetry cabinets
ATTRIBUTED TO ANDRÉ-CHARLES BOULLE, LATE SEVENTEENTH CENTURY, height 127cm (50in)
New York $1,652,500 (£1,124,150). 19.XI.93

This pair of cabinets contain the technical and stylistic features generally associated
with the work of André-Charles Boulle and can be dated from *circa* 1690, when the
cabinet-maker's career was reaching its apogee. They would have been used to show
vases, pieces of sculpture or clocks and to house jewellery or medals. Engravings by
Marietre, after Boulle, show variations for a cabinet virtually identical to the present
pair, and suggest that these cabinets originally stood on bases. It is possible that, since
they had probably become old fashioned by the end of the seventeenth century, the
cabinets went into storage, in the course of which they could have become separated
from their stands. (ABOVE)

One of a pair of Louis XV japanned corner cupboards

ATTRIBUTED TO B.V.R.B., *c.*1750, height 101cm (39¾in)
Monaco SF5,450,000 (£641,200:$990,900). 18.VI.94

B.V.R.B is the stamp of Bernard II Vanrisamburgh who, from 1730, had a workshop in the rue de Reuilly. He had a succession of three partners who were responsible for selling his furniture. These cupboards probably date from 1750–58, when Vanrisamburgh was working with Lazare Duvaux. Duvaux's records show that the cabinet-maker fulfilled three commissions for such japanned corner cupboards during this period, for M. La Fresnaye, M. Fabus and Mme de Pompadour. (LEFT)

An early Louis XV parquetry commode

ATTRIBUTED TO CHARLES CRESSENT OR ANTOINE-ROBERT GAUDREAUS, *c.*1740, height 93cm (36½in)
London £177,500 ($268,025). 10.VI.94

This commode is part of a group usually attributed to Cressent, but re-attributed by Francis Watson to Antoine-Robert Gaudreaus, supplier to the *Garde-Meuble Royal*. Watson based his re-attribution on an entry in Gaudreaus's inventory for such a piece, which was commissioned for the king's apartments at the Château de la Muette. The group, however, has all the stylistic features usually associated with Cressent's work and it is possible that Gaudreaus commissioned the la Muette commode from a colleague, in this case Cressent. Although there is no proof to support this, such practice was not uncommon at the time. (RIGHT)

A Louis XVI ormolu-mounted tulipwood, kingwood, fruitwood and parquetry commode
SIGNED *G. BENEMAN*, LAST QUARTER OF EIGHTEENTH CENTURY, height 89.9cm (19½in)
New York $1,674,500 (£1,139,100). 19.XI.93

In 1785 Marie Antoinette decided to redecorate her *Salon des Nobles* at Versailles. This commode, made for the room by Joubert in 1771, was sent to the *Garde-Meuble* in Paris. It was restored by Beneman and delivered to the King's palace at Compiègne on 28 August 1786, for use in his private apartments. When the monarchy fell, paintings and furniture not sold on behalf of the Revolution were sent to the *Garde-Meuble* to be registered and redistributed. Among them was this piece which was used in the apartments of one of the Directors at the Palais du Luxembourg. (LEFT)

An armchair from a suite of Louis XVI giltwood seat furniture
SIGNED *I. POTHIER*, LAST QUARTER EIGHTEENTH CENTURY
New York $690,000 (£469,400). 19.XI.93

This armchair was part of a suite consisting of two *canapés*, or sofas, and six armchairs. Of these one of the *canapés* and two armchairs have been lost. Although this suite bears the stamp of Jean-Jacques Pothier, it is possible that he was working with Georges Jacob. The pair are known to have collaborated during the 1770s and a set of eight similar chairs, stamped by Jacob, are now in the collection of the Château de Fontainebleau. (RIGHT)

An Italian walnut bureau cabinet
VENICE, MID-EIGHTEENTH CENTURY, height 260cm (102⅜in)
Milan L150,000,000 (£60,050:$90,075). 13.XII.93

This bureau cabinet comes from the period in Italy when the late baroque was merging almost imperceptibly with the rococo. The balance and solidity of the work is typical of earlier furniture, but the delicate glass engraving and light curves herald the new. (ABOVE)

A Roman polychrome marble and *pietre dure* table top
LATE SIXTEENTH CENTURY, 164 x 104cm (64½ x 41in)
London £183,000 ($272,670). 10.XII.93
From St Mary's Episcopal Church, Hamilton

The ancient Roman mosaic can be regarded as the antecedent of the sixteenth-century *commesso,* a kind of sectional mosaic executed in hard stones or *pietre dure* and soft stones such as marble. The tradition of working stones continued throughout the Middle Ages and Renaissance, taking inspiration from the classical models of the past and often reusing hard stones from ruined temples and monuments. From the end of the sixteenth century the two main centres for *commessi* were Florence, where naturalistic patterns with birds, flowers, figures and landscapes were mainly developed, and Rome, where the geometric and more abstract motifs, such as those seen in this table top, were highly fashionable. (BELOW)

NINETEENTH-CENTURY FURNITURE

An English marquetry side table
STAMPED *MH* BELOW A CROWN, AND *HOLLAND & SONS*, *c.*1865, width 160cm (63in)
London £122,500 ($183,750). 11.III.94

The initial MH surmounted by the royal crown of England indicates that this cabinet once formed part of an important collection of royal furniture at Marlborough House, St James's. Built at the beginning of the eighteenth century the London mansion was designed for the Duke of Marlborough and passed to the Crown in the nineteenth century. In preparation for the occupation by Albert Edward, Prince of Wales, later King Edward VII, and his bride Princess Alexandra of Denmark the house was extensively remodelled in 1863 under the direction of the architect Sir James Pennethorne. A suite of fashionable new reception rooms was created and quantities of furniture ordered, including the above cabinet. The cabinet, veneered with burr-yew within sycamore, boxwood and walnut crossbandings, is typical of the very high quality of furniture being produced by Holland & Sons during the 1860s and 1870s and incorporates elements of both Grecian and Louis XVI styles. The *en camaieu* central panel is painted with a putti waking Cupid and is flanked by portrait heads of Shakespeare and Chaucer. (ABOVE)

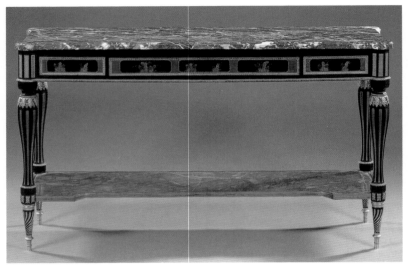

A French lacquer side table
STAMPED *HENRY DASSON 1882*, WITH A 'G' BELOW THE PRINCE OF WALES FEATHERS AND A LABEL PRINTED *ON HER MAJESTY'S SERVICE* AND TYPED *THE PROPERTY OF THE LATE QUEEN MARY*
height 93.5cm (3ft 1in)
London £54,300 ($81,450). 11.III.94

This console furnished Marlborough House during the occupation of the Prince and Princess of Wales, later King George V and Queen Mary, between 1901 and 1911. It is possible that it was purchased from Dasson in 1882 by the Prince's father, Edward VII, during one of the then Prince of Wales's frequent trips to Paris. (ABOVE)

A pair of 'Viennese' enamel and gilt-bronze mounted urns on pedestals
THIRD QUARTER OF NINETEENTH CENTURY, height 1.83m (6ft)
New York $112,500 (£75,000). 24.III.94

Most of the goldsmiths familiar with the art of enamelling – a technique related to glass production – were to be found in Bohemia, Prague and Vienna. The decoration on these urns and their pedestals distinguishes them as having been produced in Vienna during the second half of the nineteenth century. (LEFT)

The Barber of Seville piano; a French gilt-bronze and tulipwood *bombé* piano

BRONZES SCULPTED BY LÉON MESSAGÉ, CASE BY FRANÇOIS LINKE, MOVEMENT BY ERARD OF PARIS, 1890s, length 2m (6ft 6¾in)
London £155,500 ($103,000). 27.V.94

François Linke was born in Austria in 1855 and died in Paris in 1946. He established his name at the Paris *Exposition Universelle* of 1900, where he risked his fortune to put on a magnificent display of fine furniture, which included a similar piano. Linke's earlier work appears to consist entirely of copies of important eighteenth-century furniture. He soon became frustrated with this practice, however, and with his collaboration with the little-known sculptor Léon Messagé created a new and distinctive style, which fused the rococo with the flowing lines of art nouveau. (RIGHT)

A Louis XV style gilt-bronze mounted mahogany cylinder desk

SECOND HALF NINETEENTH CENTURY, height 1.78m (5ft 10in)
New York $195,000 (£127,450). 17.IX.93
From the Joseph M. Meraux Collection

From the Second Empire onwards many of the finest Paris makers were producing furniture reminiscent of the Louis XV style. The cylinder of this highly ornate desk is decorated with a shield issuing implements of war and berried branches, and is flanked by elaborately cast figural two-light candelabra. (LEFT)

AMERICAN DECORATIVE ARTS

A Chippendale carved mahogany tilt-top tea table
PHILADELPHIA, c.1765, height 71.1cm (28in)
New York $596,500 (£397,600). 30.I.94

This piecrust tea table was carved by an unknown, but highly important, carver who arrived in
Philadelphia, probably from London, during the early 1760s. It is possible that it was ordered
by David Deshler of Philadelphia, who is known to have commissioned other fine pieces of
Chippendale furniture, and descended through his daughter to the Canby family. (ABOVE)

A classical brass-inlaid rosewood, satinwood and mahogany swivel-top card table
ATTRIBUTED TO CHARLES HONORÉ LANNUIER, NEW YORK, c.1815, height 78.7cm (31in)
New York $211,500 (£144,000). 24.X.94

This card table is one of a pair (the other is now in the collection of the Metropolitan Museum of Art) made for Philip Hone, a prominent businessman, diarist and Mayor of New York in 1826. The tables were probably purchased for his house at 44 Cortlandt Street, which was, in his own words, 'one of the most genteel residences in the city.' (LEFT)

A Chippendale carved mahogany lowboy
PHILADELPHIA, c.1755, height 78.4cm (30⅞in)
New York $387,500 (£258,300). 30.I.94

According to tradition this lowboy has been in the Biddle family of Philadelphia since the mid-eighteenth century. Its most famous owner was Nicholas Biddle (1786–1844), whose cultural and economic leadership of Philadelphia in the second quarter of the nineteenth century resulted in impressive growth and prosperity for the city. (LEFT)

A Chippendale block- and shell-carved mahogany kneehole dressing table

ATTRIBUTED TO EDMUND TOWNSEND, NEWPORT, RHODE ISLAND, 1765–85, height 83.8cm (33in)
New York $519,500 (£337,675). 24.VI.94

This dressing table has been attributed to the master craftsman Edmund Townsend on
the basis of comparisons with a labelled example in the Museum of Fine Arts, Boston, and
another signed example in a private collection. Each of these three desks share distinctive
construction characteristics. (ABOVE)

A collection of Pennsylvania-German miniature wallpaper
bandboxes and fabric sewing birds on a maple shelf
PENNSYLVANIA, c.1820, height of shelf 88.9cm (35in)
New York $40,250 (£27,400). 23.X.93
From the Collection of Burton and Helaine Fendelman

This maple shelf, then partially assembled, was purchased by the artist
Barry Cohen along with a smaller collection of birds and boxes. The
pieces were then arranged by Cohen, who made numerous additions.
The resulting assemblage, so characteristic of Cohen's refined passion
and affection for jewel-like small objects, bears a marked resemblance
to many of the constructions he created as an artist. (ABOVE)

Six nesting Nantucket lightship baskets
LABELLED DAVIS HALL, NANTUCKET, MASSACHUSETTS, LATE NINETEENTH CENTURY,
heights 11.4cm to 19.1cm (4½in to 7½in)
New York $118,000 (£79,200). 29.I.94
From the Bertram K. Little and Nina Fletcher Little Collection

The technique of Nantucket basket-making derives from that of
casks, barrels and wooden kegs made by coopers for whaling ships.
Ribs of white oak were notched into a wooden base and woven
with rattan or fine calibre cane. Baskets were made in every shape
and size, with a weave fine enough to hold flour. No Nantucket
home or pantry was complete without them. (ABOVE)

EUROPEAN TAPESTRIES AND CARPETS

JACOB BENNE
An Oudenarde wild park tapestry
*c.*1550, 295m x 505cm (9ft 8in x 16ft 6in)
London £58,700 ($88,637). 20.V.94

This hunting scene shows a fallen deer being attacked by a lion and a griffin. On either side can be seen a wyvern, a leopard, a running stag, two wild horses, a bear and a giant lizard, while the Calydonian boar hunt is depicted in the background. Included in the border decorations are the allegorical figures of Justice, Music and Dominion. The tapestry was sold to the Oudenarde museum and so returns to its place of origin. (ABOVE)

An Empire Savonnerie carpet
FRANCE, FIRST QUARTER NINETEENTH CENTURY, approximately 5.84 x 4.62m (19ft 2in x 15ft 2in)
New York $233,500 (£154,110). 20.V.94
From the Estate of Wendell Cherry

The design of this carpet shows the influence of Napoleon's first wife, Joséphine de Beauharnais, on French decoration in the early 1800s. In 1799 Napoleon gave Malmaison to Joséphine. Many of the furnishings she had made for the palace reflected the magnificent rose garden there, which was designed by Redouté. (RIGHT)

APPLIED ARTS

**A Majorelle gilt-bronze mounted carved mahogany fireplace
surround:** *Les Orchidées*
*c.*1903, height 2.15m (7ft ½in)
New York $255,500 (£172,600). 26.XI.93
From the John and Katsy Mecom Collection

Prior to 1898 Louis Majorelle's furniture designs were dependent upon sinuously
carved elements and inlaid marquetry techniques representing organic or landscape
details. During the last two years of the century, however, he expanded his atelier to
include a foundry to produce gilt- and patinated-bronze mounts for his furniture.
Les Orchidées (The Orchids) was his second series of pieces in this new style. (ABOVE)

The Tiffany Parakeets and Goldfish Tea Screen
Signed *Tiffany &Co.PP*, *c*.1914, height 18.1cm (7⅛in)
New York $134,500 (£88,770). 19.III.94
From the Collection of Raymond and Lenore Grover

Louis Comfort Tiffany based this screen upon the 'Parakeets and Goldfish
Bowl' window shown in the 'Dark Room' of his exhibit at the 1893 World's
Columbian Exposition in Chicago. The mark 'PP' was used by Tiffany to
denote those articles chosen for his display at the Panama Pacific Exhibition.
Tiffany received a gold medal for this display, which included jewellery and
decorative arts. (BELOW)

ÉMILE GALLÉ
'La giroflée des murailles' glass vase
c.1900, ENGRAVED *GALLÉ*, 20cm (7 ⅞ in)
Monaco FF444,000 (£54,150:$83,000). 17.X.93

Émile Gallé's ambition was to raise the complex
science of glass production to a new, hitherto
unimagined, artistic status. In this he succeeded
most impressively, by experimenting for thirty
years, until his death in 1904, to devise ever
more challenging possibilities for this most
difficult of media. He created a wide palette of
colours with rich internal and surface effects,
evolving brilliant polychrome enamels and new
techniques of inlaying glass and of working it
into sculptural forms with high-relief decoration.
Gallé's motifs were primarily derived from
nature, and include the wallflower, the subject of
the present vase. (ABOVE)

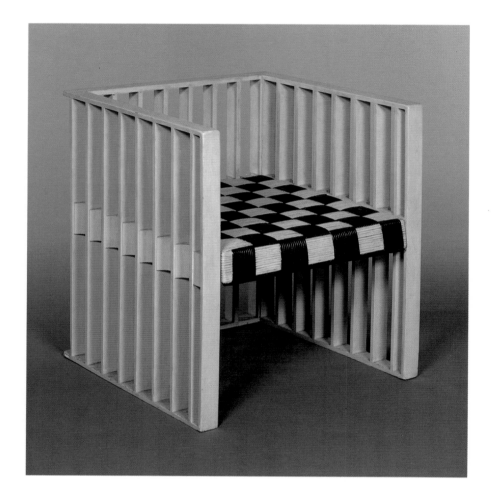

KOLOMAN MOSER, EXECUTED BY PRAG RUDNIKER
A painted beech and woven cane armchair
FOR THE PURKERSDORF SANATORIUM, 1903, height 72cm (28 ⅜ in)
London £85,100 ($128,939). 23.IX.93

This armchair was one of several to this design which were used in the entrance hall
of the Purkersdorf Sanatorium. The design of the sanatorium was perhaps the most
important architectural and interior project undertaken by the Wiener Werkstätte in
their early functionalist mode, and this armchair is arguably the most dramatic piece
created within the scheme. (ABOVE)

CHARLES RENNIE MACKINTOSH
An oak, ceramic tile and leaded glass washstand for the
blue bedroom, Hous'hill
1904, height 160.5cm (63¼in)
London £243,500 ($362,800). 22.IV.94

This washstand was part of the furnishings created by Mackintosh for the blue
bedroom at Hous'hill, which he was commissioned to redecorate and furnish in
1903–04 by Miss Cranston. Miss Cranston was Mackintosh's most important
single patron, allowing him complete freedom to transform a series of tea rooms in
Glasgow as well as the Hous'hill commission. When the house was broken up in
1933 much of the furniture was sold at auction and the majority of the furniture
from the blue bedroom was assumed lost. Several of the pieces have re-emerged over
the past twenty years, however, and have been sold by Sotheby's. (ABOVE)

A carved wood stool,
designed by Pierre
Legrain

c.1920–25, height 33.7cm (13¼in)
New York $98,750 (£65,175). 15.VI.94

Legrain created this stool for
Mme Jeanne Tachard for her
villa at La Celle-Saint-Cloud,
after an introduction from her
close friend Jacques Doucet.
Legrain had made an identical
stool for Doucet and although
the designer would normally
create only unique pieces for
his important clients, he
made an exception in this
case because of the friendship
between Doucet and Tachard
and their shared taste for the
avant-garde. (LEFT)

DESNY

A modernist tea and coffee service
MARKED *DESNY*, *c*.1930, width 34.5cm (13⅜in)
London £23,000 ($34,270). 22.IV.94

This dramatic geometric service of rosewood
and electroplated metal comprises a teapot,
coffee pot, milk jug, sugar pot and tray formed
as a mechanistic cylinder. (RIGHT)

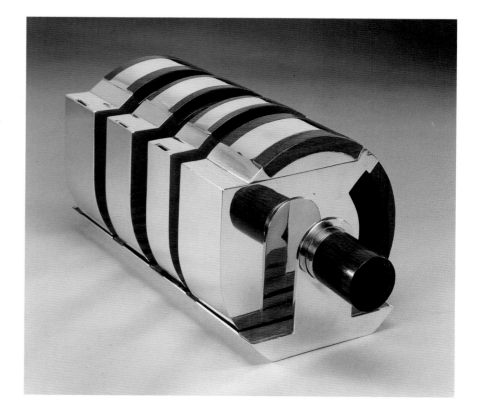

**A Jean Desprès modernist
hammered silver and ivory
necklace**
SIGNED *J. DESPRES*, *c.*1930
New York $57,500 (£37,950). 15.VI.94
From the Collection of Michael Chow

Although Jean Desprès trained as a
goldsmith, during World War I he
worked in an aircraft factory. The
impact of this engineering experience
is evident in the mechanistic forms
which he developed as a craftsman-
designer. (LEFT)

**A Maurice Marinot internally decorated
acid-etched glass-stoppered bottle**
INSCRIBED *MARINOT*, *c.*1930, height 9.2cm (3⅝in)
New York $35,650 (£23,529). 15.VI.94
From the Collection of Michael Chow

After a visit to the Viard workshops Maurice Marinot
became enthralled by glass and it was in this small
studio in 1911 that he began learning the techniques
of the medium. Marinot produced around 3,000
glassworks in a career which peaked for little more
than a decade from the early 1920s to the mid 1930s.
During that period, however, he changed direction
several times, developing new techniques to blow very
heavy-walled vessels and devising new methods of
decoration. He would also use acids to cut deep into
the surface of the glass giving it the appearance of
jagged chunks of ice, as in this remarkable bottle and
stopper. (RIGHT)

CERAMICS AND GLASS

A pair of Dutch delft 'flower pyramids'
ADRIANUS KOEKS' FACTORY, 1695–1710, heights 109cm and 90cm (43in and 35½in) London £287,500 ($437,000). 15.VI.94

The first pagoda vases of this type were designed by Daniel Marot to a commission from Queen Mary II (1662–94), and were intended for the ornamental dairy at Hampton Court Palace. There followed a brief fashion for these magnificent and extravagant display pieces among members of the English court, with other examples being recorded at Chatsworth and Dyrham Park. (LEFT)

A Staffordshire creamware tea party group

1750–60, height 17.5cm (6⅞in)
New York $453,500 (£304,350). 20.X.93

This superbly modelled group offers a unique reflection of eighteenth-century 'genteel' life and is significant, not only as a study in contemporary costume and furniture design, but also as a comment on English social custom. The figures are the epitome of gracious sobriety, with two couples politely partaking of afternoon tea. This piece achieved a record price for European ceramics sold at auction. (LEFT)

A London delftware group of lovers

PROBABLY SOUTHWARK, 1670–85, height 13.4cm (5¼in)
New York $82,250 (£55,200). 20.X.93

English delftware figures are highly rare as their production in the late seventeenth and eighteenth centuries was restricted by the nature of the coarse clays and the thick tin glaze used. The figures in this group may possibly represent popular characters of the period, in which case a mould would have been adapted from a readily available print. Based on the costumes of the two figures, this group must have been one of the earliest attempts at figure-making by the London delftware potters. (RIGHT)

A Chelsea octagonal small bowl
1752–54, width 10.5cm (4 ⅛ in)
New York $24,150 (£16,200). 22.IV.94

This small octagonal bowl is based on *The Round Dance* (1617), an etching by Jacques Callot (1592–1635). Callot was a celebrated etcher who produced designs for the Medici glassworks in Florence. *The Round Dance* is one of a series of fifty etchings, first published in 1617, which covers a variety of subjects including landscapes, single figure studies of noblemen, duellers, grotesques, figures from the *Commedia dell'Arte* and studies of public Florentine games. The etchings were quickly copied, not only during Callot's life, but also during the succeeding centuries. The lively figures seen here are typical of Callot's style at this period and probably depict members of the Italian Comedy. These actors or *zanni* not only acted from an unwritten script but were also jugglers, gymnasts, buffoons and anything else that appealed to their audiences, both courtly and popular. (LEFT)

A Sceaux faïence soup tureen, cover and stand
CHAPPELLE PERIOD, *c.*1755–60, 33.5cm (13¼in)
London £11,500 ($17,100). 1.III.94

The design of this earthenware tureen is based upon that of the elaborate rococo silverware fashionable in mid-eighteenth-century France. It is decorated in enamels with sprays dominated by blown roses and double tulips entwined with convolvulus and forget-me-not trails. The naturalistic knop depicts a cut cauliflower head, asparagus and a mushroom. (RIGHT)

A Du Paquier gold- and diamond-mounted gaming set

*c.*1740, the gaming box 16.7 x 14.7cm (6⅝ x 5¹³⁄₁₆in)
New York $255,500 (£172,600). 21.X.93

This extraordinary box must be one of the first gaming boxes to be made in porcelain and is one of only two other Du Paquier examples known. Formerly in the Imperial Hermitage Collection in St Petersburg, it is possible that the box was a gift from the Austrian Emperor to Catherine the Great of Russia. (ABOVE)

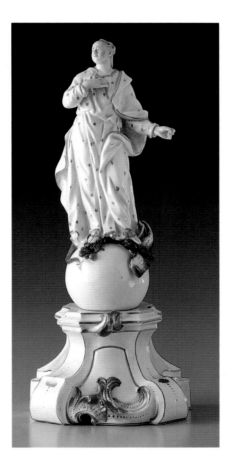

A Fulda figure of the Madonna of the Immaculate Conception

MODELLED BY WENZEL NEU, *c.*1770, 37.5cm (14¾in)
Zürich SFr80,500 (£37,975:$57,500). 1.VI.94

Belief in the Immaculate Conception was for centuries the subject of controversy in the Catholic church, but was generally accepted from about the sixteenth century onwards and became particularly associated with the Counter-Reformation. This figure was modelled after a sculpture by Ignaz Günther in the church of Attel in Bavaria. (LEFT)

A documentary Meissen part tea service
MARCOLINI PERIOD, c.1775–80
London £29,900 ($44,500). 2.III.94
From the Collection of the late Joseph A. Wilby

When the Elector Friedrich Augustus III took power in 1774, the Meissen factory was put under the control of Count Camillo Marcolini. It was during the Marcoloni period (1774–1814) that this neo-classical part tea service, painted with panels, was produced. The panels depict cherubs in the various stages of porcelain production from the chemical process at the outset to firing and painting. The fourteen-piece set was painted by Johann Georg Loehnig and Johann Gottlieb Matthäi. (ABOVE)

An Ott and Brewer Belleek potpourri vase and cover
TRENTON, NEW JERSEY, c.1889, height 34.2cm (13½in)
New York $25,300 (£16,850). 28.I.94

In 1882 William Bromley, Jr, of the Irish Belleek factory, arrived in America to work at the Trenton porcelain manufactory, Ott and Brewer, producing the first Belleek porcelain in America. When the line made its début in 1883, the firm was criticized for their use of Irish forms and decoration. By adapting the line for an American market, however, they went on to win a gold medal at the 1889 Philadelphia Exhibition of Art Industry. (ABOVE)

A Viennese transparent-enamelled beaker

ATTRIBUTED TO GOTTLOB SAMUEL MOHN, SIGNED AND DATED *1812*, 9.8cm (3⅞in)
London £21,850 (32,300). 9.XI.93

The panel of this beaker is amusingly painted with a vignette set in a library. Two petitioners, one standing, one seated, have come to put their case before a lawyer. The lawyer appears to be considering the case fairly, but his left hand is stretched behind his back to accept a bribe from a friend of one of the petitioners, while his feet are trampling over a copy of *Corpus Juris* beneath the table. In an alcove behind the lawyer stands the headless statue of Justice. (ABOVE)

A St Louis upright bouquet-in-basket weight

Diameter 7.5cm (2¹⁵⁄₁₆in)
New York $29,900 (£19,900). 6.XII.93

The firm of St Louis was one of the leading French paperweight makers of the nineteenth century. Their upright bouquet in a basket is extremely rare and, according to Geraldine J. Casper 'represents the achievement of a mas-ter artisan as well as displaying a refreshing awareness of the compositional potential of paperweight design.' (LEFT)

A Silesian engraved armorial goblet and cover

WARMBRUNN, *c.*1760, height 26.5cm (10⅜in)
London £7,705 ($11,700). 15.VI.94

This armorial glass dates from the period after the Second Silesian War (1744–45) when Frederick the Great of Prussia revived an antiquated claim to the province and forced Austria to yield the territory. The glass is decorated on one side with a coat of arms and inscription below a large gilt palmette. Also depicted is the Greek god Amphitrite flanked by sea-nymphs and a dolphin. (ABOVE)

PRECIOUS OBJECTS *by David Bennett*

S ales of Precious Objects at Sotheby's have always attracted a wide and glamorous following, and this was certainly the case during the 1993–94 season. A truly international field of collectors, dealers and museums vied for beautiful and historical pieces from categories as varied as jewels, objects of vertu, clocks and watches and silver in our salerooms.

Sotheby's hold major jewellery sales in New York, Geneva, St Moritz, Hong Kong and London and have established the world auction records for the sale of diamonds, cultured pearls and major coloured stones. We have also conducted the four highest-value jewellery sales in history. This season all areas of the market showed considerable strength, including antique and period jewellery, modern and twentieth-century jewellery and especially major diamonds and coloured stones. The most vivid illustration of this strength was provided during an historic two-day sale in Geneva in November, at which the total of SFr102.75 million established a world record for any jewellery sale. The top lot was a spectacular 100.36-carat diamond, the second largest D-colour, internally flawless diamond ever to have been sold at auction, which achieved $11,882,300. (Sotheby's sold the largest D-colour diamond in November 1990 for $12,760,000 – the world record price for any jewel at auction.) As was to be the case throughout the year, international dealers from Europe, the United States, South America, Asia and the Middle East bought actively, as did private collectors.

Jewellery auctions in New York were also highly successful this season. The October sale totalled $26.2 million and included a sapphire and diamond strap bracelet by Van Cleef & Arpels ($332,500) and an enamel, ruby and diamond orchid brooch, made by Tiffany & Co. for the 1889 Exposition Universelle in Paris ($415,000). A sapphire and diamond necklace by Ostertag ($937,500) was included in the April sale, which brought $29.5 million, a 49% increase over the same auction last year. The undoubted highlight of this sale was a magnificent diamond necklace by Harry Winston,

A miniature gold-mounted rock crystal terrestrial globe on a silver-gilt stand
FABERGÉ, WORKMASTER
E. KOLLIN, ST PETERSBURG,
LATE NINETEENTH CENTURY,
height 11.5cm (4½in)
Geneva SFr124,500
(£56,100:$83,000) 18.V.94.
(ABOVE)

Sapphire and diamond necklace (detail)
OSTERTAG, c.1935,
approx. 40.6cm (16in)
New York $937,500
(£633,450). 14.IV.94. (LEFT)

which achieved a record $4,402,500. In London, the centre for specialized sales of antique and collectors' jewellery, our sale in June featured a ruby and diamond brooch/pendant from the French Crown Jewels (£62,000).

Few things are as personal to the owner as jewellery, and the 125 exquisite pieces collected by Hélène Beaumont and auctioned in Geneva in May provided an elegant statement of her style, collecting interest and above all fascinating life on the French Riviera. The quality and size of Mme Beaumont's collection inevitably called to mind the jewels of the Duchess of Windsor, a personal friend. Both collections shared the complete absence of antique jewels, favouring modern and contemporary designs instead, such as the magnificent ruby and diamond necklace by Van Cleef & Arpels, which sold for SFr820,000. Perhaps the most important piece in the collection was the Jonker Diamond No. 2, the second largest stone to be cut from the famous 726-carat Jonker stone (SFr2,600,000).

The term 'objects of vertu' is derived from the seventeenth-century 'man of vertu' – a man with a special interest in the fine arts – and is now used to

A gold hunter cased double dialled minute repeating chronograph with alarm, split 30-minute register, dual time zone and Vernier tachometer
BY A. LANGE & SÖHNE, DRESDEN, c.1907
diameter 6.3cm (2½in)
New York $101,500 (£68,600).
26.X.93 (ABOVE)

describe those exquisite small items once also referred to as bibelots or objets de vitrine. Sotheby's hold sales of miniatures, vertu and Russian works of art regularly in Geneva, New York and London. This season has seen a number of fine examples from the Fabergé workshop, including a miniature gold-mounted rock crystal terrestrial globe on a silver-gilt stand which achieved SFr124,500 in Geneva in May.

Sales of pocket watches were particularly strong this year. In New York a gold hunter cased, double dialled minute repeating chronograph, the first watch with alarm to be manufactured by Lange & Söhne, was sold for $101,500, while in Geneva the first of only three examples of the 'Universal Uhr', described by the makers as 'the most complicated watch in the world', brought SFr883,500. Quality wristwatches are still in demand, such as the Patek Philippe world time wristwatch which achieved $121,300 in New York in October.

The Moller Collection, sold in London in November, featured a distinguished group of English clocks and barometers including a walnut longcase clock by John Ellicott (£122,500) and a walnut angle barometer and perpetual regulation of time (£58,700). The most fantastic creation to appear in our October sale in London was an eighteenth-century automaton, organ and carillon clock, shaped as a jewelled pagoda, which was built in response to a demand for mechanical curiosities from the Chinese court (£353,500).

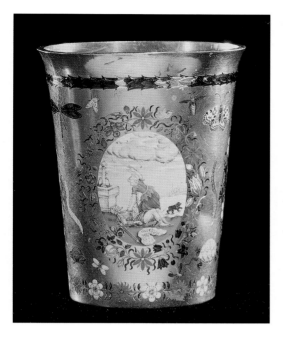

A Continental enamelled gold beaker
EARLY SEVENTEENTH CENTURY
height 10.5cm (4⅛in)
New York $189,500
(£128,900). 22.X.93 (ABOVE)

One of the finest collections of silver formed in North America since the war was that of the late Richard George Meech, Q.C., the first part of which was sold in New York in October. Featuring English silver dating from the reign of Elizabeth I to that of Queen Anne, the auction catalogue mirrored the changing fortunes and fashions of England during those turbulent but exciting times. Among the many extraordinary pieces in the sale were a Charles II parcel-gilt large tankard which previously belonged to Henry St John, notorious for his murder of Sir William Escott at the Globe Tavern in 1684 ($233,500), and a James II silver two-handled basket, made for the Chapel family in 1686, which achieved $398,500.

Historically important silver from the Continent appeared in our May sale in Geneva, when a pair of Swiss parcel-gilt silver tazzas, commissioned by a fraternity in Altdorf and depicting the tale of William Tell, were sold for SFr421,500. Also included was a Belgian silver-gilt toilet mirror, made by Joseph-Germain Dutalis, which brought SFr432,500, while in New York in October a seventeenth-century enamelled gold beaker achieved $189,500.

George I is not remembered as a great patron of the arts in England, as he preferred to reside in Germany for much of his reign. The appearance at auction in London in June of a rare silver-gilt salver, commissioned for the King and engraved with his arms, reflected this when it sold for £78,500, more than three times its low estimate.

This season at Sotheby's, sales of Precious Objects of the highest quality and rarity have attracted bidders from around the world, further strengthening the market. As always, association with a respected collector, craftsman or historical figure has increased competition in the salerooms, while items of great intrinsic worth have also been highly sought after. We look forward to further achievements within the Precious Objects categories next season.

A George I silver-gilt salver
BY NICHOLAS CLAUSEN, LONDON, 1720, ENGRAVED WITH THE ROYAL ARMS OF GEORGE I
diameter 28.6cm (11¼in)
London £78,500 ($118,500). 9.VI.94 (ABOVE)

JEWELLERY

A sapphire and diamond strap bracelet
VAN CLEEF & ARPELS, *c.*1939
New York $332,500 (£223,150). 21.X.93

Bold three-dimensional strap or *jarretière* bracelets are typical of late 1930s style. The Duke of Windsor chose a similar bracelet to this one, also designed by René-Sim Lacaze for Van Cleef & Arpels, to give to Wallis Simpson in celebration of their marriage contract. The Duchess was photographed by Cecil Beaton on her wedding day wearing her bracelet at the window of the Château de Candé in France (*see* p.279). (BELOW)

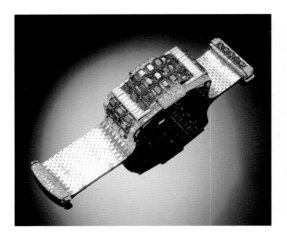

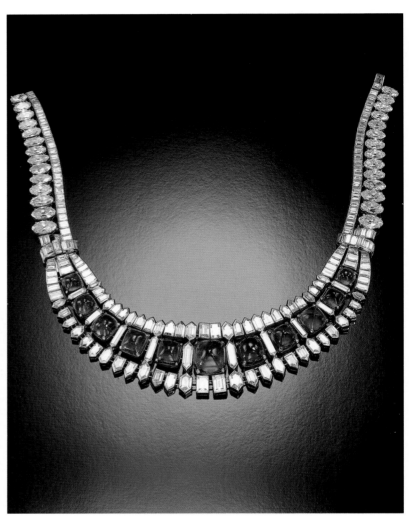

An emerald and diamond necklace
*c.*1935, approx. 36cm (14in)
Geneva SFr1,500,000 (£704,200:$1,063,800). 18.V.94
From the Collection of Mme Hélène Beaumont

In antiquity one of the most common forms for coloured stones in jewellery was the cabochon cut, consisting of a rounded polished surface rather than facets. But with the development of new techniques in the seventeenth century, all fine gemstones came to be faceted. It was not until the 1920s that jewellers began to re-use the cabochon cut for important stones, such as the emeralds in this magnificent necklace. (ABOVE)

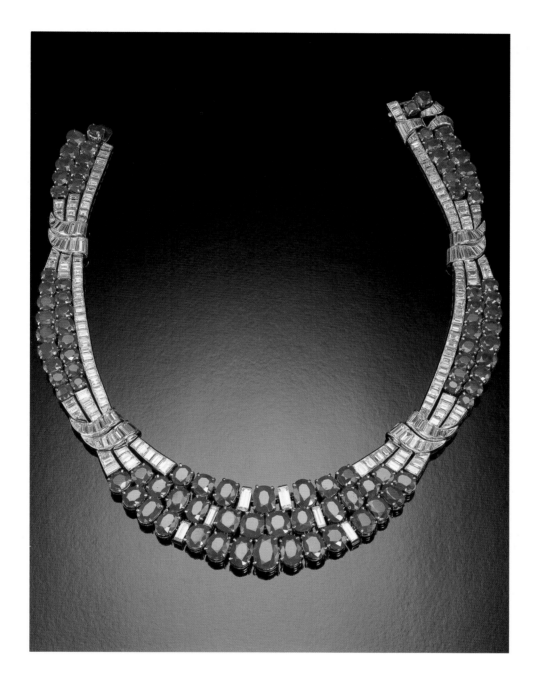

A ruby and diamond necklace
VAN CLEEF & ARPELS, c.1935
Geneva SFr820,000 (£385,000:$581,500). 18.V.94
From the Collection of Mme Hélène Beaumont

This necklace is very similar both in design and quality to a ruby and diamond necklace commissioned in 1936 by the Duke of Windsor, then King Edward VIII, from Van Cleef & Arpels, and given to Mrs Simpson on her fortieth birthday. The first version of that necklace, which was later remodelled, also consisted of a triple festoon of rubies and diamond-set motifs at the sides. (ABOVE)

A rectangular shaped diamond
Geneva SFr17,823,500 (£8,028,600:$11,882,300). 17.XI.93

Weighing 100.36 carats, this is the second largest D-colour, internally flawless stone ever to have been sold at auction. Throughout the world there are very few diamonds weighing over 100 carats, and those that exist are hardly ever of such fine quality. The purchaser of this stone will have the privilege of naming it. (ABOVE)

A diamond ring
HARRY WINSTON, New York $2,147,500 (£1,417,350). 14.IV.94

This emerald-cut diamond, weighing 33.60 carats, is signed *Winston* and is accompanied by the original working diagram which states that the D-colour stone may be potentially flawless. (ABOVE)

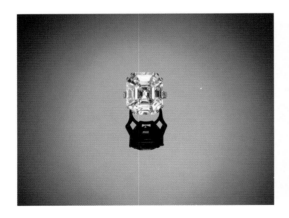

The 'El Mansour' Diamond
MOUNTED AS A RING WITH DIAMOND SHOULDERS
Geneva SFr3,743,500 (£1,686,300:$2,495,700). 17.XI.93

The origin of this spectacular diamond, which weighs 50.82 carats, is shrouded in mystery. It was sold twenty years ago by the late Louis Arpels, a founder of Van Cleef & Arpels, who said that the diamond had been purchased from a European royal family, who wished to remain incognito. They did, however, reveal the stone's name as 'El Mansour', which is best translated as 'The Victorious' or 'The Triumphant', a title sometimes used by rulers in the Islamic world. (ABOVE)

The Jonker Diamond No. 2
MOUNTED AS A RING
Geneva SFr2,600,000 (£1,220650:$1,844,000). 18.V.94
From the Collection of Mme Hélène Beaumont

At 40.46 carats the Jonker No. 2 is the second largest diamond to be cut from the original 726-carat Jonker, which was mined in South Africa on 17 January 1934. The stone was named after Jacobus Jonker, a sixty-two-year-old digger whose luck turned after eighteen years prospecting in the country. It was bought in 1935 by Harry Winston, who divided the Jonker into thirteen emerald cuts and one marquise. (ABOVE)

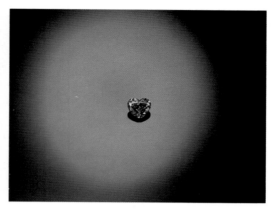

A fancy blue diamond
New York $4,237,500 (£2,796,750). 14.IV.94

Although historically blue diamonds were mined in India, by the end of the nineteenth century these mines were nearly exhausted, making South Africa the primary source of coloured diamonds this century. The rarity of blue diamonds, particularly larger ones such as this 13.22 carat stone, makes them highly desirable. (ABOVE)

A heart-shaped fancy blue diamond
Geneva SFr4,953,500 (£2,231,300:$3,302,300). 17.XI.93

Fancy blue diamonds are extremely rare in nature and thus are highly sought after. The present 8.92-carat stone is outstanding for its shape and size (according to our records it is the largest such diamond ever sold at auction), its exceptionally rich deep blue colour and for the fact that it is internally flawless. (ABOVE)

A pair of diamond bracelets
HERZ-BELPERRON, DESIGNED BY SUZANNE BELPERRON, c.1935
New York $222,500
(£146,850). 13.IV.94

After studying at *L'École des Beaux-Arts* in Paris, Mme Belperron began a ten-year collaboration with René Boivin. In 1933 she joined pearl merchant Bernard Herz and later formed Herz-Belperron with his son, Jean. She had complete artistic control of the business, using outside workshops to make her creations. Refusing to compromise, she never signed her jewellery, feeling that each piece was easily recognizable as her own. (LEFT)

A diamond necklace
HARRY WINSTON, New York $4,402,500 (£2,905,650). 14.IV.94

According to Laurence Krashes in his book *Harry Winston: The Ultimate Jeweler*,
Mr Winston once remarked, 'Ever since I was quite young, jewels have fascinated me.
I think I must have been born with some knowledge of them.' This self-evaluation
was proved correct not only by his phenomenal success in business, but also by his
keen sense of aesthetics that resulted in some of the world's most beautiful jewels.
This diamond necklace is the quintessential Harry Winston jewel, featuring ten pear-
shaped D-colour diamonds which hang gracefully from the centre and weigh nearly
100 carats. Its unmatched quality combined with the mastery of its execution and the
elegance of its design result in a classic Winston masterpiece, which achieved a world
record for a diamond necklace sold at auction. (ABOVE)

The Arcot No.1 diamond and diamond necklace
VAN CLEEF & ARPELS
Geneva SFr2,038,500 (£918,200:$1,359,000). 17.XI.93

This magnificent and historically important stone is one of a pair of diamonds
known as the Arcots after the Nawab of Arcot, who made a gift of them to Queen
Charlotte, consort of King George III, in 1777. The jewels were sold in 1830 to the
Crown Jeweller John Bridge of Rundell & Co., who allowed them to be used in the
coronation crown of Queen Adelaide the following year. In 1837 the jewels were
bought by the Marquess of Westminster, and remained in his family until 1959,
when they were bought by the renowned New York gem dealer Harry Winston. The
diamonds were recut and sold separately, this one, the Arcot No.1, being mounted as
a pendant drop suspended from a wonderful necklace by Van Cleef & Arpels. (ABOVE)

A ruby and diamond flower brooch
VAN CLEEF & ARPELS
Geneva SFr267,500 (£120,500:$178,300). 17.XI.93

A sapphire and diamond flower brooch
VAN CLEEF & ARPELS
Geneva SFr201,500 (£90,750:$134,300). 17.XI.93

Each of these brooches is set at the centre with a cluster of brilliant-cut diamonds, surrounded by eight petals invisibly set with its respective calibré-cut coloured stones. (RIGHT)

A diamond and coloured stone bead bracelet
CARTIER, c.1940
New York $145,500 (£96,000). 14.IV.94

As a result of Jacques Cartier's journeys to India to purchase rubies, sapphires and emeralds, Cartier's designers were able to create unique jewels, such as the present bracelet, which sparkled with clusters of colourful gems and diamonds. (LEFT)

A sapphire and diamond ring

CARTIER, SIGNED, *c.*1920, MOUNTED IN PLATINUM, ENHANCED WITH
SQUARE-CUT AND SMALL OLD EUROPEAN-CUT DIAMONDS
New York $827,500 (£555,300). 21.X.93

The superb cushion antique mixed-cut sapphire in this
important ring weighs 33.34 carats. According to the
A.G.L. certificate which accompanies the piece, the
stone is of Kashmir origin, Kashmir being the source
of the world's finest sapphires. Its extraordinary colour
and brilliance make it an exceptional example. (LEFT)

An enamel, ruby and diamond orchid brooch

TIFFANY & CO., *c.*1889
New York $415,000
(£278,523). 20.X.93

This brooch is one of
twenty-five orchids
made by Tiffany & Co.
especially for the Paris
Exposition Universelle
of 1889, and is of the
Indian *phalaenopsis
schillerianum* variety.
The brooches are the
first objects that can
be safely attributed to
the designer Paulding
Farnham. Tiffany's
won the Gold Medal
for jewellery at the
Exposition largely due
to the success of the
enamelled orchids,
which were praised by
French and American
jewellers and critics
alike. (LEFT)

A ruby and diamond brooch/ pendant
BAPST, *c.*1825
London £62,000 ($94,850).
23.VI.94

This brooch/pendant formed part of the ruby and diamond set created by Ménière using designs by his son-in-law, Bapst, who was to replace him as Crown Jeweller. It was made for Marie-Thérèse, the sole surviving child of Louis XVI and Marie-Antoinette, using stones from an earlier set which had been commissioned by Napoleon in 1810 for his second wife, Empress Marie-Louise. (LEFT)

A gold and micromosaic brooch
CASTELLANI, LATE 1880s, INSCRIBED *VICTORIA EMPRESS FREDERICK TO MISS NASH BERLIN 1890*
London £13,800 ($21,100). 23.VI.94

Princess Victoria, eldest daughter of Queen Victoria, married Frederick, Crown Prince of Prussia (later German Emperor and King of Prussia) in 1859. She patronized Castellani from the 1850s onwards. (ABOVE)

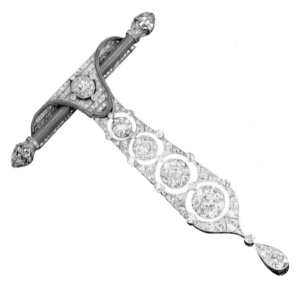

An enamel and diamond art deco brooch
*c.*1920
London £14,950 ($22,300). 14.XII.93
From the Elton John Collection

Much of Elton John's jewellery is commissioned by the singer from makers such as Cartier and Tiffany. His collection also contains many earlier fine quality pieces, however, such as this art deco brooch, designed as a green enamel thyrsus with rose diamond finials supporting a drop panel pierced with four circular motifs, decorated with circular swing panels and a pear-shaped drop. As Elton himself has said, 'Collecting is my passion. I love wearing my jewellery and I can't stop buying more and more.' (ABOVE)

A gold, enamel, sapphire and diamond bangle
CARLO GIULIANO, *c.*1870
London £19,550 ($29,700). 7.X.93

The arched centre of this gold Egyptian-style bangle is set with a row of cushion-shaped sapphires between borders of black and white enamel. These are held at either side by Nubian heads, whose features and wings are delicately portrayed with enamels and whose white-plumed headdresses are banded by a row of rose diamonds. (ABOVE)

MINIATURES, VERTU & RUSSIAN WORKS OF ART

MORITZ MICHAEL DAFFINGER
Portrait of Countess Sidonie Potocka (1786–1828)
*c.*1830, height 8.5cm (3⅜in)
London £14,950 ($22,575). 9.VI.94
From the Collection of H.S.H. the Prince de Ligne

Daffinger was the pre-eminent miniaturist of the important early nineteenth-century Vienna School. Following the visit of Sir Thomas Lawrence to Vienna in 1819, Daffinger developed a new pictorial style which was greatly indebted to the large-scale works of the English master. Daffinger succeeded in translating Lawrence's remarkable *esprit* and bravura into the more contained technique of miniature painting. The present miniature is an excellent example of his work. (BELOW)

A Viennese silver-gilt and enamel nef
RUDOLF LINKE, *c.*1885
New York $27,600 (£17,950). 21.VI.94

Rudolf Linke worked at various addresses in the VII district of Vienna from 1885. His mark, however, is found less frequently on this type of work than that of the more prolific Böhm or Ratzersdorfer. The stem of this piece is formed by a figure of Neptune upon an enamelled base of elephant heads and shells, while the hull and open sails of the ship are enamelled with mythological and allegorical scenes. (ABOVE)

A Russian silver-gilt
and shaded enamel
kovsh
FYODOR RÜCKERT, MOSCOW,
*c.*1900, length 34.3 cm (13½in)
New York $34,500 (£22,425).
21.VI.94

The revival of the
technique of cloisonné,
incorporating traditional
decorative motifs on
such objects as *kovshi,
bratini* and *charki,* was a
reflection of Pan-Slavism
which developed
throughout the second
half of the nineteenth
century. (LEFT)

A monumental icon
of the Mother of
God Hodigitria
CIRCLE OF DYONISII, *c.*1500,
108 x 82cm (42½ x 32¼in)
London £100,500 ($152,750).
16.VI.94

The Hodigitria, literally
'the Guide, the One who
leads the way', is perhaps
the most venerated icon
of the Mother of God.
Ascribed by tradition to
a painting of the Virgin
by Luke the Evangelist,
the original icon was
held in Constantinople
by the middle of the fifth
century, but mysteriously
disappeared when the
city fell to the Turks in
1453. (RIGHT)

A gold and hardstone desk calendar
FABERGÉ, WORKMASTER H. WIGSTRÖM, STRUCK WITH MAKER'S MARK
A. FABERGÉ, ST PETERSBURG, 1899–1908
Geneva SF223,500 (£100,676:$149,000). 18.XI.93

Henrik Wigström succeeded Michael Perchin as
Fabergé's head workmaster, following Perchin's death
in 1903. His incumbency saw the most productive
period of the House's output. His workshop produced
a wide range of *objets de vitrine* made of gold,
hardstone and enamel. (ABOVE)

A jewelled and
enamel minute
repeating timepiece
with gold mounts
FABERGÉ, WORKMASTER
H. WIGSTRÖM, ST
PETERSBURG, 1899–1908,
height 21cm (8¼in)
Geneva SF251,000
(£113,050:$167,350).
18.XI.93

From 1904 until 1917
all the Imperial Easter
Eggs were produced
under the personal
supervision of Henrik
Wigström, although
they do not all bear his
hallmark. (LEFT)

CLOCKS AND WATCHES

An ormolu quarter-striking automaton, organ and carillon pagoda clock
ATTRIBUTED TO JAMES COX, *c.* 1775, height 151cm (59½in)
London £353,500 ($537,300). 8.X.93

In China during the second half of the eighteenth century there was a great demand for complicated automaton clocks, which stimulated the English clockmakers of the period to make many fantastic creations for export to the Far East. The present clock is the only known example with a rising nine-tier pagoda, four simulated waterfalls and a peacock which moves its head, wings and tail – this performance made to the accompaniment of an organ and a bells musical mechanism. (LEFT)

A walnut longcase clock

JOHN ELLICOTT, *c.*1740, height 256.5cm (8ft 5in)
London £122,500 ($181,300). 18.XI.93
From the Moller Collection

John Ellicott, one of the greatest eighteenth-century clockmakers, was a Fellow of the Royal Society from 1738 and later became clockmaker to George III. He is best known for his invention in 1752 of a compensated pendulum which bears his name. The present clock pre-dates this invention, but incorporates an earlier form of pendulum compensation. (LEFT)

A walnut angle barometer and perpetual regulation of time

*c.*1730, height 102cm (42in)
London £58,700 ($86,900). 18.XI.93
From the Moller Collection

This rare barometer engraved *'A Perpetual Regulation of Time'* appears to be the earliest recorded example of its kind. Although its form is usually associated with Francis Watkins, this celebrated maker completed his apprenticeship in 1746, about sixteen years after this example was made. A possible attribution is to the optical instrument-maker John Cuff (1708–72). (BELOW)

A small marine chronometer

LOUIS BERTHOUD, *c.*1810,
diameter of bezel 8.4cm (3⅜in)
London £29,900 ($45,450). 7.X.93

With the expansion of merchant fleets during the eighteenth century, the need to determine an accurate position at sea became paramount. In 1713 the English government offered three prizes for the discovery of a method to determine longitude accurately, but it was not until John Harrison built a marine chronometer in 1761, capable of determining the ship's position, that the prize was claimed. (ABOVE)

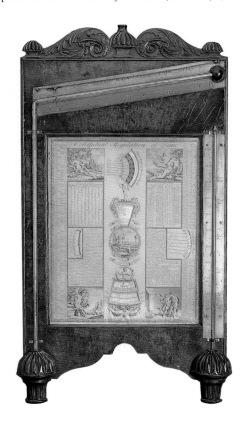

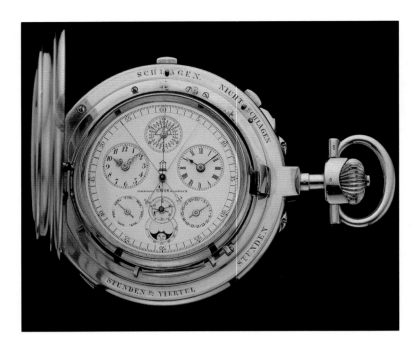

A silver and pink gold hunter cased watch with up-and-down indicator
LANGE & SÖHNE, GLASHÜTTE BEI DRESDEN, c.1910, diameter 6.8cm (2¹¹⁄₁₆in)
Geneva SFr20,700 (£9,300:$13,800). 18.XI.93

Lange's up-and-down indicator was patented on 18 May 1879 and eighty-eight watches with the movement were produced from 1879 to 1940. (ABOVE)

A 'Universal Uhr' gold hunter cased carillon clockwatch
UHRENFABRIK UNION, MOVEMENT SUPPLIED BY AUDEMARS PIGUET, c.1899, diameter 8.35cm (3¼in)
Geneva SFr883,500 (£397,975: $589,000). 18.XI.93

Described by the makers as 'the most complicated watch in the world', this is the first of only three examples ever made. The model was the outcome of a collaborative effort between Louis Elisée Piguet, Audemars Piguet and the Uhrenfabrik Union. (ABOVE)

A gold, enamel and pearl openface quarter-repeating musical watch
c.1800, diameter 5.8cm (2¼in)
New York $96,000 (£63,350). 13.VI.94

The scene of this watch depicts a woman holding a child and being consoled by her husband, who is about to embark upon a naval journey. It is of the highest quality of Swiss enamel painting, found on such pieces in the early part of the nineteenth century. (ABOVE)

A gold and enamel pair case watch
HENRY ARLAUD, THE CASE SIGNED *HUAUD LE PUISNÉ*, c.1675, diameter of inner case 3.25cm (1¼in), outer case 3.9cm (1½in). Geneva SFr48,300 (£21,750:$32,200). 18.XI.93

Huaud Le Puisné is the signature of Jean-Pierre Huaud, found on his work between 1675 and 1682. (LEFT)

A gold and enamel openface watch
OMEGA, 1925, length 5cm (2in)
Geneva SFr46,000 (£21,600:$32,600).
19.V.94

This is one of a series of watches made by Omega for the Paris Exhibition of Modern Decorative and Industrial Art in 1925. (LEFT)

A gold dual crown world time wristwatch

PATEK PHILIPPE & CO., SIGNED, *c.*1953
New York $121,300 (£81,959). 26.X.93

This watch has a dual crown system, meaning the crown at 3 o'clock rotates the inner chapter ring while the crown at 9 o'clock rotates the inner bezel, thus eliminating the necessity to hand set the world time ring. (ABOVE)

A gold rectangular backwind bracelet watch

CARTIER, SIGNED, *c.*1935, length 3.4cm (1⅜in)
Geneva SFr27,025 (£12,700:$19,150). 19.V.94

Cartier wristwatches are highly prized particularly those from the first half of the 20th century, for their case, dial and, in the present example, strap designs. The bracelet of this 18 carat gold watch has a concealed deployant clasp. (ABOVE)

A gold and diamond-set centre seconds calendar wristwatch

ROLEX, SIGNED ON BEZEL, *c.*1986,
diameter of bezel 3.6cm (1⁷⁄₁₆in)
London £14,950 ($22,575). 3.VI.94

According to Messrs Rolex only a limited number of this model with the named bezel were made in 1986. (ABOVE)

A platinum minute repeating self-winding perpetual calendar chronograph wristwatch

INTERNATIONAL WATCH COMPANY, SIGNED, 1991
diameter 4.5cm (1¾in)
New York $90,500 (£60,738). 14.II.94

The present watch is part of a limited production of fifty watches. (ABOVE)

A pink gold skeletonized reverso calendar wristwatch with wind indication

JAEGER LE COULTRE, SIGNED, 1991,
length 4.2cm (1¹¹⁄₁₆in)
New York $37,950 (£25,650). 26.X.94

This is number 65 from a limited edition of 500 watches, manufactured in 1991 to commemorate the sixtieth anniversary of the Reverso wristwatch. (ABOVE)

A gold rectangular wristwatch with retractable dial

CARTIER, SIGNED, 1960, length 2.4cm (¹⁵⁄₁₆in)
New York $18,975 (£12,500). 13.VI.94

This watch appears to have been made to order in 1960 from a design which was first produced in the early 1940s. Its rectangular case slides beneath a spring-loaded cover and frame, concealing the dial. (ABOVE)

SILVER

A Charles II parcel-gilt large tankard
JACOB BODENDICK, LONDON, *c.*1670, height 23.5cm (9¼in)
New York $233,500 (£158,800). 22.X.93
From the Meech Collection

The cover of this tankard is mounted with the embossed arms of the Henry St John who, with a Col. Webb, was found guilty of murdering Sir William Escott in 1684 at the Globe Tavern, Fleet Street. Each man pleaded the King's pardon and was discharged. It is said that the pardon cost £16,000, half of which went to the King and the other half being divided between two ladies then in great favour. (ABOVE)

The Capel Basket
A James II silver two-handled basket
PETER HARACHE I, LONDON, 1686, length over handles 57cm (22⅜in)
New York $398,500 (£271,100). 22.X.93
From the Meech Collection

The arms are those of Henry Capel, son of Arthur, 1st Baron Capel of Hadham, and
his wife Dorothy Bennet. This form of basket was sometimes used in England and
Holland to hold the clothes and linen of a newborn baby. It is unlikely, however,
that this was the present example's purpose as the couple were childless. (ABOVE)

A George I silver sauceboat

PAUL DE LAMERIE, LONDON 1726, length 19.5cm (7½in)
London, £67,500 ($99,900) 11.XI.93

This sauceboat is similar in shape to two known plain examples, but employs the flat chased *régence* ornament which appears on de Lamerie's magnificent Treby toilet service now in the Ashmolean Museum, Oxford. (ABOVE)

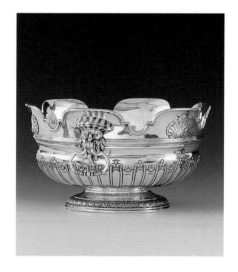

A Dutch silver monteith

CORNELIUS VAN DIJCK, DELFT, 1714,
width 33.5cm (13¼in)
Amsterdam, Dfl172,500 (£61,200:$92,250) 8.VI.94

The earliest known Dutch example of this type of bowl was made in Amsterdam in 1708. (LEFT)

A French silver teapot

JEAN-CHARLES GORDIÈRES, PARIS, 1763, height 18cm (7in)
Monaco FF199,800
(£23,500:$35,600) 19.VI.94

Spirally fluted tea and coffee pots with spouts terminating in animal masks were popular across Europe during the third quarter of the eighteenth century. The spout of this magnificent teapot is in the form of a bird. (LEFT)

The Van Wyck Salver
An American rococo silver salver

MYER MYERS, NEW YORK, *c.*1768, INSCRIBED *IN TESTIMONY OF EXEMPLARY JUSTICE & AS A SMALL ACKNOWLEDGEMENT FOR KINDNESSES RECEIVD* (SIC), *THIS PLATE IS HUMBLY PRESENTED TO THEORS: VAN WYCK BY HIS FRIENDS. SAML. SCHUYLER. WILLM. LUPTON & CORNS. SWITS* AND *GRATIOR AMICO VENIENS IMMOBILE VIRTUS* (VIRTUE COMING MORE WELCOME FROM A STEADFAST FRIEND) AND *AMICITAE PIGNUS PRO BENEFICUS RECEPTIS* (A PLEDGE OF FRIENDSHIP FOR KINDNESS RECEIVED), diameter 30.5 cm (12in)
New York, $255,500 (£170,300) 28.I.94
From the Collection of Philip Van Rensselear Van Wyck III

This salver was commissioned *circa* 1768 from Myer Myers as a gift of thanks to Theodorus Van Wyck (1718–76) for helping his sister, Magretta Van Wyck Schuyler, raise her children after the death of her husband. The catalogue *American Rococo 1750–1775* states 'the size, quality and rococo design of the engraving is the most arresting of any American silver of the period.' (RIGHT)

A pair of German parcel-gilt silver Torah finials
PETER VON LOHE, HAMBURG, 1650–55, height 41cm (16⅛in)
Geneva, SFr630,500 (£284,000:$420,300) 15.XI.94

These finials are very early examples of Jewish silver from the city of Hamburg made soon after the founding of the Ashkenazi community there in 1627. Peter von Lohe, the maker of these finials, is recorded in Hamburg until 1655 when he moved to the town of Schwerin. He was appointed Court Goldsmith to Duke Christian of Mecklenburg-Schwerin in 1657. (LEFT)

One of a pair of Swiss parcel-gilt silver tazzas
(MARTIN) ADAM TROGER, ALTDORF IN URI, 1597, INSCRIBED *DIE HERREN UND STUBEN GESELLEN ZUM STRUSEN,* height 13.7cm (5⅜in)
Geneva, SFr421,500 (£197,900:$298,900) 16.V.94

The *Gesellschaft zum Straussen* was a fraternity established in the late fifteenth century, whose philanthropic and political aims were reflected in the motto *Fortior Ferro* (stronger than iron). These tazzas depict the legend of William Tell, which is linked with the founding of the Swiss confederacy. (RIGHT)

A Belgian silver-gilt toilet mirror

JOSEPH-GERMAIN DUTALIS, BRUSSELS, 1814–31
118 x 87 cm (46⅞6 x 34¼in)
Geneva, SFr432,500 (£203,050:$306,700) 16.V.94

Little is known about Joseph-Germain
Dutalis whose maker's mark first appears
during the period 1814–31, when Belgium
was part of the Kingdom of the Netherlands.
It is presumed that he was the son of the
silversmith Petrus-Gabriel-Germain Dutalis,
who became a master in 1775. The quality
and dimensions of this mirror indicate that it
was either a royal commission or at least one
from a person of comparable wealth. (BELOW)

A pair of Victorian silver-gilt six-light candelabra

MARY & RICHARD SIBLEY AND RICHARD SIBLEY, FOR
MAKEPEACE & WALFORD, LONDON, 1839, height 62.5cm
(24½in). London, £68,800 ($102,900). 10.III.94
From the Collection of the late Mrs Vera Hue-Williams

These candelabra were made for John, 2nd
Earl of Eldon the year after he succeeded to
the title. He stood as Tory M.P. for Truro
from 1829 to 1832 and as Lord Eldon
continued his political career in the House of
Lords. He was also President of the Pitt Club
in 1842. In January 1853 he was declared of
unsound mind and died at his seat, Shirley
Park, Surrey, on 18 September 1854. (LEFT)

COLLECTORS' CATEGORIES *by David Redden*

T he Collectors' Categories sold at Sotheby's offer an extremely broad array of property, ranging from the finest vintages, to ancient Roman coins and German bisque dolls. Record prices continue to be achieved in these categories, with new areas regularly being developed, adding to the intrigue they offer to the collector at auction.

Coin sales at Sotheby's go back to 1775, the year after the company's founding, which makes us the oldest coin auctioneers in Europe, and through our predecessor firm in New York which held its first coin sale in 1841, also in America. Top-quality coins generated much interest in the auction room this season. In December 1993, the final part of the Athena Fund Greek and Roman coins were sold in New York and Zürich for approximately $6.4 million. In London, the Strauss Collection, one of the finest collections of British gold coins in private hands, was successfully sold in May, bringing £821,128. A significant number of American medals was consigned this year, including a rare Tuesday Club in Annapolis Medal, 1746, struck in silver (of which perhaps only five examples are known), sold for $28,600, and a small Thomas Jefferson Indian Peace Medal, silver, from 1801, the rarest of this type of Jefferson Peace Medal, fetching $16,500.

Stamp sales at Sotheby's began in 1872, thirty-two years after the first stamp, the Penny Black of Great Britain, was published. Stamp collecting has always had a large group of followers and today it remains the most popular hobby in the world. A number of significant stamps have passed through our salerooms in the last ten years: in London we offered the Rhodesia 1910–1913 'Double Head' from the Collection of Robert M. Gibbs in October 1987; in New York in June 1993, the Otto Kallir Collection of Aviation History; and in May, Postage Stamps of the Far East, sold in Hong Kong.

In 1977 the Collectors' Department opened at Sotheby's in Belgravia, concentrating on toys and dolls. Today Sotheby's has departments in London and New York holding three sales of toys and dolls a year.

Voskhod 2,
Berkut Spacesuit:
Alexei Leonov's
training suit for the
first spacewalk on
18 March 1965
PROPERTY OF ZUEZDA
New York $255,500
(£170,300). 11.XII.93. (LEFT)

Thomas Jefferson,
Indian Peace medal,
1801
SMALL SIZE, SHELL TYPE
IN SILVER
New York $16,500 (£11,000).
10.XII.93. (ABOVE)

Violin by Giovanni
Francesco Pressenda
TURIN, 1831,
length of back 35.5cm (14in)
London £161,000 ($247,900).
21.VI.94. (ABOVE)

The earliest record of sales of musical instruments at Sotheby's was in April 1805. However, sales devoted to musical instruments were not initiated until 1969, when the department was founded in London. Prices fetched by musical instruments at auction are far from predictable. The highlight of the June 1994 sale was a violin in near-perfect condition by Giovanni Francesco Pressenda, which sold for £161,000 ($247,900), setting a world record for the sale of a nineteenth-century violin.

In 1970 Sotheby's Wine Department was founded in London and is set to expand with first sales in New York in October and in Zürich in December this year. In the June sale this year Sotheby's was honoured to sell a large number of bottles from the personal holdings of the Baroness Philippine de Rothschild, owner of the Château Mouton Rothschild. Three nebuchadnezzars of Château Mouton Rothschild sold for £35,300, more than seven times their combined pre-sale estimate. These giant bottles are extremely rare and have never before been released from the vineyard's cellar.

At the turn of the century an emerging interest in War Medals put them on the block, but it was not until the late 1960s that a specialist department was founded. In the last decade we have sold a large number of famous awards, as collectors vie for pieces of tangible evidence of human accomplishment. During the 1980s the Polar Medal awarded to Captain Lawrence Oates, who sacrificed his life on Scott's ill-fated Antarctic Expedition in 1910–1913, fetched £55,000. This season a Great War Victoria Cross group for the Salonika campaign, awarded to Private H. W. Lewis, Welch Regiment, was sold for £26,450.

Sales of Militaria, Arms and Armour have been held at Sotheby's in Sussex since 1979, where nineteenth- and twentieth-century items were auctioned, while the salerooms in London sold earlier militaria and antique firearms. All categories of firearms and militaria are now sold at Billingshurst, with three sales held a year.

Beginning in 1965 Sotheby's was the first of the fine art auction houses to put Veteran, Vintage and Classic cars on the block. Sales have grown from two to over ten sales a year, and have been held in Johannesburg, Monza, Perth, Melbourne, Canberra, Sydney, Ireland, Cleveland, Palm Beach, Zürich and Monte Carlo, in addition to regional sales throughout the United Kingdom.

Over the past decade Animation Art has developed into a very popular collecting area, and we now sell many types of animation artwork including pre-production concept art. We hold two various-owner animation art sales a year. In addition, our continuing relationship with The Walt Disney Company which began in 1989 has given rise to the sale of cels from Who Framed Roger Rabbit?, The Little Mermaid, Beauty and the Beast *and*

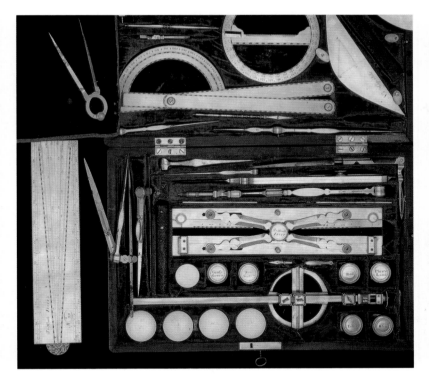

A casket set of
drawing instruments
by Thomas Heath
(detail)
ENGLISH, MID EIGHTEENTH
CENTURY, SIGNED *T Heath
FECIT No 39,*
case 45 x 30.5 x 15cm
(17¾ x 12 x 6in)
London £36,700 ($55,000).
4.III.94. (ABOVE LEFT)

Detective Comics
No. 27
MAY 1939, D.C. PUBLICATIONS
New York $48,875 (£32,260).
18.VI.94. (ABOVE RIGHT)

this season Aladdin. *We will be continuing our tradition of Disney sales with the sale in 1995 of art from their latest blockbuster hit,* The Lion King.

Sales of Sports Memorabilia commenced at Sotheby's in 1991 with a baseball card making a world record of $451,000 for an item of sporting memorabilia. Memorabilia of favourite players continues its tradition as a strong collecting field. In our New York sale in April this year, Babe Ruth's historically significant Home-Run Bat, which saw his record of fifty-six home runs, fetched an auction record of $63,000.

The desire to collect 'classic' entertainment memorabilia has been demonstrated during the past season's Collectables sales. The year commenced with a sale of Hollywood memorabilia which included Vivien Leigh's Oscar for her performance as Scarlett O'Hara in Gone With the Wind, *which fetched a remarkable price of $563,500. Sales of Rock 'n' Roll memorabilia began in 1981 in London, and we now hold sales on both sides of the Atlantic.*

In New York in 1991 we held our first Comic Art and Comic Book sale. Prices for Silver Age comics and comic art (1956–1969) have been surpassing those from the Golden Age (1939–1945). In the 1993 sale we sold an Amazing Fantasy No.15 *comic book (the first appearance of Spider-Man) by Steve Ditko from the Silver Age for a record price of $37,400. Overall prices continue to go beyond our expectations at auction in this collecting area.*

Seldom has the sense of historical discovery been stronger in the saleroom than last December, when, in an extraordinary auction event,
mankind's first faltering steps into space were intimately chronicled
in the wonderful artifacts of the Russian Space History sale. At
the same time, the sale was, in its own right, a leap into the
unknown. Were there, indeed, ready buyers for the space capsules,
Gagariana, moon rocks, and engineering drawings consigned to
Sotheby's by the people and industries of Russia? Under the
intense scrutiny of a packed auction room and television crews
from all over the world, the sale began.

The first twenty lots told the story of Yuri Gagarin – the first
man in space – and Vostok I – his tiny space ship. These same
lots, too, told the story of the sale. Estimated at between
$400,000 and $600,000, the twenty lots of space suits,
engineering logs and flight reports were sold for double their
high estimate. If the success of a sale could be measured by its
slow pace, this one took six hours of earnest bidding for 200
lots. Nearly $7 million changed hands. Items which had once
been disregarded, through the alchemy of historical insight, now
became treasure.

Who were the buyers? They were almost entirely private collectors, and mostly from America. For many, this was their first essay into space
collecting, although not their first visit to Sotheby's. While no institutions
were among the major buyers, at least one institution may have benefitted
handsomely from the sale. This American institution, yet to be publically
named, has been promised the long-term loan of many of the most
significant artifacts from the sale.

One artifact which will not be displayed anywhere
has to be a candidate for the most unusual item
Sotheby's has ever sold. This, lot 68a, was literally 'out of this world' – the Luna mission
descent stage and 'Lunakhod' lunar surface rover, described in the catalogue as
'now resting on the surface of the
moon'. When title changed hands
for this currently unrecoverable
artifact for $68,500, Sotheby's had
achieved another auction first, the
sale of a man-made object on an
extra-terrestrial body.

The Cosmonaut
mannequin
'Ivan Ivanovich'
FLOWN IN SPACE,
23 MARCH 1961
New York $189,500
(£126,300). 11.XII.93 (ABOVE)

Kosmos 1443
space capsule
FLOWN IN SPACE ON THE
KOSMOS 1443 MISSION FROM
2 MARCH TO 23 AUGUST 1983
New York $552,500
(£368,300). 11.XII.93 (BELOW)

WAR MEDALS

A Great War V.C. group for the Salonika Campaign awarded to Private H.W. Lewis, Welch Regiment

Billingshurst £26,450 ($39,400). 30.XI.93

On the night of 22 October 1916 the 11th Welch were ordered to mount a raid on German trenches situated on the heights of Dorsdale outside Salonika. The raiding party was spotted by a German sentry and subjected to forty minutes of enemy fire, during which time Private Hubert William 'Stokey' Lewis was shot in the arm, but refused medical attendance. Eventually the 11th Welch reached the German trenches and in the ensuing counter-attack Lewis was again wounded, but for a second time refused medical attention. At this point three Germans were seen approaching, and Lewis attacked them single-handedly, defeating them all. Subsequently, during the retirement, he went to the assistance of a wounded man, and under heavy fire carried him on his shoulders to safety, before collapsing himself. He was awarded the Victoria Cross on 15 December 1916. (RIGHT)

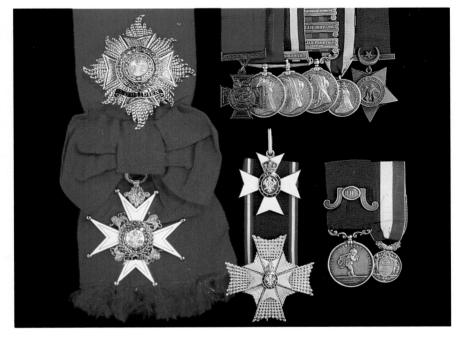

A Victorian V.C., G.C.B., K.C.V.O. group awarded to General Sir Reginald Hart, Royal Engineers

From the direct descendants of General Sir Reginald Hart

Billingshurst £23,000 ($34,300). 30.XI.93

On 31 January 1879 Reginald Hart joined a force of 500 men of the 24th Bengal Native Infantry Regiment, escorting a supply column in Afghanistan. That afternoon the convoy was attacked by between thirty and forty Afghan tribesmen, who concentrated their offensive on a wounded man. Having gained permission to go to the aid of the sowar, Hart with ten sepoys ran 1,200 yards into a storm of fire. Directing some of his sepoys to keep the tribesmen at bay, Hart, with assistance, succeeded in carrying the wounded man under the cover of a cliff, for which he was awarded the Victoria Cross. Hart received the medal from Queen Victoria who, according to his son, further tested his bravery by pushing the pin into his chest. (LEFT)

ARMS AND ARMOUR

A German cased percussion sporting rifle
BY SPANGENBERG, SAUER & STURM, *c.*1850–55, length 80.2cm (31½in)
Zürich SFr71,300 (£33,600:$50,900). 1.VI.94

This sporting rifle is a splendid example of mid-nineteenth-century
German craftsmanship. It was one of many luxurious presents given
by foreign gunmakers to Tsar Nicholas I, who actively collected arms
for the Imperial Collection. Other foreign presentations to Nicholas I
are still preserved in the Hermitage, St Petersburg. (ABOVE)

A German silver-encrusted swept-hilt rapier
LATE SIXTEENTH CENTURY, blade: 115.6cm (45½in)
New York $28,750 (£18,975). 6.VI.94
From the Metropolitan Museum of Art

The rapier is a light, slender sword especially designed for thrusting.
The hilt of the present example is finely decorated with engraved
designs of scrolling flowers and foliage, grotesque masks, birds and
putti heads, all encrusted in silver. (LEFT)

SPORTING GUNS

GARDEN STATUARY

A marble planter

LATE NINETEENTH CENTURY, height 114cm (45in)
New York $21,850 (£14,200). 30.VI.94

The long sides of this rectangular planter are decorated with carved foliate swags containing nuts, fruit and shells, linked to a central lion's head. Similar swags adorn the shorter sides, with male masks at the four corners. The planter is raised on four circular turned columns. (BELOW)

A pair of 12-bore single-trigger assisted-opening sidelock ejector guns

BY BOSS & CO., London £58,700 ($87,600). 17.V.94

These guns were built in 1924, the zenith period in English gun-making, and they conform to all the original specifications in the maker's records. They appear to be virtually unused retaining all their original finish. It is becoming apparent that market demands are for such guns in their original condition. (ABOVE)

COINS AND MEDALS

Silver dedication medal from the city of Nuremberg to Charles V

BY ALBRECHT DÜRER AND HANS KRAFFT THE ELDER, 1521
London £55,000 ($84,700). 5.VII.94

One hundred of Dürer's medals were struck in 1521 in Nuremberg to honour the newly-crowned Charles V, who was to visit the city. The visit was postponed, however, evidently due to an outbreak of the plague in the city, and the majority of the medals were melted, with only ten recorded examples surviving today. (ABOVE)

Marriage Schauguldiner of Maximilian I and Maria of Burgundy

BY ULRICH URSENTALER,
AFTER 1511,
London £35,200 ($54,208).
5.VII.94

With his marriage to the heiress Maria in August 1477, the nineteen-year-old Maximilian I gained Burgundy and Flanders. The marriage only lasted five years, as Maria was accidentally killed while hunting in 1482. This medal is derived from an earlier 'marriage medal' by Giovanni Candida.

(ABOVE)

Silver medal of The Tuesday Club in Annapolis

STRUCK IN 1749–50
New York $28,600 (£19,050). 10.XII.93

The Tuesday Club of Annapolis, Maryland, was established on 14 May 1745 by eight worthies of the city to serve as a *locus* for social gatherings. Membership was by invitation only and at its height there were fewer than 20 members. Silver medals were made in 1749–50 in England to replace the paper badges worn since the club's first anniversary in 1746. (LEFT)

Double sovereign of the 'Fine' issue of Edward VI

THIRD PERIOD (1550–53)
London £88,000 ($132,900). 26.V.94
From the Strauss Collection of British Gold Coins

With British gold coins dating from before the Roman invasions to the present day, the Strauss Collection catalogues the island's history over the last two thousand years. This coin dates from a period when 'Fine' and base (where the gold is mixed with base metals) versions of the same coin were simultaneously in circulation; a practice begun by Edward VI's father, Henry VIII, to raise money quickly. (BELOW)

Marcus Junius Brutus gold coin

L. PLAETORIUS CESTIANUS MONEYER, 43–42BC
Zürich SF528,000 (£241,050:$356,750). 26.X.93

This is one of only two known examples of this gold coin. It declares an astonishing message from Marcus Junius Brutus, seen on the obverse, who acknowledges the part he played in the assassination of Julius Caesar, giving the reason for the murder (the Cap of Liberty), the means (the two daggers) and the date (EID MAR or 15 March) on the reverse. (ABOVE)

Hong Kong dollar

UNDATED (1935)
London £28,600 ($43,472). 8.X.93

The introduction of a Government paper dollar in Hong Kong became possible following China's abandonment of the silver standard in November 1935. The Colony's currency had to be tied to that of China and the notes issued by its Chartered and Private Banks had hitherto been based on large and unwieldy reserves of silver dollars. This example is arguably the very first Hong Kong banknote issued. (BELOW)

Gold crown of George III

BY WILLIAM WYON, 1817
London £56,100 ($84,700). 26.V.94
From the Strauss Collection of British Gold Coins

In 1816 Great Britain, triumphant the previous year at Waterloo, proclaimed its supreme power in finance as well. The face value of gold coins ceased to be tied precisely to the intrinsic worth of the bullion they contained and a new coinage was introduced. This extremely rare Pattern crown of 1817 is one of only an estimated five to have been struck. (ABOVE)

STAMPS

THE OBSERVER, SUNDAY, JANUARY 23, 1938

FAMOUS STAMP FORGERY

NEW LIGHT ON AN OLD SCANDAL

FORMER OFFICIAL'S STORY

DISCOVERY 40 YEARS AFTERWARDS

The other week THE OBSERVER published the story of the great stamp forgery of 1871-72 (the only known forgery on any scale of British stamps). We now publish the story of Mr. A. J. Waldegrave, honorary secretary of the Institute of Public Administration, and formerly deputy Comptroller and Accountant-General of the Post Office. Mr. Waldegrave sheds new light on an old mystery.

It fell to me while I was in the Accountant-General's Department of the Post Office to help in investigating the circumstances of the forgery. This, if I remember rightly, was in 1912, the forgery having come to light forty years after the event, and not twenty-five.

The stamps came on the stamp market, not by purchase from 'the Government (the Post Office does not augment its income by the undignified procedure of marketing old stamps—a procedure to which the stamp-dealers would no doubt object), but by purchase from some workmen engaged on repairing the roof of an

Great Britain
1871–72 1s. green
FROM A FULL-LEATHER GODDEN ALBUM, RELATING THE DISCOVERY AND INVESTIGATION OF THE STOCK EXCHANGE FORGERY
London £64,200 ($95,650). 17.XII.93
From the Collection of Dr Ian Ray

From June 1872 to June 1873, and very possibly for much longer, the United Kingdom Post Office was the victim of a huge fraud. Unidentified officials in the telegraph office of the London Stock Exchange successfully defrauded the authorities of an estimated £50 per day. The principal evidence of this, the Stock Exchange Forgery, resides in a group of around 650 surviving counterfeit 1s. green Victorian postage stamps, 160 of which are in the collection compiled by the nuclear physicist Dr Ian Ray. Before 1876 the law demanded that each of the 2,000 broker's messages dispatched daily by the telegraph office of the Stock Exchange were franked with an ordinary postage stamp, which was then cancelled. The fraud was simple: the official on duty in the telegraph office affixed a forged stamp to the telegraph form and pocketed the genuine article, which could be exchanged for cash at any post office or licensed stationer. Discovery was unlikely as the books were always in order and all telegraph forms were routinely pulped after being in storage for three months, thus destroying the evidence. In fact the fraud did not come to light until 1898, and despite an eighteen-year long police investigation no-one was ever charged. (LEFT)

China
1897 $1 on 3c. red revenue surcharge
Hong Kong HK$1,670,000 (£144,600:$216,600). 5.V.94

In 1897 the National Post Office of China found itself short of higher denomination stamps and it was decided that the 3 cent revenue stamp would be surcharged. The type first used was found to be too small and was replaced with larger Chinese figures. This initial printing of the 'small' one dollar is the most valuable stamp of China with just thirty-two recorded. (ABOVE)

Malaysia-Straits Settlements
1912–23 $500 purple and orange-brown
London £10,350 ($16,050). 10.IX.93

High face value stamps of the British Empire from the early years of this century have been accorded rarity status since their date of issue. When first issued in 1906 the Straits Settlements $500 was the world's highest priced stamp, having a face value of £62.50. Not surprisingly few collectors purchased them as new issue, hence their value today. (ABOVE)

Great Britain
The Inland Revenue exhibition volume dating from about 1900
London £40,000 ($62,000). 8.VII.94

Until 1915 senior Inland Revenue officers were permitted to form official reference stamp collections using samples overprinted with the word 'Specimen' or later, 'Cancelled'. This volume was originally the property of Mr Birtles, a senior official, and contains a comprehensive showing of the Official and Public issues of King Edward VII and King George V, several with unique or very rare overprints, including the rarest stamp of Great Britain overprinted 'Specimen': the King Edward VII 6d. 'I.R. Official', which was issued in May 1904, the last month in which such overprinting was permitted. (ABOVE)

Philippines
1899 50c. orange plate number block
New York $10,925 (£7,300). 23.III.94

Following the American occupation of the Philippines on 1 May 1898, after Admiral Dewey's fleet entered Manila Bay, military postal stations were established as branch post offices. American stamps overprinted 'PHILIPPINES' were placed on sale in Manila on 20 June 1899. This fifty cent stamp was the highest face-value in the series and it is remarkable that a block of ten with the marginal imprint and plate number should have survived in pristine condition. (LEFT)

MUSICAL INSTRUMENTS

A two-manual harpsichord by Antoine Vater

PARIS, SECOND QUARTER OF THE EIGHTEENTH CENTURY, length 240cm (94½in)
London £67,500 ($99,900). 18.XI.93

The harpsichord was the leading keyboard instrument from the sixteenth until the late eighteenth century, when it was superseded by the piano. The case of the present example is painted green with later *chinoiserie* decorations comprising panels depicting musicians and acrobats within floral borders. (RIGHT)

WINE

A double magnum of Château Pétrus 1961
London £9,350 ($13,930). 19.I.94

Pomerol is the smallest of the great red wine districts
of Bordeaux. It measures only four by three kilometres
and covers an area of only about 730 hectares. Forty
years ago Pétrus was unknown outside a small circle of
wine-lovers in the Pomerol district of Bordeaux, but
has lately become one of the region's great names.
1961 was cold and wet during the flowering season,
and this combined with a drought later in the year
resulted in a small crop of wines, high in extract and
alcohol, which developed into the most outstanding
year since the World War II, with no rival until the
1982 vintage. (ABOVE)

Various sizes of vintage Château Mouton Rothschild wines direct from the Château cellars

Left to right: A bottle of Château Mouton Rothschild 1916, £528 ($802); a jeroboam
of Château Mouton Rothschild 1945, £14,520 ($22,070); a jeroboam of Château
Mouton Rothschild 1926, £3,080 ($4,681); a nebuchadnezzar of Château Mouton
Rothschild 1975, £9,900 ($15,048); an imperial of Château Mouton Rothschild 1971,
£638 ($970); a double magnum of Château Mouton Rothschild 1959, £2,530
($3,845); a magnum of Château Mouton Rothschild 1920, £990 ($1,504)
All London 15.V.94

Château Mouton Rothschild is regarded as the First Growth with
the most 'éclat', deep, rich, Pauillac, with intense Cabernet
Sauvignon fruit and grand presence. These extraordinary wines,
direct from the Château cellars, exemplify what the Baroness
Philippine de Rothschild and her father the late Baron Philippe
have achieved over nearly a century of wine-making. (BELOW)

VETERAN, VINTAGE AND CLASSIC CARS

1907 Mercedes 45/50hp Landaulette
California, $299,500 (£197,000). 18.VIII.93
From the Estate of B. Paul Moser

One of Daimler's first customers was Emil Jellinek, an Austrian banker, who in 1897 became an unofficial agent for the company, selling its cars to his wealthy friends and business associates. In 1900 he persuaded Daimler's directors to produce a new model, promising to take the first thirty-six cars off the line pending two conditions: that he would have sole agency for France, Belgium, Austro-Hungary and the U.S.A., and that the new cars bear the name of his ten-year-old daughter, Mercedes. (RIGHT)

1908 Rolls-Royce Silver Ghost 40/50hp
Roi des Belges Tourer
Hendon, £320,500 ($477,550). 6.XII.93

The partnership between the Hon. Charles Stewart Rolls, British adventurer, aviator, racing driver and businessman, and Frederick Henry Royce, engineer and innovator, has yet to be equalled in motoring circles. During the short time they were working together, the two men created examples of engineering brilliance with an attention to detail that was second to none. The Silver Ghost was first introduced in the autumn of 1906 at the London Motor Show, Olympia and soon earned the accolade 'The Best Car in the World'. (RIGHT)

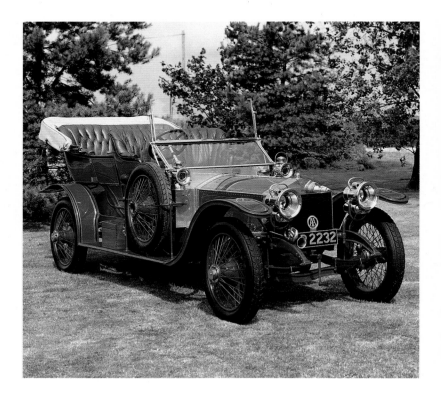

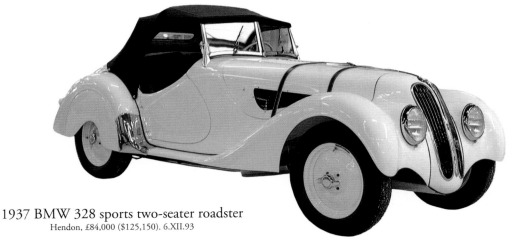

1937 BMW 328 sports two-seater roadster
Hendon, £84,000 ($125,150). 6.XII.93

As soon as it was introduced the BMW 328 began to exert a profound influence on sports car design, bringing, as it did, a new level of sophistication to the class. The BMW 328 was relatively quiet and very comfortable, well sprung and streamlined, with an engine in keeping with the product of an aero engine manufacturer. The result was a sports car which, in a single season, swept the board. (ABOVE)

1930 Bentley 4½-litre supercharged Vanden Plas Tourer
Hendon, £386,500 ($579,750). 16.V.94

The 4½-litre or 'Blower' Bentley engine was designed by Amherst Villiers for Tim Birkin, who was looking for a world beating car to run at Le Mans in 1930. The competition rules stated that a minimum of fifty cars had to be produced for the model to qualify, so fifty were built, with the first of the 'Blower' Bentleys fitted with a Vanden Plas tourer body being exhibited at the 1929 Olympia Show. At least forty of these fifty cars have survived. (LEFT)

COLLECTORS' SALES

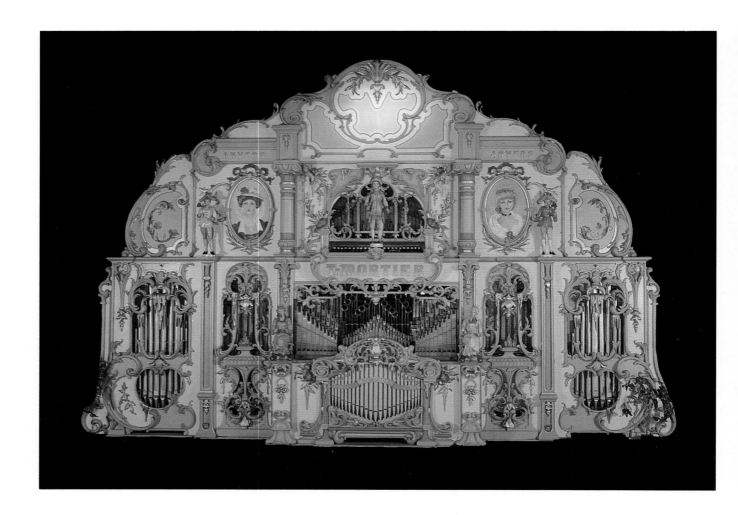

A 92-key Mortier dance organ
BELGIAN, *c*.1913, width 700cm (22ft 9in)
London £78,500 ($118,500). 8.VI.94

The man usually accredited with inventing the mechanical orchestra was Johann
Nepomucene Maelzel, for whose Panharmonicon Beethoven composed his overture
Wellington's Victory. Maelzel's Panharmonicon was the precursor of the great line of
mechanical orchestras designed to provide music for dancing, or during a banquet,
when no live orchestra was available. The 92-key movement of this dance organ plays
on many ranks of wooden pipes, a set of brass trumpets, a xylophone, bass and snare
drums, cymbals and woodblocks, and is housed behind an ornate façade. (ABOVE)

A German bisque character doll

KÄMMER & REINHARDT, IMPRESSED *K & R 108,*
*c.*1909, height 64cm (25¼in)
London £188,500 ($277,100). 8.II.94

Up to the end of the nineteenth century German doll makers had been imitating the French *bébés;* Kämmer & Reinhardt had been using the same model for twenty-three years. However, in the early twentieth century interest developed in the principle of child psychology and the new attention to children as real people had a profound effect upon doll design. A more natural and child-like doll was demanded and great excitement was created by Kämmer & Reinhardt's new 'artist' dolls, modelled from living subjects and shown at the 1908 exposition in Munich. It is possible that this doll was an experimental model, as she is the only known example of mould 108, a consideration which must have helped her to achieve a world record price for a twentieth-century bisque doll at auction. (LEFT)

A bisque 'Wunderkind' character doll with three interchangeable heads
J.D. KESTNER, *c.*1910, height 36.8cm (14½in)
New York $12,650 (£8,350). 17.VI.94

This rare doll in its original cardboard box has brown
eyes and a brown mohair wig, and is dressed in a floral
printed cream gauze dress with lace and pink ribbon
trim, socks and shoes. She has three interchangeable
heads, two with blonde hair and blue eyes, and one
with brown hair and blue eyes, enabling her to become
one of a possible four different characters. (ABOVE)

A French musical automaton
ROULLET ET DECAMPS, *c.*1910, height 89cm (35in)
London £67,500 ($104,625). 15.IX..93

This piece, one of only six, depicts 'Zulma' the Snake
Charmer, a successful act by Misses Paula and Nala
Damajanti at the Folies-Bergère in Paris in the 1890s.
On starting the musical movement her head rocks from
side to side, her chest heaves in a breathing rhythm and
her eyelids lower while she gazes at the asp. Then her
right arm draws the horn to her lips, while her left wrist
turns, causing the snake to writhe. Her rich jewellery
hides the articulation of her arm, making her the only
mechanical doll able to perform in the nude. (LEFT)

Vivien Leigh's Oscar Award for her role as Scarlett O'Hara in *Gone With the Wind*

INSCRIBED *ACADEMY FIRST AWARD TO VIVIEN LEIGH FOR HER PERFORMANCE IN 'GONE WITH THE WIND'* AND *ACADEMY OF MOTION PICTURE ARTS AND SCIENCES FIRST AWARD 1939,* height 30.5cm (12in)
New York $563,500 (£380,700). 15.XII.93
Property from the Estate of Vivien Leigh

The search by David O. Selznick for an actress to play Scarlett O'Hara in the film *Gone With the Wind* was one of the most publicized in the history of film. As well as the serious contenders, casting directors were sent around the country testing over one thousand unknowns for the role, but by December 1938 filming had already begun and there was still no Scarlett. Then the producer's brother brought a twenty-five-year-old actress from England and Vivien Leigh was cast at once as the legendary southern belle 'with a seventeen inch waist'. Leigh's performance in the 1939 epic won her the Academy Award for Best Actress at the twelfth Oscar Ceremony on 29 February 1940 and propelled her into international stardom. (LEFT)

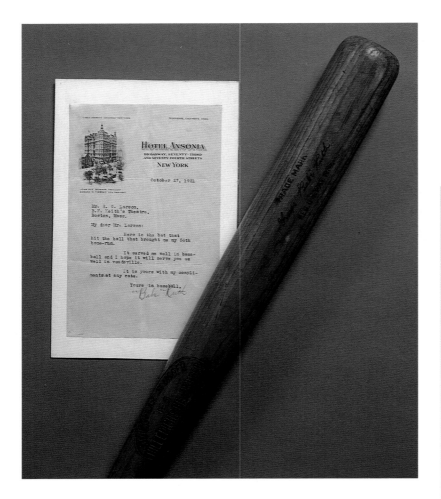

Babe Ruth game-used home run bat
HILLERICH AND BRADSBY MODEL, 91.4cm (36in)
New York $63,000 (£42,550). 9.IV.94

This bat was sent from Ruth on 27 October 1921, with a letter, to Mr R.G. Larson
of the B.F. Keith's Theatre in Boston in thanks for a stage try-out. Ruth later went
on a twenty-week vaudeville tour for B.F. Keith, making $3,000 a week as 'the
superman of baseball'. The letter reads 'My dear Mr Larson: Here is the bat that hit
the ball that brought me my 56th home-run. It served me well in baseball and I hope
it will serve you as well in vaudeville. It is yours with my compliments at any rate.
Yours in baseball, "Babe" Ruth.' (ABOVE)

A general iron
LATE EIGHTEENTH CENTURY, hosel 14.6cm (5¾in)
Ayr, Scotland £17,250 ($26,750). 11.VI.94

This late eighteenth-century golf club weighs 20oz and
has the approximate loft of a modern four iron. (ABOVE)

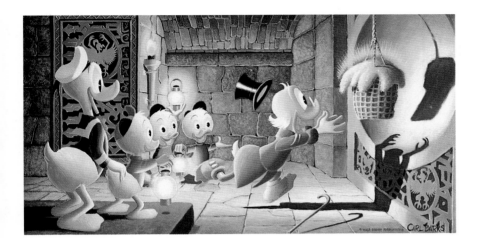

CARL BARKS
The Golden Fleece
1972, OIL ON MASONITE, 30.5 x 61cm (12 x 24in)
New York $79,500 (£52,470). 18.VI.94

Carl Barks is known to millions as the man
who wrote and drew the best Donald Duck
comic books, but he has also achieved an
international reputation as a painter. In 1966
Barks embarked on a series of oils based on
scenes from his comic books and seven years
later he produced this painting, which depicts
the five popular Disney ducks – Scrooge,
Donald Duck, Huey, Dewey and Louie – in
the caverns of ancient Colchis, where Scrooge
is about to seize the golden fleece. (LEFT)

Artwork from 'Aladdin'
1993, WALT DISNEY, SPECIALLY CREATED FOR THE CATALOGUE COVER, 37.5 x 52.7cm (14 3/4 x 20⅜in)
New York $25,300 (£16,400). 9.X.93
Proceeds donated to The Make-A-Wish Foundation
© The Walt Disney Company

'Aladdin' is Walt Disney Pictures' 31st full-length animated feature, and follows
in the Disney tradition of superb animation of classic fairy tales. This specially
created artwork depicts Aladdin and Princess Jasmine on a magic carpet journey over
the mythical city of Agrabah, as the evil-scheming Jafar and his verbose parrot Iago
menacingly watch over them. (ABOVE)

The 'Phantom of the Opera' poster
1925, UNIVERSAL, 104 x 68.6cm (41 x 27in)
New York $41,400 (£27,800). 9.XII.93

This spectacular poster promotes one of the great
horror films and depicts the elaborate underground
of the Paris Opéra with Lon Chaney, 'The Man of a
Thousand Faces', as Gaston Leroux's Phantom. (ABOVE)

III
Art
in
Collections

A MAGNIFICENT OBSESSION *by Alan Pryce-Jones*

A view of the sixteenth-century room at Hertford House, home of the Wallace Collection. (ABOVE)

To the outsider, the collector may inspire a certain amount of suspicion. Why exactly do they collect? And is the motive scholarly, or simply grasping? Snobbish or philanthropic? There are as many answers to these questions as there are collectors, and none of the answers are crystal clear.

One view is that some people, having built up a large fortune then wish to spend it on objects that are valued as priceless, and thus their own prestige will be enhanced. This is a cynical view and I do not believe it is the whole story. There are examples from history where the collecting of works of art became a true vocation. Such was the case with the nineteenth-century collectors, Lord Hertford and his illegitimate son, Sir Richard Wallace, who collected indiscriminately on their travels, but with experience developed a real taste for wonderful things. Taking the matter to its extreme, the totally dedicated collector, as was the Habsburg Emperor Rudolf I, is, not surprisingly, often a little mad to begin with.

Family pride rather than a personal affinity for objects has been the motive behind some of the greatest collections. The Medici may have set a standard here, though their acquisitiveness was matched in other lands and other centuries. The English dukes, for example, usually found it apposite to build fine houses and fill them with fine possessions. One need only look at the lifestyle of the sixth Duke of Devonshire, who was known as the bachelor duke. So prolific was his collecting that he was able to spread his treasures over a number of houses: Chatsworth, Hardwick, Chiswick House and Devonshire House in London, Lismore Castle in Ireland, and a house in Brighton, among them. The Dukes of Buccleuch and Northumberland did no less well.

Eccentrics such as the fifth Duke of Portland and the Harpur-Crewe family of Calke Abbey added fresh spice to the notion of a collection. The Harpur-Crewes formed their collection by the simple technique of never throwing anything away. When one room became overcrowded with belongings they merely moved to the next in their very large house. On inheriting even greater splendour, the Duke of Portland adopted the opposite practice. He abandoned his house in favour of a network of underground rooms in which he could live without coming into contact with friends or servants. The half sister of his heir, Lady Ottoline Morrell, has left a racy account of the surprises encountered by the next duke when he succeeded; large sums of money and dismantled treasures were left lying about in rooms long out of commission.

Where wealth, selectivity and passion are combined, however, the results can promote a change in style that affects countless others. Throughout his life the Duke of Windsor derived immense pleasure from collecting jewellery and precious objects, and possessed an instinctive feeling for design and period. In his quest for quality and originality he encouraged designers at Cartier and Van Cleef & Arpels to produce pieces in new and innovative styles.

It was fortunate for the Duke that the woman he loved was entirely in tune with his conception of modernism. He celebrated every occasion and every anniversary by offering his Duchess a new jewel and, in addition, the Duchess was wont to buy pieces for herself, which she carried off with elegance and aplomb. Many tried to emulate her style but few succeeded.

Throughout history there have been collectors inspired by a mixture of public spirit and personal vanity. King Charles I of England, the Empress Catherine I of Russia, Louis XIV of France and the Prince Consort shared a need to fortify and enlarge their dynasties. They were typical of an expansive age which sought to build on public success and family tradition. Likewise, those who owed their high status within society to royal patronage helped to justify that place by preserving and displaying the civilization which they adored. Only much later did a new kind of collector emerge: the subverter, the iconoclast. It is impossible to imagine an eighteenth-century Edward James, or a parallel to Burton Tremain in the accumulation of kinetic sculpture.

More spectacularly than in Europe, the public good has been a major factor in the history of collecting in the United States. It is here that endowments on the scale of those attributable to the du Pont, the Morgan or Frick families have been made possible. In Europe and elsewhere, donations to the state have been made on a much smaller scale, such as that of the Davies family in Gregynog in Wales.

A bequest is even more appreciated in a small country, which is relatively poor. Ireland, for instance, has not historically been able to afford to be generous to the arts. This drawback has, however, prompted individuals like Sir Alfred Beit and members of the Guinness family to save as much as possible of the once-splendid houses in the Republic, along with the pictures, furniture and silver which were designed to adorn them.

A portrait of the Duke and Duchess of Windsor, photographed by Cecil Beaton. (ABOVE)

The late Sir Alfred, whose family fortune had been amassed in South Africa, bought one of the finest eighteenth-century houses in Ireland and transferred to it a splendid collection of pictures and bronzes, including paintings by Goya, Frans Hals and Gabriel Metsu. The public imagination was fired when, after a lavish bequest had been made to the Irish State, he suffered not one but two sensational burglaries. Fortunately, most of the paintings were later recovered and now belong to the National Gallery of Ireland.

Some collections have transcended a private possession as those who amassed them have made them part of the national patrimony. The Annenberg collection comes to mind here; part of it once displayed in the American Embassy in London, and a still greater part now vested in the Metropolitan Museum in New York. Hardly less impressive is another ambassadorial treasure, that assembled by Mr and Mrs John Hay Whitney. Again, part of this collection was once displayed in the American Embassy in London.

FRANCISCO DE GOYA
Dona Antonia Zárata
OIL ON CANVAS, 103.5 x 87cm (40¾ x 34¼in). From the National Gallery of Ireland (ABOVE LEFT)

GABRIEL METSU
A Woman Reading a Letter
C. 1663, OIL ON PANEL, 52.5 x 40.2cm (20⅝ x 15⅞in). From the National Gallery of Ireland (ABOVE RIGHT)

FRANS HALS
The Lute Player
OIL ON CANVAS, 83 x 75cm (32⅝ x 29½in). From the National Gallery of Ireland (LEFT)

Collectors can be divided into two main categories: those who love what they own and those who thrive on the reflected glory. Loving one's treasures does not always imply that owners respect their possessions. I can recall an English peer who owned a very fine library in which he took great pride. Whenever he showed the books to a visitor he would bend them open on his knee and crack the spine so that the pages lay completely flat. The Fitzwilliam family of Wentworth Woodhouse in Yorkshire, who owned some magnificent porcelain, were in the habit of playing bowls with it on the floor of a long gallery. It is clear that some of the nobility took it for granted that they owned precious things and so took little care of them. It is only with the mounting value of works of art and the increasing cost of maintaining them that today's collectors have become more respectful. Not many, however, echo the great sensibility of the collector Harry du Pont of Winterthur who, when a maid confessed to him that she had broken a teacup, responded by falling in a faint.

If one had to elect the model collector of our time it would very possibly be the Philadelphia Maecenas, Henry McIlhenny. He outstrips other candidates on many counts. He was very rich but also very generous. He had exceptional taste, but also the knowledge needed to refine it. He made it a life work to perfect two very different houses – one a townhouse in Rittenhouse Square and one a romantic castle in Northern Ireland. In whatever he did he was a perfectionist, motivated not by snobbery but by a love of beauty and an instinct for the best possible settings. Thus, he lavished equal care on the gardens at Glenveagh and on the house and its contents. As well as adorning his own houses he was, like his father before him, an important donor to the Philadelphia Museum of Art. For thirty years he was Curator of Decorative Arts there, and both in life and in death he showed himself to be a most thoughtful benefactor.

Henry McIlhenny was a private individual, responsible only to his own volition. A somewhat similar collector was Nelson Rockefeller, about whom René d'Harnoncourt, sometime director of the Museum of Modern Art, wrote 'it is very

FRANKLIN WATKINS
Portrait of Henry P. McIlhenny
1941, OIL ON CANVAS, 119.4 x 83.8cm (47 x 33in).
From the Philadelphia Museum of Art (ABOVE)

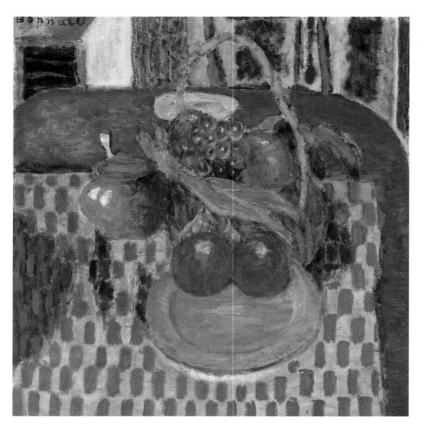

PIERRE BONNARD
The Chequered
Tablecloth
1938, OIL ON CANVAS,
85.4 x 58.4cm (33⅜ x 23in).
From the Art Institute of
Chicago (ABOVE)

have been amassing superb collections over the last two hundred years and more, in Austria, France, Switzerland and England. This family's zeal shows no sign of abating after several generations. The present Lord Rothschild has organized more than one impressive venture, among them the restoration of Spencer House in London and of Waddesdon, the creation of Baron Ferdinand de Rothschild in the late nineteenth century and now the property of the British National Trust. I have among my books a little volume published in the 1940s under Nazi auspices, which crows over the expropriation of the Rothschild family treasures from continental Europe. It certainly makes ironical reading today.

As collectors the Rothschild family has above all been associated with the eighteenth century, but in recent years at least one member, Baron Elie of Paris, has bought a number of contemporary paintings, sometimes buying an artist's entire year's work as an investment. Operations of this kind have led to close links with the auction houses of Europe and the United States, which in turn played an increasing role in the assembling and dismantling of collections. Indeed, the role of the auction house today can be compared to that of the orchestral conductor, since the procedures of buying and selling are inseparable from the forming of a collection.

In the art of collecting, fashion plays a great part. And fashion depends very much on the play of personalities. In the eighteenth century, for example, the third Lord Burlington changed the face of England by fostering an interest in Palladio, just as in the next century successive Lords Bute, operating from their great Victorian castle in Cardiff, helped to promote a response to medieval treasures, and then found their taste supplanted by collectors who had rediscovered the eighteenth century, such as the seventh Duke of Wellington and Mr and Mrs Ronald Tree.

After five centuries of collecting, it is naturally becoming hard to find collectables still available. It would be challenging to develop an interest in classical French silver, such as the work of the Germain family, because Mrs Harvey Firestone acquired many of the finest pieces a generation ago. And other once-fashionable collecting fields,

hard work to look at paintings and sculpture as intensely as he does. One simply feels he enjoys himself more profoundly when he looks at art, than in any other activity.' Although brought up in the midst of his parents' magnificent Oriental collections, his preference was for contemporary art, and he accumulated over 1,000 twentieth-century paintings, sculptures and drawings.

A collection is doubly impressive when it is the consequence of a partnership. One example of this is the collection of Mary and Leigh Block of Chicago. 'We do not buy names,' Block has said, 'and we feel no need to stay within a period.' In consequence, the Blocks have brought together masterpieces by artists ranging from Cézanne to Picasso, Fragonard to Bonnard, Chagall to Braque. Like many outstanding collectors, the Blocks did not buy art as an investment; they simply acquired what they loved.

From time to time an entire family has been engaged in collecting. A prime example here is the Rothschild dynasty, many members of which

Exterior view of the restored
Waddesdon Manor. (ABOVE)

such as portraits of the Reynolds school or Pre-
Raphaelite canvases, are by now overcrowded.
Gone are the days when Evelyn Waugh could
furnish his house with elaborate Victoriana at
minimal expense, or the late British poet-laureate,
Sir John Betjeman, could pick up drawings by
Landseer for a few shillings.

Recently there has been a revival or creation of
enthusiasm for the art of Scandinavia, and I can
imagine a latter-day collector being stimulated by
the largely untapped art of the countries of the
former Iron Curtain. But the collections of the
future are unlikely to be as wide-ranging as those
which have brought lustre to the past.

THE CULTURE OF CORPORATE COLLECTING

by Judd Tully

SAM FRANCIS
Untitled
1959, OIL ON CANVAS,
2.49 x 11.58m (8ft 2in x 38ft).
From the collection of the
Chase Manhattan Bank
(ABOVE)

Window in the Henry C.
Adams Building, Iowa,
by Louis Sullivan
1914, LEADED GLASS,
130.2 x 135.9cm
(51¼ x 48½in). From the
collection of the First National
Bank of Chicago (TOP RIGHT)

While the lavish patronage showered on artists during the Renaissance by the merchant princes of Italy is well-known, not many are familiar with the latter-day Medicis of the corporate and banking world.

Decades before corporate art patronage became accepted, or even anticipated, the pioneer innovator, Thomas J. Watson, Sr., the moving force behind the IBM Corporation, established an art collection. Starting in 1937 Watson authorized the purchase of contemporary art works from each of the seventy-nine countries with which the company was then doing business. IBM first displayed its growing art trove at the New York World's Fair in 1939, along with its latest piece of technology, the Electric Accounting Machine. 'Directly or indirectly, artists must depend on business for support,' wrote Watson in the catalogue. 'It is our opinion that mutual benefit would result if the interest of business in art and of artists in business should be increased.' That soundbite became almost a clarion call for the chieftains of American commerce to engage the visual art muse.

There is some debate about who started the modern era's stampede to acquire and commission art for the good of the corporation and its public. But it is an open-and-shut case that Diego Rivera, the famed Mexican muralist and political firebrand, caused a terrific stir in 1933 as his mural, *Men at the Crossroads looking with Hope and High Vision to the Choosing of a New and Better Future,* commissioned for the lobby of the RCA building in the new Rockefeller Center complex in Manhattan, neared completion.

The Rockefeller commission coincided with a dramatic change in the openness of Rivera's political message in paint. The artist had just completed a spectacular series of huge murals in Detroit which celebrated the modern industrial world. He had been commissioned by the Detroit Institute of Arts, then headed by Edsel Ford, president of the Ford Motor Company, and had been paid $21,000 for his Herculean labours.

Obviously impressed by the Detroit murals the Rockefeller Center matched the Ford commission, expecting a similar work. But the artist, an ardent Marxist and a vowed Communist, included a distinct portrait of Lenin on a prominent part of the mural. When Rivera refused to paint out Lenin, Nelson A. Rockefeller scuttled the project and fired the artist. The fresco was cordoned off and, nine months later, was demolished by a building crew. Rivera, in any event, was paid in full.

The episode represented a turning point in early corporate patronage. The controversy sparked by the incident was captured in a poem by E.B. White, 'I Paint What I See', published in *The New Yorker*. The poem was an imaginary account of the dialogue between Rivera and Nelson: 'And after all, It's my wall,' noted the young Rockefeller in White's biting lines.

Nelson Rockefeller, an ardent advocate of modern art, later went on to serve as president of the Museum of Modern Art. Twenty-six years after the episode his younger brother David, then president of the Chase Manhattan Bank and a trustee of the Museum of Modern Art, initiated an art-buying programme for the bank's new sixty-storey aluminium and glass-clad tower in the Wall Street area. The building was designed by Gordon Bunshaft of the renowned architectural firm Skidmore Owings and Merril.

Bunshaft was also responsible for the modernist design of Banque Lambert's sleek office tower in Brussels, which opened in 1964 – built after a fire destroyed the bank's historic headquarters. Like his American counterpart, Baron Lambert came from a line of art collectors and he embarked on an acquisitions campaign of world-class art to suit the design of the new building.

In fact, the international boom in new and modern corporate headquarters sparked the simultaneous explosion in corporate collecting that helped fuel the engine of the emerging contemporary art market. Contemporary art and architecture became inextricably linked. In the United States, at least, everyone followed the 'Chase example'.

Rockefeller assembled a blue ribbon committee of seven members which included Alfred Barr, the pioneering director of the Museum of Modern Art, and his chief curator, Dorothy Miller. Modestly, Rockefeller credits the late Bunshaft for the idea of acquiring art for the new building, a policy that was soon extended to the bank's 200 local branches and overseas offices in some fifty countries. 'I thought it was a very good idea,' recalled Rockefeller in a recent interview, 'but if we were going to do it, we should try to make sure that we bought not necessarily expensive things, but at least ones of good quality and hopefully of contemporary artists, which would also give a forward look to the building.'

During the 1960s and 1970s, Katherine Kuh, the highly regarded former curator of the Art Institute of Chicago, was employed to acquire works of art for the First National Bank of Chicago. Then Chairman Gaylord Freeman gave Mrs Kuh near total freedom in selecting the several

EMILE ANTOINE BOURDELLE
Great Warrior of Montauben
1989, BRONZE, 179 x 158.8 x 50.8cm (70½ x 62½ x 20in).
From the collection of the First National Bank of Chicago (ABOVE)

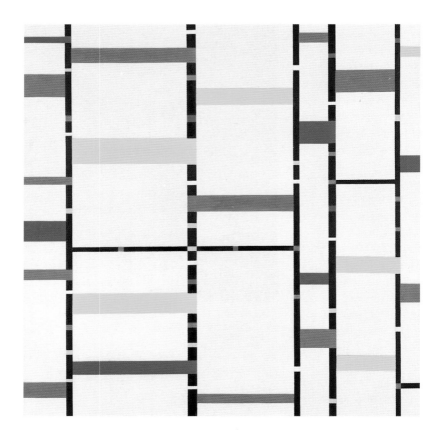

BURGOYNE DILLER
Third Theme
1944–5, OIL ON CANVAS,
106.7 x 106.7cm (42 x 42in).
From the CIBA-GEIGY
Collection (ABOVE)

thousand works of art she acquired. 'He understood that we had a direction, that we weren't just filling spaces,' recounted the late Mrs Kuh in an interview with the *Archives of American Art*. By the mid-1980s corporate art collections became as common to the workplace as a parking space or an in-house gym.

The evolution of corporate collecting in six decades of international activity is illustrated by the importance given to art in the Frankfurt headquarters of the Deutsche Bank. Starting in 1980 and focusing exclusively on contemporary German artists, the bank has amassed a superb base of several hundred works by artists such as Joseph Beuys, Anselm Kiefer, Gerhard Richter and Sigmar Polke, all of whom became celebrated artists during the late 1980s' art boom. Every artist has an entire floor devoted to their work and visitors simply select the appropriate elevator button, inscribed with the artist's name, to view each comprehensive selection. For its New York office, Deutsche Bank hired Viart Corporation, a

cutting-edge art management enterprise to advise and help acquire art for its midtown headquarters. Indeed, the services of art management companies are used by a host of blue-chip companies; Viart's achievements include the formation of a seventeenth-century British art collection for Texaco Ltd in London and an extensive collection of contemporary American drawings and prints for Merrill Lynch's headquarters in New York. 'When our clients become global, we have to be global as well,' said Barbara Missett, joint head of the company.

In another variation on the theme of regional or national-based collections, Ciba-Geigy, the Swiss giant chemical and pharmaceutical firm, started out collecting Swiss and American works for its New York operation, but was later urged by Georgine Oeri, a curator at the Guggenheim Museum, to focus on a specific period of recent American art, one that was not yet well-known to the public. After its move to the campus-like setting in suburban New York in 1959, Ciba-Geigy began acquiring New York School paintings and sculptures by the proponents of Abstract Expressionism. 'What was originally intended to give the new corporate offices an aesthetic spark gradually became a highly respected collection of contemporary art,' said Markus J. Low, Ciba-Geigy's long-time director of corporate art services.

In 1935 a United States Congress bill was passed which enabled corporations to deduct 5% of their net income before tax for charitable contributions. This legislation gave American corporations the chance to sponsor works of art and it gradually produced a surge of support for museums from a growing list of corporate sponsors eager to patronize American institutions. The Metropolitan Museum of Art, for example, has a current roster of 375 members in its corporate patronage programme, ranging from the American Express Company to the Toshiba International Foundation. Corporate patronage accounted for $2,100,000 or approximately 65% of the museum's exhibition programme budget this year. 'When corporations give this kind of money for sponsorship, they have to be able to demonstrate that its good for business,' noted Emily Rafferty, the museum's vice-president of development and membership.

The tax write-off remains a phenomenon of the United States, admired but not adopted by European or Asian parliaments. In a national survey conducted by the New York based Committee for the Arts, Inc., American businesses contributed $518,000,000 to the arts in 1991, with 18% ($93,200,000) going to museums. That figure is down from the $634,000,000 achieved in 1985. The two most frequent reasons for giving, according to the survey, were 'evidence of good corporate citizenship' and 'enhancing the corporate image'.

The bite of taxes has contributed in a different way to corporate art collecting in Britain. 'Corporate taxes were very high in the United Kingdom when I started the collection in the early 1970s,' commented Robert Hiscox of Hiscox Holdings, the fine art insurance underwriters. 'So we kept some of our profits in the company to purchase art.' Hiscox concentrates on 'unknown contemporary artists who may or may not ever be

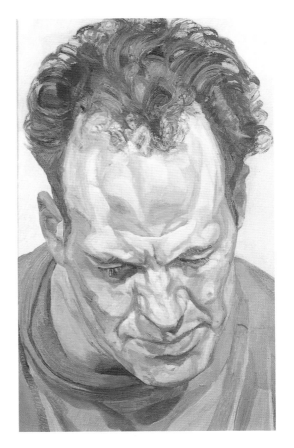

Joan Miro
The Farm
1921–2, OIL ON CANVAS,
123.8 x 141.3 x 3.3cm
(48¼ x 55⅝ x 1⅜in).
National Gallery of Art,
Washington (ABOVE)

Lucien Freud
Portrait of Frank Auerbach
1975-6, OIL ON CANVAS,
40.6 x 26.7cm (16 x 10½in).
From the collection of Hiscox Holdings Ltd (LEFT)

masters,' but also has a core group of works by the biggest names in British modern and contemporary art, including Francis Bacon, Lucien Freud and Henry Moore. However, Hiscox says that he has been tempted to sell the better-known works because of the expense incurred in having to insure them and because they didn't earn their living. But he gradually realized that the company had a marketing tool here since his business is insuring the type of art his company owns.

Another company which has recently narrowed its field of collection to works by contemporary artists is the National Westminster (NatWest) Bank. 'In earlier days, there was no defined policy towards support for the arts or forming a corporate art collection,' said Harry Morton, the bank's senior executive, Group Works of Art. 'The most recent initiative carries on into the 1990s with the formation of a collection of works by young British artists who are seen as having potential, but who have yet to achieve fame and prominence,' noted Morton. So far, sixty paintings and sculptures have been purchased and further acquisitions are planned.

At W H Smith Group, Sir Simon Hornby, the recently retired Chairman, continues to make selections for the company's collection of paintings, bronzes, mobiles and tapestries which he began in 1975. Sir Simon says he was inspired by the collection of Scottish works at another company, Robert Fleming Ltd. 'There are two rules which bind our collection,' states Sir Simon. 'First, we can only buy works by a living British artist; second, we must not exceed the budget.' He has politely rejected an offer by an American consultant to start up and operate a further corporate art-acquisition programme.

In Japan, self-contained museums bearing the names of the companies that founded them are becoming a trend among the corporate giants. Such museums are usually based in Tokyo with holdings of mainly Japanese and Chinese art. The Fukutake Publishing Company, for example, has founded a museum in Okayama devoted to Yasuo Kuniyoshi (1893–1955), a Japanese painter who became widely reputed in the United States. The company also has a second museum, the Naoshima Museum of Contemporary Art –

NICHOLAS GRANGER TAYLOR
'Caroline Ward'
1990, OIL ON CANVAS, 34.3 x 20.3cm (13.5 x 8in). From the National Westminster Bank 1990s Young Artists Collection (LEFT)

FRIDA KAHLO
Self Portrait with Monkey and Parrot
1942, OIL ON BOARD, 68.6 x 57cm (27 x 22⅜in). From the IBM Gallery of Science and Art (BELOW)

RED GROOMS
Red Square
1990, POLY-FLASH ON
ALUMINIUM WITH FOAMBOARD,
2.896 x 5.588 x 1.219m
(9ft 6in x 18ft 4in x 4ft).
Private collection, courtesy of
The Marlborough Gallery
(ABOVE)

named after the island on which it is located – which features works by Jackson Pollock, Frank Stella, David Hockney and Cy Twombly.

The Fukuoka Jishu Company and Fukuoka City Bank, owned by the Shishima family, plan to open a contemporary art museum in 1996. This time, however, the collection may well be housed at the company's head office building in Fukuoka, an important architectural statement by Arata Isozaki, winner of the Pritzker Prize.

So far, the leaner and meaner 1990s have produced a consequential paring-down of corporate art patronage. Museums cast a much wider net for new business patrons. New faces include the Florida-based Alamo Rent-A-Car Inc., which underwrote the Metropolitan Museum's recent exhibition, *American Impressionism and Realism: The Paintings of Modern Life.* In Spain, Argentaria, the country's largest financial institution, underwrote the Museum of Modern Art's blockbuster exhibition *Joan Miró* (*see* p.287) and the Metropolitan Museum's *Jusepe de Ribera – Spanish Realist in Baroque Italy.* Argentaria's private art collection includes works from the Renaissance to the twentieth century. As profits have declined, pressure from shareholders has forced some publically-owned companies to deaccession their art holdings or cut back on

acquisitions. Other reversals of fortune for some privately held companies have sparked similar measures. A number of important auctions and private sales of corporate collections have documented this sea change.

As we enter the twenty-first century, international competition is certain to become more intense, and in consequence, cultural assets will have an ever-crucial role to play. Since the Diego Rivera and Nelson Rockefeller episode in 1937, corporations have coalesced their position in the art world, to the benefit of all players. As Harry Morton at NatWest expresses, 'An art collection is a valuable string to the corporate bow.'

COLLECTIONS OF THE YEAR *by Ronald Varney*

It has often been the ambition of great collectors to reveal to the world, through a magnificent residence and splendid works of art, the prowess of their taste. Such was the case with Robert Walpole, who in the late-seventeenth century built up a princely collection through speculation in South Seas companies and then poured nearly his entire fortune into a residence suitable for displaying it. The result, Houghton Hall, took over twenty years to complete and left Walpole deeply in debt. It remained for his youngest son, Horace Walpole, to immortalize the collection and carry on the family tradition of connoisseurship. In a catalogue entitled *Aedes Walpolianae* he offered the reader precise, room-by-room descriptions of Houghton Hall and its staggering, Medici-like contents. In assessing his father's achievements as a man of taste the son

wrote glowingly, 'Your Power, and Your Wealth speak for themselves in the Grandeur of the whole Building.'

In the twentieth century the American collector Isabella Stewart Gardner felt a similar urge to house her collections in a spectacular fashion. The result, a Venetian-inspired palazzo called Fenway Court in Boston, was unveiled at a black-tie celebration held on 1 January 1903. Mrs Gardner had been specific about the design of her dream home: Fenway Court was to have an inner courtyard, roofed high overhead with glass, giving the appearance of a Venetian palace turned inward upon itself. Eight projecting balconies, with ornately-carved balustrades taken from the Ca d'Oro in Venice, were installed in the four-storey courtyard. Mrs Gardner had also embarked on a shopping tour in Europe searching out fittings and decorations for Fenway Court and returning with great quantities of pieces as diverse as choirstalls, fireplaces and tapestries.

As Fenway Court neared completion Mrs Gardner personally arranged her vast collection of paintings, furniture, textiles, ceramics and other works in a kind of 'scenographic' jumble throughout the rooms. In the Raphael Room, for example, she included not only the Raphael masterpieces *Count Tommaso Inghirami* and *Pietà*, but also objects evoking period Italian style such as a fourteen-string guitar, chasubles, mirrors, a commode, velvet wall-hangings, a fireplace and numerous Italian genre paintings.

As Mrs Gardner's guests circulated through the candlelit rooms on New Year's night the great courtyard was initially sealed off from view. After a musical soirée, the balcony doors were suddenly thrown open and the guests could see for the first time the Venetian fantasy Mrs Gardner had created at Fenway Court. The balconies hung with flame-coloured lanterns; candles flickered beyond the archways and windows, casting

ANDERS LEONARD ZORN
Mrs Gardner in Venice
SIGNED AND DATED *VENIZIA 1894*, OIL ON CANVAS,
91 x 66cm (35⅞ x 26in)
The Isabella Stewart Gardner
Museum, Boston. (RIGHT)

romantic shadows on the statuary, gardens and mosaic floors down below; the scent of tropical flowers and plants filled the air and the sound of water from the fountains recalled the soft nights of the Mediterranean. Taking all this in, Mrs Gardner's astonished guests only then must have understood why her motto for Fenway Court was 'C'est mon plaisir.'

Like that of Walpole, Mrs Gardner's collection is thoroughly catalogued, enabling historians and enthusiasts to enjoy her triumphs. If a collection is dispersed, however, the auction catalogue is the last and sometimes the only record of the owner's life work. This season has seen noteworthy single-owner sales from fields as diverse as American folk art and antiquities; English furniture and works by Picasso. What is obvious from the sales catalogues, certainly, is the passion of all these connoisseurs.

Madame Hélène Beaumont, whose magnificent collection of jewellery came to auction at Sotheby's during the 1993-94 season, was one of the great society figures of the Côte d'Azur. The American-born Hélène Thomas married Louis Dudley Beaumont, an early investor in aviation, and the couple set up residence in Cap d'Antibes at Villa Eilenroc, one of the most beautiful villas of the Riviera, situated on a twenty-two acre park at the tip of the Cap. The Beaumonts filled the neo-classical villa with many exquisite objects, including the finest eighteenth-century French furniture. In December 1992 Sotheby's Monte Carlo auctioned the contents of the Villa Eilenroc in what proved to be one of the most important sales of French furniture in recent years.

Madame Beaumont's jewels evoked all the glamour, romance and carefree extravagance of the French Riviera during the pre-war years, and they presented a magnificent record of the creativity of the Parisian jewellers during the 1930s and 1940s, in particular Van Cleef & Arpels. The highlight of the sale, which brought an impressive total of SFr11,699,300, was the fabled Jonker Diamond No.2, weighing 40.46 carats, which was purchased by a European private collector for SFr2,600,000. Another star lot, an emerald and diamond necklace, *circa* 1935, sold for SFr1,500,000. The quality and modern style

Mme Hélène Beaumont on the terrace steps of the Beaumonts' magnificent villa at Cap d'Antibes.
(ABOVE)

of the Beaumont jewels constantly brought to mind the jewels of the Duchess of Windsor, who was a longtime friend of the Beaumonts.

In the field of antiquities the importance of the Hirschmann Collection had already been recognized in 1982 with the publication of the excellent catalogue by Hansjörg Bloesch (ed.), *Greek Vases from the Hirschmann Collection*. When sold in London, under the same title, the record price of £2,201,500 was achieved for a Caeretan hydria attributed to the Eagle Painter. An extremely rare example dating from the late sixth century BC, the vase depicts a bearded and naked Hero battling with a giant sea monster, the reverse painted with a hunting scene. The

An Attic white ground Lekythos
c. 430 BC, height 41.4cm
(16⅜in) London £287,500
($428,375). 9.XII.93
From the Hirschmann
Collection. (RIGHT)

One of a pair of George II giltwood mirrors
IN THE MANNER OF
MATTHIAS LOCK, *c.*1758,
247.5 x 124cm (97½ x 49in)
London £397,500 ($588,300).
18.XI.93 From the Moller
Collection. (FAR RIGHT)

Hirschmann sale was all the more remarkable in that each of the sixty-four lots sold well above the estimated prices, bringing a total of £5,534,575, more than five times the expected amount.

The Moller Collection of English furniture, one of the most celebrated private collections of its kind formed this century, was offered in a gala evening sale in London on 12 November 1993. The ensemble comprised a breathtakingly diverse array of English furniture and clocks, many of which had been extensively published but few of which had been seen in public for more than half a century.

The collection was assembled in the main in the 1940s and 1950s by businessman and race-horse owner Eric Moller, and for many years it had graced his handsome and lovingly restored manor house at Thorncombe Park in Surrey. In forming and arranging his collection, Mr Moller had been closely advised by the leading furniture historian Robert Wemyss Symonds, who took particular pride in this collection and used it as the basis of his classic study *Furniture-Making in Seventeenth- and Eighteenth-Century England*, published in 1955. While rich in pieces from every major period of English furniture, the collection was most distinguished by a large group of mid-eighteenth-century pieces and an equally strong selection of neo-classical furniture. The lushly illustrated sale catalogue offered page upon page of eye-openers for the collector.

The auction of the Moller Collection had all the aura and buzz of a Part I Impressionist sale, with buyers coming from all over the world. The top lot was a pair of eighteenth-century mahogany commodes, attributed to the royal cabinet maker William Vile and his partner John Cobb. Formerly in the collection of the Earls of Buckinghamshire at Hampden House, these magnificent pieces were bought by a private collector for £991,500. Many other works soared above their estimates, such as the pair of George II giltwood mirrors, which also carried the Earls of Buckinghamshire provenance and sold for £397,500 to an American private collector. This landmark sale brought a total of £4,845,900 and was one of the most exciting events of the auction season.

Much was written in the press throughout the world about the sale in New York of the Stanley J. Seeger Collection of eighty-eight works by Picasso. There was rampant speculation as to whether so many works by one artist would find buyers in the current market.

In the fascinating introduction to the sale catalogue, written by John Richardson, Mr Seeger was described as an American expatriate, a graduate of Princeton in architecture and music, something of a recluse, and an obsessive collector. As Richardson commented, 'Picasso is only one of several fields in which Mr Seeger has considerable holdings. In the circumstances, who can blame this accumulator of collections for preferring to keep as far out of the public eye as possible?'

The evening sale of Mr Seeger's collection of Picassos, which had been largely acquired at public auction and covered every aspect of the artist's development, drew an enormously enthusiastic crowd, many of whom were new to the Impressionist and Modern field. The presence in the saleroom of several moderately estimated drawings by the great master caused feverish competition between buyers and seemed to carry the night along a wave of bidding assaults. To give an example, a study in pencil entitled *Etude pour l'Acteur and Deux Profils de Fernande*, a work on paper executed in 1904–05 and formerly in the collections of Gertrude Stein, Alice B. Toklas and Nelson Rockefeller, achieved more than double its high estimate, bringing $1,020,000.

Eight works went above $1 million in the Seeger sale, with the radiant *Femmes et Enfants au bord de la mer*, an oil painting of 1932, fetching the evening's top price of $4,402,500. When the bidding finally ended, all eighty-eight Picassos were sold and the $32 million total left everyone pleased and astonished.

The collection of the late Peter Jay Sharp featured a superb group of Italian Old Master paintings, European bronzes, French furniture and decorations as well as colour plate books, the works coming from Mr Sharp's Italianate Park Avenue apartment.

Peter Sharp was a renowned figure in New York business and social circles, and he was born into a family that at one time owned or managed many of New York's most prestigious buildings,

PABLO PICASSO
Verre, Bouquet, Guitare, Bouteille
SIGNED AND DATED *19*, OIL ON CANVAS, 100 x 81cm (39½ x 32in).
New York $2,312,500 (£1,562,500). 4.XI.93
From the Collection of Stanley J. Seeger. (BELOW)

GIOVANNI ANTONIO CANALE, CALLED CANALETTO

Two *Capricci*
OIL ON CANVAS,
each 150.5 x 134.9cm
(59¼ x 53⅛in) New York
$2,312,500 (£1,541,500).
13.I.94 From the Estate of
Peter Jay Sharp. (ABOVE)

including the Ritz Tower and the Stanhope. Mr Sharp added to his reputation as one of the city's leading real estate developers when in 1967 he acquired the grand and old-worldly Carlyle Hotel, a mecca of Upper East Side café society.

Mr Sharp's collection, although modest in size, was formed with meticulous care and judgement. In its almost classical definition – with masterpieces by Canaletto and Carracci complemented by allegorical bronzes from France and Italy and Louis XVI furniture – the collection conjured up the best of European civilization.

At the sale, the extraordinary quality and rarity of the property attracted very strong bidding from European as well as American collectors and dealers. The Old Master paintings were clearly in great demand, with two of the six 'Lovelace Capriccios' by Canaletto bringing $2,312,500; Girolamo Savoldo's *Portrait of a Young Man with a Soprano Recorder* achieving $1,542,500; Sir Peter Paul Rubens' *The Presentation in the Temple* selling for $1,652,500; and *Portrait of a Young Man Holding a Book* by Jan Gossaert, called Mabuse, making $1,157,500.

Perhaps the star painting of the sale was the lyrical and utterly rivetting image by Annibale Carracci, *Boy Drinking*. Created in the first years of the 1580s, a crucial moment in the history of Italian painting, it depicts a young man holding a carafe of wine in his right hand while finishing the just-filled glass in his left. The painting soared above its estimate of $700,000–$900,000, selling to the Cleveland Museum of Art for $2,202,500.

The extraordinary quality of objects in the Sharp Collection was reflected in the fact that eight auction records were achieved, and the sale total of $19,309,890 made it, along with that of Mr Seeger's, one of the most successful single-owner sales in the 1990s.

During their lifetime together, from 1925 when they married to their deaths in 1993, Nina Fletcher Little and Bertram Little of Brookline, Massachusetts, assembled the most remarkable and important collection of Americana in New England, if not the entire country. The sale of this historic collection at Sotheby's New York during the past season marked the passing of an era in the field of Americana.

Bert and Nina Little were pioneers in researching, writing about and acquiring the finest examples of American folk art. In the 1920s the Littles divided their time between their modest apartment in Cambridge and an unrestored cottage in the country north of Boston which they visited at weekends. 'Because it lacked heating, electricity, running water and a telephone,' Nina Little once reminisced about the cottage, 'I learned through experience how life was lived in the eighteenth century.' This growing interest in American history led the Littles to buy objects of rarity and intrinsic interest that looked well together and were used to furnish their home. Both Nina and Bert Little had an eye for detail and a flair for scholarship, which inclined them naturally towards pieces of high quality and historical resonance. Through the years, as their collection grew and the Littles became increasingly prominent as antiquarians, they filled two historic houses in Massachusetts with the finest examples of early American paintings, furniture and works of art.

The sale was a resounding success, the total of $7,391,293 establishing a new record for American folk art at auction. An overmantel painting attributed to Reuben Moulthrop entitled *A Pair of Portraits of Mr and Mrs James Blakeslee Reynolds* greatly exceeded its estimate in making $745,000, the top price at the sale. Most of the works exceeded, sometimes wildly, their estimates, and the saleroom was packed with buyers, many of them new to Sotheby's. The sale was aided by a week-long series of seminars and lectures about the collection, organized by the Educational Studies Department at Sotheby's in New York.

The Little Collection catalogue, with its exhaustive notes on the objects drawn from Nina Little's impeccably kept records and extensive biographies and bibliographies, will stand as one of the finest auction catalogues ever produced in the field of Americana.

Horace Walpole – and even that 'Proper Bostonian' Isabella Stewart Gardner – would have been proud of such distinguished collecting.

WINTHROP CHANDLER
An overmantel picture from the Elisha Hurlbut House, Scotland, Connecticut
OIL ON PINE PANEL,
106.7 x 151.1cm (42 x 59½in)
New York $596,500
(£400,335). 29.I.94 From the Bertram K. Little and Nina Fletcher Little Collection.
(BELOW)

A BREED OF THEIR OWN *by Geraldine Norman*

A portrait of Gerald Reitlinger, 1926,
by Christopher Wood. (ABOVE)

Overgrown lilacs and other shrubs arched over the gate from the road and pressed into the drive whose hundred-yard sweep to the house sprouted with weeds. The broken panes in the glass front door had been patched with cardboard, adding to the sense of neglect. But Woodgate House, a small, four-square Regency residence in Sussex, England, was packed from floor to ceiling with rare Oriental ceramics. As I walked through the door I saw four fifteenth-century Ming blue and white salvers arranged in a row under the hall table. Nowadays such dishes are hard to find under $100,000 and rare patterns can reach $1,000,000.

I have been lucky enough to meet many fascinating collectors over the years, but that visit to Gerald Reitlinger at Woodgate House in the early 1970s stands out in my memory as defining what collecting – real obsessive collecting – is all about. He was deep in his seventies, a small, bent figure with a wizened face, his sharp intelligence and humour unimpaired. A traveller and author, Reitlinger had been collecting and studying Oriental porcelain since the 1920s. In the pre-war years he had helped with excavations in Iraq and had brought back many shards. These items were exhibited in a room devoted to Islamic pottery, which he called 'the museum', along with complete lustre dishes and bowls of the twelfth and thirteenth centuries.

The drawing room was, on the other hand, exclusively polychrome Chinese, with every surface crammed with rarities from the Ming and Qing periods. The dining room was Japanese with tall Imari vases and other seventeenth- and eighteenth-century porcelains. In the bedrooms every horizontal surface was covered with ceramic figures, bowls or plates, and yet more plates hung on the walls. Some bedrooms were exclusively blue and white, and others polychrome. In Reitlinger's own room, a seventeenth-

A Chinese vase,
_c._ 1690-1710,
height 25.5cm (10in).
From the Reitlinger
Collection, now in the
Ashmolean Museum,
Oxford. (LEFT)

recovered from the shock. He died three weeks later, apparently from a broken heart. In fact, some seventy-five per cent of the collection was eventually rescued and passed, under his will, to the Ashmolean Museum in Oxford. It was exhibited at Sotheby's in London in 1981 before it was transferred to the museum.

The term 'collector' is often used loosely to describe any private individual who chooses to spend his or her money on art. Real collectors, however, are a breed of their own. They are not interior decorators, though many, like Reitlinger, choose to display their treasures at home: their art is bought for its own sake, not because it will look good in the living room. Neither are they scholars, though many scholars collect, and many collectors know more about their own narrow field of collecting than any art historian. Real collectors are driven by an inner compulsion to amass every possible example of a particular art form; they longingly desire rarities, whether or not they have any visual appeal. It seems this instinct for collecting is something they are born with; indeed many great collectors started with stamps, marbles or dinky toys as children. It is not absolutely necessary to be eccentric to be a collector – but few serious collectors manage to avoid it.

The most extreme example of this breed that I have come across is Lothar-Günther Buchheim. In the years immediately after World War II, he formed the world's greatest private collection of German Expressionist paintings, drawings and prints. This was the art that Hitler had dubbed 'degenerate' and had banned from German museums. The aftertaste of public disgrace lingered in the minds of German curators, and no-one wanted these works, enabling Buchheim to buy them for next to nothing. He recalls, 'Often I bought out of anger, sheer rage, because nobody else did.'

Buchheim was born in 1918 in Chemnitz in Germany, the illegitimate son of a young artist, Charlotte Buchheim. Encouraged by his mother, he started life as a painter, holding his first exhibition in Leipzig at the age of fourteen. At nineteen he wrote his first bestseller – a book about his experiences of paddling a canoe from the source of the Danube to its delta on the Black Sea coast

century dish hung between the shaving mirror and the basin; the bathroom was decorated with Iznik tiles. Indeed, I have it on the authority of a regular visitor that there were 260 pieces of blue and white Chinese porcelain in the spare bedroom alone.

Reitlinger belonged to that generation of collectors whose researches sorted out the history of ceramic production across Asia. They met at the Oriental Ceramic Society in London to discuss the dating and origins of their finds and held exhibitions to share with others what they had discovered. Reitlinger had formed his collection by tirelessly haunting the junk shops and auction houses, knowing more about what he was looking at than did anyone else. He claimed never to have spent more than £50 on any individual item.

The Reitlinger story has a tragic ending, however. In 1978 Woodgate House was severely damaged in a fire started accidentally. Initially, it was believed that the entire collection had been destroyed and Reitlinger, who had spent the night wandering around in the smoke, never

of Romania. He later became a war artist and reporter and used his wartime experiences aboard a submarine to write a novel, *The Boat* (1973), which brought him worldwide recognition: the very successful film version made Buchheim a millionaire. After the war he worked for three years as an art dealer, and states, 'There's nothing to making money in the art trade, *if* you know something about art. Not many people do.'

Buchheim has written three of the standard reference works on German Expressionism – one on *Die Brücke* movement, one on *Der Blaue Reiter,* and another on Expressionist graphics. Expressionist art is, however, only the small but distinguished core of his collecting activity. He has some fifty separate collections, including glass paperweights, carved wooden fairground figures of animals, Chinese snuff bottles, art nouveau glass, African carvings, shells, fossils and mail order catalogues.

When I met with him in 1991 he was planning a museum for his collections that was to be sited on an island in the river Isar at Munich.

ERNST LUDWIG-KIRCHNER
Interior with Painter
1920, SIGNED, OIL ON CANVAS,
90.5 x 150cm (35⅝ x 59in).
Expressionist painting
now in the L.G.
Buchheim Collection.
(ABOVE)

ERICH HECKEL
Pechstein Sleeping
1910, SIGNED, OIL ON CANVAS,
110 x 74cm (43⅜ x 23¼in).
Expressionist painting
now in the L.G.
Buchheim Collection.
(LEFT)

The museum was to be built as a cathedral: his most treasured items, the Expressionist works, were to be placed in the centre aisle while the side altars were to accommodate his other collections. His idea was to show a collection in the kind of environment in which it grows, in a space filled with a miscellany of objects which have taken a collector's eye.

Nothing has come of this dream. 'The Bavarian authorities did not even turn the idea down,' he told me recently. 'They just did nothing about it.' He considers Bavarian politicians to be philistines; 'they still find Expressionism disturbing,' he says. He is currently negotiating for a museum in another region of Germany.

The most distinguished collector I have met, who has amassed works of art on a similar scale to that of Buchheim, though more narrowly concentrated on great paintings and sculpture, is Paul Mellon. Mellon has given 800 of them to the National Gallery of Washington; in addition, he has founded the Yale Center for British Art and made many smaller donations to museums, besides filling three homes with pictures. Important Impressionist works were mainly acquired to furnish his homes or as bequests to museums. It is his passionate pursuit of British art in general, and sporting art in particular, that qualifies him to be counted as a truly fervent collector.

He can't help being a little out of the ordinary, having inherited one of the largest fortunes in America from his father, who was Secretary of the Treasury under three presidents, and founder of the National Gallery in Washington. Mellon farms and breeds racehorses in Virginia and has a love of the country and country sports which he first discovered during his visits to England as a child. His determination to build a great collection of British art was a corollary of his sporting interests and was born over lunch at Claridges in London in 1959.

Mellon had been asked to negotiate loans from British friends for the Virginia State Museum's exhibition *Sport and the Horse* held in 1960; the catalogue was to be written by Basil Taylor, a British art historian who worked at the Royal College, and Mellon invited him to lunch. Over an indifferent meal – food was still rationed then,

even at Claridges – the two men discovered a natural sympathy. Before the end of the meal Mellon had been inspired to form the first American collection of British art and Taylor had agreed to help him. Mellon gives a vivid picture of their collaboration in his autobiography, *Reflections in a Silver Spoon*:

'Photographs and transparencies, to say nothing of real drawings and paintings, shuttled across the Atlantic by the boatload and planeload, and the overseas telephone knew no rest. Basil's letters were typed on airmail blue paper on a portable typewriter that had seen better days. The carriage and the patten slipped, so the typeface was subject to both pitch and roll. Further, the content, which might be described as "stream of consciousness", wandered from one subject to another. It was full of amusing anecdotes and of critical judgements on the pictures he had seen. Sometimes the typing ran off the bottom of the paper, so that the signature had to be superimposed in the corner. I looked forward to these missives with the intense pleasure that some people experience as they pick up the morning paper.'

JAN WYCK
A Hawking Party
1690, OIL ON CANVAS,
52 x 68.5cm (29½ x 27in).
From the Yale Center for British Art, Paul Mellon Collection.
(ABOVE)

Mr Wilder admiring the *View on East Bergholt Church* by John Constable, which he bought for £60 in 1970. Mr Wilder developed a real passion for English paintings and put together a collection of unrecorded paintings which he believed to be the work of Constable. (LEFT)

JOHN CONSTABLE

View on East Bergholt Church
1811-15, 35.5 x 21.6cm (14 x 8½in). (ABOVE)

The result of this curious collaboration was the establishment of the Yale Center – after the Tate Gallery in London, the best collection of British art in the world. Mellon may have the highest recognition among collectors of British art, but there are two others whom I particularly admire: the late Mr F.L. Wilder, formerly of Sotheby's London, and the Hon. David Thomson, son and heir of Lord Thomson of Fleet.

Mr Wilder was the longest serving expert ever employed by Sotheby's; he died in 1993 at the age of 100½, having worked for Sotheby's from 1911 to 1983. He was primarily a print expert and helped found *Print Prices Current*, a reference work published annually from 1918 to 1939. After World War II he wrote an invaluable handbook entitled *How to Identify Old Prints*. His experiences as a collector embody two fundamental truths about the art market: that prices can go down as well as up, and that an expert is only as good as his own eyes.

In the inter-war years Mr Wilder formed a distinguished collection of English mezzotint portraits. These were high fashion at the time, as were the eighteenth-century portraits by Reynolds, Gainsborough and other artists on which these prints were based. World War II killed the fad for mezzotints and prices have never recovered; Wilder's collection became virtually worthless.

Much more important to him, however, than his interest in mezzotints was a passion for the work of the English landscapist John Constable. Constable's reputation as a landscape painter is second only to that of Turner and any work by Constable has always fetched a high price. But Mr Wilder put together a collection which cost him next to nothing.

Mr Wilder bought from auctions and junk shops paintings that experts had failed to identify as the work of Constable, including a study of Constable's famous painting *The Leaping Horse* for £80 in 1925, a Constable copy of a Teniers landscape for £22 in 1959 and *View on East Bergholt Church* for £60 in 1970. He acquired a total of about eighty paintings that he believed to be the work of Constable, although art historians who have made a special study of Constable's work only accept a handful of them as genuine.

I have a vivid memory of walking into Sotheby's London Print Department one lunchtime in the 1970s to find Mr Wilder with a small cloud study, painted on board, lying on the desk in front of him; he was peering at it with passionate interest. 'What is it?' I asked. 'A cloud study by Constable,' he replied, touching it lovingly with his hand. He had bought it at that morning's picture auction where it had been catalogued as 'English School'. 'It's his brushwork without any doubt,' Mr Wilder told me, 'but I shall never get anyone else to believe it.' Had the picture experts agreed about the artist, Mr Wilder would not, of course, have been able to afford it.

David Thomson is another Constable enthusiast but, as the scion of an immensely wealthy Canadian family which owns the Hudson Bay Company and several hundred newspapers, he can afford paintings and drawings whose authenticity is already established. Moreover, he is a close friend of the leading Constable scholar Ian Fleming-Williams. The two friends make a formidable but curious team – a young tycoon in his thirties and a retired schoolmaster in his seventies. Fleming-Williams used to teach painting at Charterhouse and retired in 1970 to devote his time to studying Constable. Both he and Thomson are painters themselves which may help to explain their affinity.

John Constable died in 1837, but his sparkling landscape studies, made directly from nature, only became famous later in the century. As a result, many of his works went into circulation undocumented and an extraordinary number of paintings and drawings have been 'rediscovered' over the twenty-year period during which Thomson has been collecting. By 1991 he owned some

A portrait of the Baron Hans-Heinrich Thyssen-Bornemisza in profile against a painting of a Renaissance woman.
(LEFT)

eighty drawings and Fleming-Williams was able to write a unique type of visual biography based on the collection. *Constable and His Drawings* demonstrates how the struggles of the artist's personal life are reflected in the mood and subject matter of his drawings.

Owners of extraordinary treasures exist in many guises – the French painter Arman, for instance, who collects Japanese armour, African wood carvings, old radios, pistols and cars, or Baron Thyssen who is a passionate collector of antique silver and carpets as well as the Western oil paintings for which he is best known and which now fill a museum next to the Prado in Madrid. It takes no more than ten minutes in the presence of a collector to discover whether they are a serious collector or just an art appreciator. The 'real' collector can't survive without a fix; they are driven by their passion to collect. There was a time when Thyssen had to purchase at least one picture a day.

Art collecting is, however, a benign addiction. The general public profits at the end of the day through the creation of new museum collections and the publication of art historical studies whose groundwork has been laid by the collector's enthusiasm. Moreover, the eccentricities of the collectors themselves enhance the lives of those fortunate enough to come into contact with them.

THE EIGHTEENTH-CENTURY HOUSE RESTORED

SPENCER HOUSE *by Joseph Friedman*

West front of Spencer House, St. James's Place, London. (BELOW)

John, 1st Earl Spencer, by Thomas Gainsborough. (OPPOSITE ABOVE)

The restored Palm Room. (OPPOSITE BELOW)

Only a short time ago the future of Spencer House looked bleak. This great eighteenth-century palace stood empty, the interior stripped of its original contents and fittings, the exterior disfigured by obtrusive modern additions. So it might have continued, but in 1985 the lease of the house was acquired by the J. Rothschild group of companies and, under the direction of its chairman, Lord Rothschild, work began on one of the most remarkable restoration projects of recent times.

Spencer House was built in 1756-66 by John, 1st Earl Spencer, head of one of England's most illustrious and aristocratic families, and from the time of its construction was hailed as a masterpiece. The building was begun by the architect John Vardy, a follower of William Kent, and

completed by another architect, James 'Athenian' Stuart. Both men produced work of pioneering importance. The exterior and ground-floor apartments by Vardy clearly presaged the transition from the Palladian style to neo-classicism, while the first-floor apartments by Stuart were among the earliest fully-developed neo-classical interiors in Europe and some of the first to feature elements derived from the architecture of ancient Greece, marking an important step in the development of the Greek Revival. The magnificence of the building itself was matched by that of its contents. The 1st Earl Spencer was an avid collector and filled the house with specially-commissioned furniture, Old Master paintings, antique sculpture and other treasures.

As the residence of the Spencer family, Spencer House played a vital role in the social, cultural and political life of London, providing the setting for grand receptions attended by Royalty, statesmen, and eminent figures from the world of art and science. The Spencers continued to live at Spencer House until the late nineteenth century, when the building was leased to a succession of tenants, including the Duke and Duchess of Marlborough. The family returned to Spencer House shortly before World War I, but in 1920 the building was let again to Prince and Princess Christopher of Greece, and in 1927 the Spencers moved away for good, signing a long lease with the Ladies' Army and Navy Club.

Over the years Spencer House had undergone a series of alterations but these were principally of a decorative rather than a structural order. While most great houses of the eighteenth century in London had either been largely rebuilt or demolished, Spencer House preserved the greater part of its original fabric and decoration. Sadly, however, this was shortly to change. Directly the lease was signed with the Ladies' Army and Navy Club, all the original contents of the house were

removed to Althorp, the Spencers' country seat, and in the years that followed extensive alterations were made, including the construction of an unsightly two-storey extension above the south and east wings. Worse was to come, for with the outbreak of war, the interior was also stripped of its fittings, including chimney-pieces, doors, doorcases, dados and skirting boards, all of which were transported to Althorp for safekeeping and later installed there. The Blitz caused further damage, and by the time the war had ended the house was in a state of utter dereliction.

A hasty clean-up operation was put in hand, and the house was briefly occupied by Christie's, with auctions being held in the Dining Room. In 1956 the house was leased to the British Oxygen Company and completely overhauled, emerging as a modern corporate headquarters, the state apartments fitted out with swing doors and partitions, the internal courtyard crammed with lift shafts and machinery. The house was still in this condition almost thirty years later when the lease was offered for sale and was acquired by the J. Rothschild group of companies.

Lord Rothschild admits that the decision to take on Spencer House was largely a romantic one, inspired by the love of a great historic building he had known since childhood. His primary aim was to rescue the house from decline and restore it in a manner consistent with its unique architectural importance. However, he also wanted to show that the project could be accomplished within a commercial framework. Indeed, he had to. As chairman of a public listed company, with responsibilities to over 15,000 shareholders, he had to ensure the project paid its way.

The odds were daunting: even among Lord Rothschild's colleagues there was considerable scepticism. But for Lord Rothschild himself the challenge was irresistible, combining as it did his two great passions, business and the arts, and he eventually won the backing of the board.

It was first necessary to find a function for the building. The existing grant for office use was due to expire in 1997, but through feasibility studies it soon became apparent that office use remained the only viable scheme which would guarantee the building's long-term future. When

approached on this point, the authorities indicated that if a scheme of exceptional merit was advanced, they might grant an extension of office use. On this basis work began on the development of a detailed plan.

The challenge could hardly have been greater. The brief, in essence, was to restore Spencer House to the appearance of a nobleman's palace, while equipping it for use as an office building that would meet the needs of the twentieth and even twenty-first centuries.

Lord Rothschild appointed a team of expert advisers drawn from every branch of the building industry, together with a panel of leading architectural historians. Extensive structural surveys were undertaken; research was carried out in libraries and archives; scrapes were taken from the paintwork in the state apartments to determine the original allocation of colour and gilding; and visits were made to Althorp to examine the contents and fittings removed from Spencer House in the 1920s and 1940s. Advice was sought from amenity groups, and the authorities, too, were consulted at every step.

In October 1986, Lord Rothschild and his team were ready to submit their plan. The solution they proposed was an ingenious scheme combining state-of-the-art technology with strict historical authenticity. The building would be fitted with every modern device and the structure substantially reinforced, yet traditional building methods would be used throughout and all alterations and additions would be made with no visible disturbance to the historic fabric. The courtyard would be cleared and the extensions of the 1920s replaced by a light-weight structure of suitable Georgian design. The exterior of the building would be restored to its original appearance, allowing for the alterations carried out by the architect Henry Holland in the late eighteenth century, and the same approach was taken to the state apartments.

The cost of the scheme was such that only by securing a long lease and a perpetual grant for office use could Lord Rothschild commit the necessary funds. These conditions were met, and by June 1987 workmen were on site.

In size and complexity the restoration of Spencer House was as great an undertaking as the building's original construction, and it was to be another two and a half years before the project reached completion. The state apartments called for particular sensitivity. It had been intended that these would serve as directors' offices but, once the project was underway, it was proposed instead that they be used as banqueting rooms, to be hired out on a commercial basis, so enhancing the viability of the overall scheme. The idea was gladly welcomed by the Spencer Trustees and the authorities. It had been agreed that the state apartments would be opened to the public, and Lord Rothschild now saw the possibility of restoring them to museum standard. New oak floorboards were laid throughout, cut to eighteenth-century widths and polished with natural wax to achieve an authentic pale finish. Paint was carefully removed from mouldings, although in every room an area was left unstripped so as to preserve the 'archaeology' of the interiors for future study. In the Dining Room the shafts of the columns were stripped and the underlying scagliola coating polished to its original marble

finish. For the decoration, traditional white flat oil paint was used, mixed by hand with pure pigment, while the gilding was of the best 23.25 carat gold. In the Painted Room, specialist conservators were brought in to clean and retouch the murals and inset panels. Silk for the hangings, window curtains and chair covers was specially produced on genuine Jacquard looms, woven to the original 21-inch width. Perhaps the most impressive aspect of the project was the recreation of the missing architectural fittings, including chimney-pieces, decorative joinery and gilt-metal door furniture, all of which was reproduced exactly using impressions taken from the original fittings at Althorp.

To furnish Spencer House Lord Rothschild and his colleagues adopted a three-part strategy. With the cooperation of museums and other public institutions they were able to borrow a number of items originally produced for the house but subsequently sold by the Spencers. The Victoria and Albert Museum supplied a giltwood console table originally from the Dining Room, while Temple Newsam supplied the pair to this table. The Victoria and Albert Museum, with the cooperation of English Heritage, also agreed to

The Dining Room of Spencer House with restoration in progress. (TOP)

Restoration of the scagliola coating to columns in the Dining Room. (ABOVE)

lend the remarkable suite of neo-classical seat furniture designed by Stuart for the Painted Room, previously displayed at Kenwood House. Where the original furniture could not be borrowed, replicas were commissioned, including such key pieces as the side tables and pier glasses from the Great Room. In addition, a fund was established to purchase furniture of suitable character, including a set of chairs attributed to John Gordon, a craftsman patronized by the 1st Earl Spencer. To accompany this furniture the company also acquired a collection of antique carpets together with a magnificent modern copy of a seventeenth-century Persian carpet, specially woven in Turkey for the Great Room.

Paintings and other works of art were likewise borrowed and purchased. Particularly significant was the loan from the Tate Gallery of Gavin Hamilton's *Agrippina with the Ashes of Germanicus,* a painting commissioned by the 1st Earl Spencer, almost certainly for Spencer House. Other works of art were lent from the Royal Collection and the Royal Academy.

The restoration programme continues. Appropriate late eighteenth-century planting is underway in the garden, while the decoration of the state apartments constantly evolves as fresh opportunities arise to purchase and borrow suitable contents. But already one can talk of lasting achievements. In architectural terms the project has been hailed as one the most successful ever undertaken; once again the house achieves that perfect fusion of the fine and decorative arts to which the 1st Earl Spencer and his architects first aspired. Now, as in the eighteenth century, the state apartments provide a showcase in which it is possible to admire some of the finest works of art and furniture anywhere on public display, in an architectural setting of incomparable beauty and sophistication. Equally important, the house now has a role, a living function. While retaining the atmosphere of a private residence, it serves as a place of business and a focus for social, cultural and political activity, just as it did originally. In December 1989 the Great Room provided the setting for a dinner held by the Society of Dilettanti, of which the 1st Earl Spencer had been a member. The dinner was attended by the

Princess of Wales, a direct descendant of the Earl, and it was the Princess who re-opened the house officially in 1990, since which time there have been countless receptions and other events.

The success of the Spencer House project clearly demonstrates that high-quality restoration can be achieved within a commercial framework and points the way to greater cooperation between architects and historians, planners and developers. Valuable discoveries have been made and existing techniques and ideas refined, while vital training has been provided in traditional craft skills. The restoration of Spencer House, no less than its construction, is a paradigm of what can be achieved through architecture and offers hope to all who love historic buildings.

The Dining Room in 1992, restored and furnished to evoke the style of the eighteenth century. (ABOVE)

THE EIGHTEENTH-CENTURY HOUSE RESTORED

MILES BREWTON HOUSE *by J. Thomas Savage*

The sobriquet 'America's best preserved city' is often applied to Charleston, South Carolina. The peninsular city contains over 3,500 rated historic structures which have survived the ravages of wars, fires, hurricanes and an earthquake in 1886 and are protected by America's earliest historic zoning ordinance that created Charleston's Old and Historic District in 1931. Within this district is a remarkable collection of late colonial dwellings representing the synthesis of British architectural traditions and regional American contributions to rococo design. Chief among these is the Miles Brewton house, completed in 1769.

By the third quarter of the eighteenth century, Charleston's burgeoning wealth, based on the bounty from rice and indigo and the mercantile fortunes fostered by shipping, exhibited itself in

new public buildings and grand private dwellings. Indeed, in grandeur and splendour of buildings the city was said to have surpassed anything ever seen in America. Enjoying the greatest per capita wealth of any colonial American centre, Charleston attracted a stream of British artisans and imported consumer goods of all types to which its inhabitants availed themselves in the creation of their town houses.

Charleston's golden age of trade was paralleled by the economic ascendancy of Miles Brewton. As part owner of eight commercial vessels and South Carolina's largest slave dealer, Brewton was at the pinnacle of the city's mercantile élite. His marriage in 1759 to Mary Izard brought him within the sphere of South Carolina's leading planter families and the royal colony's aristocratic British officials.

Street façade of the Miles Brewton house on King Street, Charleston, South Carolina, completed in 1769. (RIGHT)

Both within and without, the Brewton house reflects the eighteenth-century's use of architectural hierarchy. Raised on a high English basement that houses domestic offices and work spaces, the house is entered by way of two elegant stone stairs with half turns and double landings leading to the projecting portico. Here, the single order porticoes with columns rising from ground floor to pediment follow the classical temple form: Doric lower porch and Ionic upper gallery surmounted by an Ionic pediment and entablature. This impressive façade lends the appearance of a sixteenth-century Italian country villa of the sort identified with Andrea Palladio and contrasts markedly with the more conservative single houses then prevalent in Charleston.

Inside, the architectural hierarchy established on the portico is consistently repeated. The two rooms which face onto the street are larger than the rooms behind them, are fully panelled and feature carved elements while those facing the garden have simpler panelled chimney walls and plaster above the wainscot, indicative of their original use as library and butler's pantry below and bedchambers above.

No architect for the house is known but it is likely that Brewton and his general contractor, Richard Moncrieff, collaborated on the design, perhaps aided by the abundance of architectural design sources available in Charleston in the 1760s. One of the craftsmen employed by Moncrieff was the English carver Ezra Waite. In August 1769 he advertised his involvement in the Brewton house, proclaiming that he had 'finished the architecture, conducted the execution thereof, viz, in the joiner way, all tabernacle frames, (but that in the dining-room excepted), and carved all the said work in the four principle rooms.'

The dining room referred to by Waite is the grand southeast Drawing Room with a cove ceiling situated on the second floor, and is the most sumptuous of Charleston's surviving eighteenth-century rooms. Here, John Bivins, the leading authority on Charleston carving, has proposed that the two candidates capable of carving the elaborate overmantel placed at the centre of one of the walls were carver and gilder John Lord and mastercraftsman Thomas Woodin. Like Waite,

The mahogany staircase on the first floor occupies the rear passage, with its original floor of Purbeck stone imported from Dorset in England. (LEFT)

The southeast Drawing Room on the second floor, *circa* 1895. Four of the upholstered British 'French' or elbow chairs, made in *circa* 1770, are visible, each upholstered in a different textile. Edward Savage's portrait of Mary Brewton Motte Alston hangs above the carved console table with *pietra dura* top. (BELOW)

Detail of the carved wood decoration restored to its original crispness. (TOP)

A carved bird emerges from the overmantel of the house's primary reception room. (ABOVE)

Alston carried out numerous architectural changes including the addition of the fine neo-classical leaded oculus in the pediment of the portico and the installation of the formidable barbed iron spikes to the eighteenth-century iron fence on the street front – a tangible response perhaps to the attempted slave insurrection of 1822. In the same year, Alston's daughter married William Bull Pringle.

The Pringles inherited the house in 1839 and saw much of their considerable fortune swept away during the Civil War. Their spinster daughter Susan received the house at the time of the mother's death in 1884 and in 1917 it was inherited by Susan Pringle's three nieces, the Misses Frosts, all born in the house. Undaunted by the genteel poverty that characterized much of Charleston during the Depression years, the Misses Frosts cherished and protected the family house, and shared it with interested visitors who received memorable tours from them. In the 1960s, the house was inherited by the Manigault family, the present owners Mr and Mrs Peter Manigault representing the eighth generation in the succession of family ownership.

Fate could not have provided more sympathetic, dedicated or patient stewards for the house and its collections. From 1988 to 1991, the Manigaults committed themselves to one of the most comprehensive restoration projects ever attempted on a private residence in America. The mission was to conserve the original architectural structure and restore all the decorative features including any missing elements which could be replicated. An initial structural survey of the house revealed the perilous condition of the portico, which had shifted during the earthquake of 1886 leaving the bulk of its weight to rest on one column. Modern equipment and materials were brought in to remedy the problem, after which the house was transformed into a laboratory for the study of decorative finishes and conservation techniques. Restoration architects Charles Phillips, Joseph Oppermann and the late Paul Buchanan were commissioned to analyse the evolution of the structure, install non-obtrusive climate control systems and prepare specifications for the physical restoration.

these well-connected London craftsmen may have been lured to Charleston by the building boom in the city or perhaps had found it necessary to leave England as a result of the economic depression that followed the Seven Years' War.

In August 1775 Miles Brewton, his wife and children set sail for Philadelphia where Brewton had been elected a delegate to the second Provincial Congress. Their ship was lost at sea. Since then, the property has passed into the careful hands of Brewton's descendants, with each generation adding its own collections. The first to inherit were Brewton's sisters, Rebecca Brewton Motte and Frances Brewton Pinckney. In 1791 Colonel William Alston of the wealthy family of Carolina rice planters married Mary Brewton Motte, the daughter of Rebecca, and bought the house from his mother-in-law and her sister.

Analyses of the paints and finishes in each room, conducted by Frank Welsh, have enabled the first period colours to be replicated and are used throughout the house. For two-and-a-half years a team of highly-skilled women worked to remove up to twenty-six layers of paint from interior and exterior wooden surfaces, returning the delicate carving to a level of crispness unseen since Miles Brewton's occupancy. Ninety-eight per cent of the carving was intact and missing elements were carefully copied by the master carver John Bivins. The removal of paint also revealed ghost marks indicating the original locations of decorative features and furnishings. A remarkable survival, the only known architectural console table in a colonial American house, was returned to its original position in the South Parlour as a result of this process. Carved from New England white pine, as is all of the interior and exterior carving, the console has a *pietra dura* top of the sort secured on the Grand Tour.

The archaeological approach to the interior restoration has yielded much new evidence regarding the transmission and emulation of fashionable English schemes of interior decoration in the American colonies. The house is rich, for example, in papier-mâché ornament, an easily exportable alternative to stucco and supplied by Charleston upholsterers, as revealed in the advertisement placed by John Blott in 1765: 'Machee Ornaments for Ceilings & c. to imitate stocowork'. Long thought to be plaster, the applied ceiling ornament in the South Parlour is an intact example of this ephemeral form of decoration, as are the gilded fillets bordering a plaque showing the god Apollo on the ceiling of the stair landing.

Documentary evidence from a journal entry of 1773 suggested that there were also gilt fillets in the second-floor Dining Room. However, physical evidence for this had eluded the investigative team until one afternoon when the removal of an interior column capital spilled forth the contents of an eighteenth-century rat's nest. The rodent had furnished his rococo lair with nut shells, a chair splat, half a watch case, a lorgnette, bits of newspaper, wallpaper, upholstery stuffing, shreds of glazed chintz and a few flecks of glittering papier mâché – enough to reconstruct a full repeat

of the fillet. A further 170 feet of gilded fillet was replicated using materials and techniques as close as possible to the original, with modifications dictated by contemporary understanding of material permanence. The creation is now reinstalled against the brilliant Prussian blue of the cove ceiling, a colour determined by the discovery of a tiny fragment of original ceiling plaster.

Today, the portrait of the young Miles Brewton, painted by Joshua Reynolds in 1756, surveys an again familiar sight from its place of prominence within the overmantel in the southeast Drawing Room. No doubt, he would approve of the accomplishments of his industrious progeny. The magnificent British glass chandelier – the survivor of an earthquake and a ceiling collapse – casts a warm glow in the room which is enhanced by soft light from discreetly installed fibre-optic lighting concealed at the base of the cove ceiling. Brewton's suite of imported British elbow chairs lines the walls in eighteenth-century fashion, their contours and azure-blue silk damask restored through non-interventive techniques following careful analysis. This remarkable house is again poised to welcome succeeding generations of this American family whose equal protection of inheritance and legacy has established new standards of restoration philosophy and conservation practice.

The southeast Drawing Room on the second floor, Charleston's most impressive domestic reception room of the eighteenth century, was intended for use as a grand dining room. Miles Brewton's portrait by Joshua Reynolds, painted in London in 1756, hangs in the overmantel. The English chandelier of 1770–80 was installed in the eighteenth century. (BELOW)

HOUSING A COLLECTION *by Leslie Geddes-Brown*

Pokety Farms, Maryland, North America. (BELOW)

The sitting room at Pokety Farms. (BELOW RIGHT)

It is a well-known saying that great things come in small packages, but sometimes in a collection the largest and most inspiring item may go virtually unnoticed. The house a collector chooses for himself must, at the very least, be in harmony with the collection. Occasionally it is the building which acts to transform the collector's interest in a particular style or period, and therefore directs the path a collection will take.

By their very nature, the collectors who attend Sotheby's salerooms are the same people who are searching for beautiful homes in which to house their works of art. Sotheby's International Realty was started in 1976 to meet this requirement, specializing in properties of distinction across a broad price band. Specific to these houses is the aesthetic appeal they would have for art-lovers in terms of their design or location.

Bernice Chrysler Garbisch and her husband, Colonel Edgar Garbisch, became the owners of one of the finest collections of American naïve paintings and furniture. But if they had not inherited Pokety Farms in 1941, a hunting lodge on Maryland's eastern shore, this might not have been so. In the process of renovating the charming clap-board and porticoed building, the couple began to buy the traditional folk art and antiques that it demanded, and at a time when few people were interested in such works. The Garbisches bought pieces for their charm and entertainment value rather than their academic importance, once writing, 'the true measure of the worth of any art is the extent to which it is enjoyed.' They also got great satisfaction from the chase (which took them from specialist dealers to obscure shops across America), from living with their

finds, and from the knowledge that much of their naïve paintings collection would eventually hang in the National Gallery in Washington.

John L. Marion, Chairman of Sotheby's North America, remembers the couple well, for they were favourites of his. 'They were childhood sweethearts, they did everything together. When it came to collecting, they went to exhibitions together and picked the paintings and the furniture together.... Fittingly, they died within hours of each other, on 26 December 1979.' Five years earlier Sotheby's had handled the auction of almost 600 pieces from the Garbisch collection; now they were asked to sell the remaining pieces and the house which had been the collection's inspiration. The auction of the contents was held on site, for it was realized that to view the pieces in their correct surroundings would have a powerful effect on prospective buyers. But Pokety Farms refused to be laid bare again, and the buyer of the bulk of the collection subsequently acquired the house as well.

If a collection is inspired by a house, then it will resist a change of location on the whim of its guardians. It is for this reason that so many collectors decide to sell their treasures when they move house – they simply would not work as well anywhere else. Jaime Ortiz-Patiño, on the other hand, was inspired by his collection. He began collecting quite modestly in 1956 with enamelled snuff boxes. But the passion was surely in his blood. His grandfather Simon Patiño, known as the Tin King of Bolivia, had a deep love of the arts, while his parents passed on the tradition of collecting objects of great quality.

Soon Ortiz-Patiño's interests extended to mediaeval manuscripts, fine bindings, French furniture, French and English silver, Old Master and Impressionist paintings. The collection became so vast that he felt the only way it could be sympathetically and safely shown was in a purpose-built house with state-of-the-art security and conservation systems. In 1965, Jacques Regnault was commissioned to build a large house on a hillside in Vandoeuvres, near Geneva. Though the quiet Île de France building is unremarkable from the outside – the needs of the collection took precedence over architectural pyrotechnics – inside it

provided a glittering setting for the works of art. Nothing was spared to create a fitting environment for the collection; the dining-room walls were covered in early nineteenth-century French wallpaper, while Louis XV *boiseries* were adapted to fit the drawing room. Nor were the gardens neglected: a spring garden and a French garden of pleached limes and white roses were created, as was a nine-hole golf course – golf being another of the collector's obsessions.

In the twenty-five years that Jaime Ortiz-Patiño lived in Vandoeuvres his collection continued to grow. Thus, when he moved to London to become Bolivia's advisor in Europe, much of it had to be sold. The quality of those pieces which he selected for sale caused enormous excitement during the three-day auction at Sotheby's New York, while the house proved equally covetable and fetched a record price in 1992.

Any person interested in Renaissance art surely dreams of living in a villa designed by the world's most famous architect, Andrea Palladio. Only some twenty examples were ever built, and one of these was commissioned by the Venetian admiral Giorgio Cornaro in 1551 to be built at Piombino

The drawing room of the Ortiz-Patiño house near Geneva. (BELOW)

Front view of the Villa Cornaro in Piombino Dese in the Veneto. (RIGHT)

One of the rooms in the Villa Cornaro showing the decorative plaster-work by Bartolomeo Cabianca and the biblical frescoes by Mattia Bartoloni. (BELOW)

Dese in the Veneto. By 1554 the family was living in the eighteen main rooms of Villa Cornaro (it later acquired an equal number of secondary rooms) and had commissioned the six monumental statues of illustrious members of the Cornaro family, which still stand in the Great Hall. In the early seventeenth century Mattia Bartoloni painted 114 frescoes on its walls while Bartolomeo Cabianca created the superb stucco work on the walls and ceilings. This was the house-as-work-of-art with a vengeance.

In 1969 Villa Cornaro came up for sale. For years the Miami businessman Richard Rush and his wife Julie had been searching for a grand, European home in which to display their collection of Old Master paintings, Venetian glass and antique furniture. They were tipped off by Peggy Guggenheim about the sale and, undeterred by the state of complete disrepair in which they found it, they purchased the villa and spent the next twenty years restoring it to its former glory.

The work completed, they decided to move on. 'It's a beautiful place,' admitted Richard Rush, 'but after a while it simply became my home. While I still have a certain amount of my youth left … now's the time to close this chapter.' In truth, he probably tired of his Italian project once it had reached perfection.

The Rushes made sure that their efforts were not wasted and that Villa Cornaro remained in careful hands. Palladio enthusiasts from America, Germany and Canada were desperate to buy, but the successor was chosen for his custodianship rather than for placing the highest bid. As a result, the villa achieved a lower price than the fine Titian, *The Penitent Magdalen,* owned by the Rushes and sold through Sotheby's in 1988.

Just as it is absurd even to try to furnish a Palladian villa with anything other than the appropriate antiques, so it is with the work of the more original modern architects. When Sotheby's agreed in 1989 to sell the New York *pied-à-terre* created by the architect Philip Johnson for Mrs John D. Rockefeller III in 1949–50, they realized that they would need to seek out a connoisseur.

Johnson had studied architecture with Walter Gropius and Marcel Breuer and was a disciple of Mies van der Rohe. In 1932 he published *The International Style* with Henry-Russell Hitchcock, thus coining the popular term. The townhouse was described by the architect as 'primarily a place to display Mrs Rockefeller's art collection which was too big and too modern to be anywhere else.' Warhol called it 'the original New York loft', for Johnson was an early proponent of unadorned brick, steel beams, white vinyl tiles and industrial fixtures, and the building's floor-to-ceiling windows were some of the earliest in the city. Mrs Rockefeller gave the building to the Museum of Modern Art in 1958, but it returned to private ownership seven years later when acquired by the collector, Robert Walker, who amassed an important collection of twentieth-century furniture. The furniture looked wonderful *in situ,* but what else would?

With the knowledge that those interested in the furniture collection would also be attracted to the building, Sotheby's took the unprecedented step of auctioning the house and its contents

together. As Stuart Siegel, President of Sotheby's International Realty, explained, 'an auction would present the townhouse as a masterwork of twentieth-century art and attract clients who valued its aesthetic merit as well as its prestigious early history.' Before the sale, a model of the building and contents went on tour worldwide.

There were eight serious bidders for the house. As the house had previously failed to find a buyer when offered at $1,650,000, the estimate was reduced to $1,400,000–$1,500,000. It was sold to two dealers in twentieth-century works of art for $3,500,000, confirming that the house and furniture were of specialist interest and needed to be seen in context to be fully appreciated.

Such events are a salient reminder that the finest building, whether a Renaissance villa or an American farmhouse, a New York loft or a purpose-built showcase, when matched sympathetically to both owner and works of art, can become the unsung hero of that collection.

Interior of the Philip Johnson townhouse.
(ABOVE)

PRINCIPAL OFFICERS AND SPECIALISTS

Diana D. Brooks
President and Chief Executive
Officer, Sotheby's Holdings, Inc.

Simon de Pury
Chairman, Sotheby's Europe

Henry Wyndham
Chairman, Sotheby's
United Kingdom

John L. Marion
Chairman, Sotheby's North
and South America

Julian Thompson
Chairman, Sotheby's Asia

William F. Ruprecht
Managing Director, Sotheby's
North America

George Bailey
Managing Director,
Sotheby's Europe

American Decorative Arts
Leslie B. Keno
New York (212) 606 7130
William W. Stahl, Jnr
New York (212) 606 7110
Wendell Garrett
New York (212) 606 7137

American Folk Art
Nancy Druckman
New York (212) 606 7225

American Indian Art
Ellen Napiura Taubman
New York (212) 606 7540

American Paintings
Peter B. Rathbone
New York (212) 606 7280

Animation and Comic Art
Dana Hawkes
New York (212) 606 7424
Stephen Maycock
London (071) 408 5206

Antiquities and Asian Art
Richard M. Keresey (antiquities)
New York (212) 606 7328
Carlton Rochell (Asian)
New York (212) 606 7328
Felicity Nicholson (antiquities)
London (071) 408 5111
Brendan Lynch (Asian)
London (071) 408 5112

Applied Arts from 1880
Barbara E. Deisroth
New York (212) 606 7170
Philippe Garner
London (071) 408 5138

Arms, Armour and Medals
David Erskine-Hill
London (071) 408 5315
Gordon Gardiner
Sussex (0403) 783933
Margaret Schwartz
New York (212) 606 7260

Books and Autograph Manuscripts
Stephen Roe
London (071) 408 5286
David N. Redden
New York (212) 606 7386
Paul Needham
New York (212) 606 7385

British Paintings 1500-1850
David Moore-Gwyn
London (071) 408 5406
Henry Wemyss (watercolours)
London (071) 408 5409
James Miller
London (071) 408 5405

British Paintings from 1850
Simon Taylor (Victorian)
London (071) 408 5385
Susannah Pollen
(twentieth-century)
London (071) 408 5388

Ceramics
Peter Arney
London (071) 408 5134
Letitia Roberts
New York (212) 606 7180

Chinese Art
Carol Conover
New York (212) 606 7332
Gong Jisui (paintings)
New York (212) 606 7334
Julian Thompson
London (071) 408 5371
Colin Mackay
London (071) 408 5145
Mee Seen Loong
Hong Kong (852) 524 8121

Clocks and Watches
Tina Millar (watches)
London (071) 408 5328
Michael Turner (clocks)
London (071) 408 5329
Daryn Schnipper
New York (212) 606 7162

Coins
Tom Eden (ancient and Islamic)
London (071) 408 5315
James Morton (English
and paper)
London (071) 408 5314
Paul Song
New York (212) 606 7391

Collectors' Department
Dana Hawkes
New York (212) 606 7424

Hilary Kay
London (071) 408 5205

Contemporary Art
Anthony Grant
New York (212) 606 7254
Tobias Meyer
London (071) 408 5400

European Works of Art
Elizabeth Wilson
London (071) 408 5321
Margaret Schwartz
New York (212) 606 7250

Furniture
Graham Child (English)
London (071) 408 5347
Mario Tavella (Continental)
London (071) 408 5349
Larry J. Sirolli (English)
New York (212) 606 7577
William W. Stahl
New York (212) 606 7110
Phillips Hathaway (Continental)
New York (212) 606 7213
Alexandre Pradère
Paris 33 (1) 42 66 40 60

Garden Statuary
James Rylands
Sussex (0403) 783933
Elaine Whitmire
New York (212) 606 7285

Glass
Simon Cottle
London (071) 408 5135
Lauren K. Tarshis
New York (212) 606 7180

**Impressionist and Modern
Paintings**
David J. Nash
New York (212) 606 7351

Alexander Apsis
New York (212) 606 7360
Marc E. Rosen (drawings)
New York (212) 606 7154
Melanie Clore
London (071) 408 5394
Michel Strauss
London (071) 408 5389
John L. Tancock
Tokyo 81 (3) 3503 2944

Islamic Art and Carpets
Richard M. Keresey (works of art)
New York (212) 606 7328
Mary Jo Otsea (carpets)
New York (212) 606 7996
Prof. John Carswell (works of art)
London (071) 408 5153
Jacqueline Bing (carpets)
London (071) 408 5152

Japanese Art
Neil Davey
London (071) 408 5141
Yasuko Kido (prints)
London (071) 408 2042
Suzanne Mitchell
New York (212) 606 7338
Ryoichi Iida
New York (212) 606 7338

Jewellery
John D. Block
New York (212) 606 7392
David Bennett
Geneva 41 (22) 732 8585
Alexandra Rhodes
London (071) 408 5306

Judaica
David Breuer-Weil
Tel Aviv 972 (3) 22 38 22
Camille Previté
London (071) 408 5334
Paul Needham (books)

New York (212) 606 7385
Kevin Tierney (silver)
New York (212) 606 7160

Latin American Paintings
August Uribe
New York (212) 606 7290

Musical Instruments
Graham Wells
London (071) 408 5341
Leah Ramirez
New York (212) 606 7290

Nineteenth-Century European Furniture and Works of Art
Elaine Whitmire
New York (212) 606 7285

Nineteenth-Century European Paintings
Michael Bing
London (071) 408 5380
Nancy Harrison
New York (212) 606 7140

Old Master Paintings and Drawings
Alexander Bell
London (071) 408 5485
Gregory Rubinstein
(drawings)
London (071) 408 5416
George Wachter
New York (212) 606 7230
Scott Schaefer (drawings)
New York (212) 606 7222
Nancy Ward-Neilson
Milan 39 (2) 7600471
Etienne Breton
Paris 33 (1) 42 66 40 60

Oriental Manuscripts
Marcus Fraser
London (071) 408 5033

Photographs
Philippe Garner
London (071) 408 5138
Beth Gates-Warren
New York (212) 606 7240

Portrait Miniatures, Objects of Vertu, Icons amd Russian Works of Art
Gerard Hill
New York (212) 606 7150
Haydn Williams
(miniatures and vertu)
London (071) 408 5326
Ivan Samarine (Russian)
London (071) 408 5325
Heinrich Graf von Spreti
Munich 49 (89) 291 31 51

Postage Stamps
Richard Ashton
London (071) 408 5224
Robert Scott
New York (212) 606 7288

Pre-Columbian Art
Stacy Goodman
New York (212) 606 7330
Fatma Turkkan-Wille
Zürich 41 (1) 422 3045

Prints
Nancy Bialler (Old Master)
New York (212) 606 7117
Mary Bartow (19th & 20th C.)
New York (212) 606 7117
Robert Monk (contemporary)
New York (212) 606 7113
Jonathon Pratt
London (071) 408 5210

Silver
Kevin L. Tierney
New York (212) 606 7160
Peter Waldron (English)

London (071) 408 5104
Harold Charteris (Continental)
London (071) 408 5106

Sporting Guns
Adrian Weller
Sussex (0403) 783933

Tribal Art
Jean G. Fritts
New York (212) 606 7325

Trusts and Estates
Warren P. Weitman
New York (212) 606 7198

Veteran, Vintage and Classic Cars
Malcolm Barber
London (071) 408 5320
David Patridge
Rumney NH (603) 786 2338

Western Manuscripts
Dr Christopher de Hamel FSA
London (071) 408 5330

Wine
Serena Sutcliffe MW
London (071) 408 5050

INDEX

ACKNOWLEDGMENTS

PROJECT EDITOR Slaney Begley
ART EDITOR Ruth Prentice
ASSISTANT EDITOR Nella Guagenti
DESIGNER Alistair Plumb
PICTURE RESEARCH Abigail Ahern

PUBLISHER'S ACKNOWLEDGMENTS
The publisher would like to thank Ronald Varney, William F. Ruprecht, Luke Rittner, Amanda Brookes, Michel Strauss, Lynn Stowell Pearson, Elizabeth Thorpe, Melanie Brownrout, David Lee, Nicki Marshall, and all the Sotheby's departments for their help with this book.

Thanks are also due to Ron Bowen for the illustrations to Ian Fleming's 'The Property of a Lady', which appear on pages 14, 18, 22-3 and 27. Ron Bowen is an American artist and teacher living in London. His work, which has appeared in international exhibitions, also includes book illustrations and set designs for theatre and dance. He is currently Senior Lecturer at the Slade School of Fine Art, University College, London.

Prices given throughout this book include the buyer's premium applicable in the saleroom concerned. These prices are shown in the currency in which they were realized. The sterling and dollar equivalent figures, shown in brackets, are based upon the rates of exchange on the day of the sale.